TOWARDS THE BORDERS OF THE
BRONZE AGE AND BEYOND

TOWARDS THE BORDERS OF THE
BRONZE AGE AND BEYOND

Mycenaean Long Distance Travel and
its Reflection in Myth

Jörg Mull

© 2022 Jörg Mull

Published by Sidestone Press, Leiden
www.sidestone.com

Imprint: Sidestone Press

Lay-out & cover design: Sidestone Press
Photograph cover: Replica of "Argo", the mythical ship of Jason and the Argonauts at the port of Volos town, Magnessia, Thessaly, Greece. Photo: Iraklis Milas (stock.adobe.com)

ISBN 978-94-6426-077-9 (softcover)
ISBN 978-94-6426-078-6 (hardcover)
ISBN 978-94-6426-079-3 (PDF e-book)

Contents

Abstract	**7**
Acknowledgements	**9**
1. Preface	**11**
2. Introduction	**13**
3. References to Time and Dates in the Bronze Age	**17**
4. The Historical and Archaeological Framework of Travel and Mobility in the Bronze Age	**21**
5. The Economic Background of Bronze Age Long Distance Travel	**33**
6. Shipbuilding in the Bronze Age	**43**
7. Evidence for Mycenaean Long Distance Journeys in the LBA	**49**
8. Reflections of Mycenaean Long Distance Travel in the Mythological Record	**57**
8.1 Definitions, Structures and Functions of Myth	57
8.2 Myth and History	58
8.2.1 Approaches to the Historicity and the Origins of Myths	58
8.2.2 The Transmission Processes During the 'Dark Ages'	60
8.2.3 Transposition and Re-Interpretation of Myth during the Archaic Age of Greek Colonial Expansion	61
8.2.4 Epic Poetry, Canonization and Local Variants	62
8.2.5 Early Geography and the 'Historization of Myth' in the Archaic, Classical and Hellenistic Periods	64
8.3 Genealogies – Mythical Timekeeping	70
8.4 The Content and Narrative Style of Greek Travel Myths – Quests and Journeys in the LBA	72
8.5 The Historicity of Greek Travel Myths – Conclusions and Vantage Point	75
9. Mycenaean Contacts with the Civilizations in the Eastern Mediterranean	**77**
9.1 Mycenaean Contacts with Anatolia	77
9.1.1 Archaeological and Historical Evidence of Mycenaean Contacts with Anatolia	77
9.1.2 Reflections in Greek Myths	79

9.2 Mycenaean Contacts with the Levant — 82
    9.2.1 Archaeological Evidence of Mycenaean Contacts with the Levant — 82
    9.2.2 Reflections in Greek Myths — 84

9.3 Mycenaean Contacts with Cyprus — 87
    9.3.1 Archaeological Evidence of Mycenaean Contacts with Cyprus — 87
    9.3.2 Reflections in Greek Myths — 88

9.4 Mycenaean Contacts with Egypt — 89
    9.4.1 Pictorial, Historical and Archaeological Evidence of Mycenaean Contacts with Egypt — 89
    9.4.2 Reflections in Greek Myths — 95

10. Mycenaean Contacts with the Central and Western Mediterranean — 105

10.1 Evidence of Mycenaean Journeys to Italy and Sicily — 105
    10.1.1 Archaeological Evidence — 105
    10.1.2 Reflections in Myths — 108

10.2 Evidence of Mycenaean Contacts with Sardinia — 109
    10.2.1 Archaeological Evidence — 109
    10.2.2 Reflections in Myths — 110

10.3 Mycenaean Contacts with the Iberian Peninsula — 111
    10.3.1 Archaeological Evidence — 111
    10.3.2 Reflections in Greek Myths — 116

11. Mycenaean Journeys to the Black Sea Area — 123

11.1 The Historical, Archaeological and Epigraphic Evidence of Mycenaean Contacts with the Black Sea Area — 123

11.2 Reflections of Mycenaean Journeys to the Black Sea Area in Greek Myths — 126

12. The Mysterious Countries 'Beyond' — 131

12.1 The Far South and East – The Ethiopians, the Red Sea and the Indian Ocean — 131

12.2 The Far West – 'The Isles of the Blessed' — 133

12.3 'Hyperborea' – The Mysterious 'Far North' — 135
    12.3.1 The Archaeological Evidence of Contacts from Mycenaean Greece with Northern Europe — 135
    12.3.2 The Mythical Record of Mycenaean Contacts with Northern Europe — 141

13. Summary and Conclusions — 147

14. References — 151

Abstract

The Late Bronze Age from about 1600 to 1150 BCE was a time of unprecedented economic activity in human history based on the supply and production of the eponymous alloy bronze on an almost industrial scale. The supply networks for copper and tin, the components of true bronze, during this period stretched over large parts of western Eurasia and included long distance maritime transport.

The palatial centres of Mycenaean Greece were positioned at a unique geographical interface between the cultural centres of the eastern Mediterranean as well as the metal supply sources in the western Mediterranean, northern Europe and the Black Sea area. There are archaeological, historical and epigraphic indications that the Mycenaeans somehow contributed either directly or indirectly via intermediaries to the exchange of goods in the second half of the 2nd millennium BCE. However, and partially due to limitations of archaeological and historical evidence, the degree to which the Mycenaean Greeks conducted long distance commercial journeys themselves to participate in the metal trade of the period is still disputed.

Joerg Mull analyzes the large corpus of the Greek myths, many of which are likely to go back to Bronze Age roots and which contain evidence of long distance journeys of Mycenaean pioneering adventurers. Mull, after an education in classical languages, became a trained economist with almost 30 years of experience in international business. From this unusual vantage point he provides a fresh perspective on what is known about travel and trade during the Late Bronze Age, a discipline so far dominated by archaeologists, historians and linguists.

In his new volume, the transmitted mythical stories of Mycenaean explorers on the metal trading routes of the Late Bronze Age are used as supporting evidence to answer the still controversially discussed question regarding the Mycenaean involvement in the exchange of goods, especially metals, during the Late Bronze Age. The analysis shows that there is clear evidence of Mycenaean long distance travel and exploration contained within the corpus of Greek myths with a focus towards the metal supply centres of the age in Sardinia, southern Iberia and the Black Sea area.

Regarding the economic networks of the Late Bronze Age, within which these mythical journeys likely took place, the academic and professional background of the author as an economist and long-time business professional sometimes leads to new questions being asked and new perspectives given on the existing archaeological and historical research. With respect to the references contained in the myths, the book takes the ancient mythological tradition serious to an extent that the strictly scientific reader from an archaeological or historical provenience will find unorthodox or even provocative. Yet in this way the historical and archaeological background for mythical protagonists like Heracles or Perseus becomes accessible to a broader audience.

Acknowledgements

The composition of this paper took up a considerable amount of time in the years 2018 to 2021 and would not have been possible without the support of many benevolent contributors.

For the archaeological, historical and linguistic background of the paper I owe a lot to Eberhard Zangger, Ivo Hajnal, Jeffrey Spier and the 'Zurich boys' for a continuous and gentle coaching, but most of all to Jorrit Kelder for his frequent feedback and mentorship throughout the entire process. Valuable crosschecks on methods and interpretations have been provided by Tobias Muehlenbruch.

I also would like to thank Karsten Wentink for the professional management of the publication process and his patient advice esp. on the Bell Beaker phenomenon as well as Olav Odé for his wonderful map making. Max Araujo Rentsch did a great job in his creative illustration management.

Max, Ann-Michelle, Tiane, Vivian, Ivan, Miguel, Carol, Xiaoding, Lillian and Shuang deserve credit for downloads and myriad contributions.

Last but most importantly I would like to thank my wife Tracey for an incessant support during the entire project.

1

Preface

This book develops ideas around the question, where the Bronze Age Mycenaeans travelled and what may have been their motivations for journeys to far-away places. To answer this type of questions, scientific work over the last few centuries has developed in specialized disciplines.

Archaeology analyzes the material remains of ancient times and interprets them. Over a century of modern archaeology has helped tremendously in many places of the world to form a relatively consistent picture of the ancient past. Great progress has been made for instance in the last years in terms of modern analytic technologies in order to identify the origins of metals in weapons and tools as well as the clay used in ceramics.

An important limitation of archaeology however is that it *'does not suffice for proving historical events but serves at most to present the cultural milieu.'* (already Persson Nilsson 1932, 18) and thus serves only as a *'proxy measure for demographic mobility and change'* (Knapp 2021, 47). The result of archaeological analysis regularly leads to relative chronologies and rarely to absolute and precise information.

Another related problem of archaeological research in particular with respect to the analysis of (trade) relations between distant groups of people in the past is that the absence of material remains in a certain area does not always mean that people did not visit the place. The 'absence of evidence' is thus not to be equated with 'evidence of absence', as this problem is often described. The visitors may just have not left anything behind or the remains may have been made of organic materials and long since vanished.

To complicate the situation even further, the presence of material finds of a known origin, *e.g.* Mycenaean ceramics, in a distant location does not automatically prove that Mycenaeans visited the place. The pottery found could also have been delivered by traders of a different provenience or consist of local copies.

Nevertheless the overall picture archaeological finds are able to produce at the very least gives a good overview about the potential geographical reach and – by and large – the intensity of exchange between different groups of people.

Historical research tries to understand and interpret ancient texts as well as their context. With respect to the analysis of the relationship between distant groups of people, we are sometimes in the lucky position that a few texts and references get transmitted over the centuries, which provide some information. A few wall paintings and papyri as well as tablets inscribed with contemporary languages with reference to the 'Mycenaean age' have survived the test of times. The content needs to be interpreted carefully, since the representations are often biased or equivocal. Yet, for a time as long gone by as the Bronze Age textual or pictorial references overall are naturally rare.

Linguists analyze the structure of different languages or words, their development over time and relationships between them, systematize them and interpret the results. A lot of progress has been made to understand the origins and regional distribution of ancient languages. Linguistics can thus help to provide a broad-brushed picture of the relationship between the speakers of different languages and sometimes their spatial movements. The difficulty here lies in the problem to associate identified language groups with specific material remains.

Overall, then, for the disciplines briefly listed here, the enormous distance in time as well as the problems and gaps in each research area make the evidence available subject to various interpretations. Final proof is difficult and elusive, which creates room for speculation and many interesting books.

Modern research now embraces other disciplines as well to fill the gaps, such as palaeo-genetics, palaeo-geography, archaeo-botany and anthropology, just to name a few. This relatively new approach is driven by the insight that only a multi-disciplinary scope is able to provide a comprehensive and somewhat conclusive picture of events as far distant in time as the Bronze Age (*e.g.* Bellwood 2013 in Knapp 2021, 46).

Within the 'classical' disciplines, there is still a considerable hesitation to be felt to include the mythological heritage in this multi-disciplinary approach. Reasons for this hesitation probably lie in the required interpretation of the complex mythical language in general as well as in the ebb and flow of mythical enthusiasm generated within the last century. The hype of expectations generated by Schliemann and his excavations in Troy and Mycenae initially seemed to prove some key contents of the Greek myths. Later this exuberance cooled down and gave way to a widespread skepticism, which moved the myths back to the realm of fairytales. These days, mythological research to some extent is beginning to be rehabilitated once more.

A specific difficulty in this context lies in the question about the 'historicity' of myths vs. a complex transmission process over long periods of time, which the myths were subject to. This paper makes the bold assumption that some key contents of the Greek myths were not invented or arbitrary and thus helpful to assist the other disciplines in their interpretation of events in the 'Mycenaean Age' (on a similar note cp. Woudhuizen 2013, 5). Given the superior importance the ancient Greeks ascribed to their mythical heritage, one is allowed to ask the question: 'Did those people of old really just invent their stories?'

This author believes that in times of migrations, commercial connections over long distances and of numerous armed conflicts, the transmission of one's own past, prowess and identity was of absolutely crucial importance for the respective peoples, especially in times when literacy was still an exception and oral traditions dominated. Even if some myths were later distorted, *e.g.* to include local traditions or recent experiences abroad, by and large these traditions were nothing to play around with.

If the Bronze Age peoples and their descendants took their mythological heritage that serious, maybe so should we.

2

Introduction

The Late Bronze Age (LBA), which lasted roughly 500 years from ca. 1600 BCE to 1100 BCE in the eastern Mediterranean, was a truly remarkable period in human history. It was the time of the emergence of great cultural centres and military powers around the Mediterranean Basin and gave a boost to the economies, architecture, arts and international travel. The rising demand for the eponymous alloy Bronze for weapons, tools and trade in the cultural centres of the time especially after ca. 2000 BCE led to quasi industrial production methods, to the emergence of transcontinental supply chains for the raw materials, copper and tin, and as a consequence to an increase in the connectivity between the peoples of this age. (Kristiansen and Larsson 2005, Latacz and Starke 2005).

Throughout the eastern Mediterranean, the major powers at this time were connected via commerce, diplomacy and travel. However the economic networks of the Late Bronze Age reached far beyond Egypt, Mesopotamia, the Levant, Anatolia and Greece. They seem to have included central Asia, the Black Sea region, northeast Africa, the western Mediterranean and northern Europe.

Whilst there are indications for indirect long-distance trade networks via caravan routes, riverine systems and major seaports like Ugarit, Troy, Amnisos and Enkomi on Cyprus as entrepots, we also have documentary evidence for direct journeys to the borders of the world as it was known. Queen Hatshepsut of the 18th dynasty in Egypt captured a trading expedition to 'Punt' in extensive wall paintings in her mortuary temple in Deir el Bahari. Punt probably needs to be located around the horn of Africa, probably in modern Somalia. (Panagiotopoulos 2006, 370) Next to pictorial evidence, archaeological finds of trading goods paint a picture of the extent of the vast trading networks in the LBA.

The LBA also saw the emergence of the Mycenaean Greeks[1] as a major power in the eastern Mediterranean from around 1600 BCE. Around 1450 BCE there is evidence for a

---

[1] The denominations 'Mycenaean' or 'Mycenaean Greeks' are modern creations and largely an 'archaeological label' rather than an ethnonym (cp. Dickinson 2019, 33). Mythical names for certain peoples or groups often differ from today's historical or archaeological terms. Often it is not known, how certain peoples called themselves in the Bronze Age. 'Greek' is a later wording derived from 'Graikoi'. Graikoi or Graeci is the word given to the settlers from Euboian Graia in Italy by the local inhabitants, for which the Graikoi formed the first point of contact with the Hellenic world. It later became the name for 'the Greeks' in general. The classical Greeks called themselves 'Hellenoi', *i.e.* descendants of the mythical 'Hellen'. For the name that 'Mycenaean Greeks' used for themselves there are only few references apart from the Homeric myths, where the terms Achaians, Danaans and Argives are found. These ethnonyms may have Bronze Age origins. The term 'Achaioi' seems to fit to the Hittite ethnonym 'Ahhiyawa' for the Mycenaeans, whereas the term 'Tanayu' is found in contemporary Egyptian sources.

Mycenaean take-over of previously Minoan-dominated trade routes. From that moment onwards, Mycenaean objects (mostly pottery) and influence is noticeable throughout the Mediterranean Basin.

Archaeologists and historians alike have tried to answer the question whether these objects and influences are evidence for a direct contact of Mycenaean mariners, or whether they reached their destinations indirectly via trade with other merchants of different origin as intermediaries. The scientific dispute as to whether Mycenaean long distance trade was more of a sporadic nature and mostly transacted via intermediaries or whether the Mycenaeans were active participants in the far reaching commercial networks of the Late Bronze Age is still ongoing (cp. the discussion in Tartaron 2013, 24). This book tries to provide supporting evidence to answer this question taken from the mythological records transmitted to us.[2]

The Mycenaeans have captured memories of heroic journeys to faraway places in their myths, which may have been verbally transmitted over centuries and seem to have been written down for the first time in the 8th century BCE.[3] The origin, historicity and interpretation of these myths are extremely complex and need to take into account very ancient roots, foreign influences and local traditions. In spite of this sometimes ambiguous heritage, this book argues that at the core of some of these myths there may have been real Bronze Age travellers, who undertook these long distance journeys and to which these ancient patterns and role models have been ascribed in mythical form and metaphorical language.

In clear view of the fact that myths do not transmit history as we understand it today and accounting for later additions, transpositions and misinterpretations, we may still get unique glimpses of Bronze Age travels when we read the stories today. If we compare the trade networks of the LBA as we can reconstruct them from archaeological research and compare these finds with the mythological sources, one is tempted to ask: How far did the people of the Bronze Age travel? What picture of their world and distant peoples did they bring home?

Against this background and these questions the key hypotheses of this book are formulated:

1. At the background of Greek travel myths are real long-distance journeys of Mycenaean travellers, who achieved heroic status at home through their pioneering adventures.
2. The travelling adventures and their heroic protagonists were embedded in long-standing narrative traditions of local and Near Eastern provenience and transmitted over centuries in metaphorical language as myths.
3. In the myths about journeys within the intense exchange networks of the eastern Mediterranean in the Late Bronze Age, commercial, diplomatic and raiding activities shine through. Motivations for the long-distance journeys of the Mycenaeans outside the eastern Mediterranean seem to lie primarily in the exploration of metal trading routes and the pioneering adventures connected with it.

---

2 See the quote by Kristiansen and Larsson (2005, 22) in section 8.2.2 on the potential of mythical transmission spanning centuries. Cp. also Schofield (2007, 188f).
3 Waal (2018, 119) argues for a parallel oral and written tradition already during the so-called 'Dark Ages', which presupposes an early adaptation of the Phoenician alphabet probably in the 11th century BCE.

4. The myths about Mycenaean travelling heroes correspond in terms of their chronology and their destinations quite well to the pattern of Mycenaean expansion in the Mediterranean as far as it can be reconstructed by archaeological, historical and pictorial evidence.
5. Knowledge about even more distant places like northern Europe or the Red Sea was available at least second hand. Mycenaean journeys along the Atlantic coastline cannot be completely excluded.

These hypotheses will be dealt with in the following chapters. In our quest, we are being helped by the later Greek historians and geographers, which transmitted to us a broad corpus of mythical and geographical information with often very ancient roots. At this point one word of warning to the strictly scientific reader may be appropriate: Due to the interpretative nature of the myths as a source of information next to archaeological and pictorial evidence, it is almost unavoidable to add a speculative element at times in order to fill the existing gaps of scientific research.

3

References to Time and Dates in the Bronze Age

In the following chapters, I am going to use references to time and chronologies of the Bronze Age as if the dates embedded therein were firmly established. However, when it comes to precise information, there are still uncertainties and interpretations (cp. the recent discussion of the problems around chronologies in Drews 2017, 235ff)

We are separated from the end of the Bronze Age by more than 3000 years. For a period as remote as this, in many instances references to time within historical documents, archaeological finds but also in the myths can often only be established in relative terms, *i.e. relative* to other events, reigns of kings etc. ('during the reign of king.., after the Deucalian flood,..). Archaeologists defined detailed relative chronologies based mainly on distinct pottery styles from certain regions, which by trade arrived in other regions and allowed to date the related finds in the respective locations (Schofield 2007, 20). There are limitations, however, to equate pottery remains with distinct peoples or cultures (Manning 2010, 15).

Egyptian dynastic lists with references to archaeologically attested rulers allow the establishment of relative chronologies as well. Further indications are provided by cross-referencing different known events, *e.g.* between Mesopotamian and Egyptian king lists, based on historical information and thus identifying synchronisms.[4] This interplay of cross-references allows the development of a relative clear and precise chronology of Late Bronze Age Egypt with a degree of uncertainty of around 10 to 20 years (Kitchen 2007, 167ff).

For Bronze Age Greece, these kinds of chronological lists are largely missing. There are several references in the works of Greek historiographers of the Classical and Hellenistic Periods to dates and chronologies, which quote events from mythical times, often with very specific – albeit sometimes inconsistent – references to dates (cp. section 8.2.5).

For a consistent chronography based on annalistic patterns and an absolute chronological system, which allow for a precise dating of events, we find the first examples in Greece only in the late 5th century BCE and the first chronological tables in the even later Hellenistic period (323 – 31 BCE) (Moeller, 2004, 170). An interesting example of a chronological table of events from this period is the so-called 'Parian

---

4 On cross-references between Egyptian and Mesopotamian chronologies cp. Kitchen (2006, 45ff and 2007, 163ff).

Marble', initially positioned on the island of Paros, which lists dates from about 264/3 BCE far back into mythical times starting with the mythical first Athenian king Kekrops and the 'Deucalian Flood'.[5]

In documents written before the 5th century BCE, historiography was not composed in annual lists but in narratives. For these earlier periods an absolute reference point to date events is missing (Moeller 2001, 241 and 2004, 171). Up to the date of the first Olympic Games in 776 BCE – sometimes considered to be the 'beginning of history' by ancient authors – and further down into mythical times ancient scholars created

> *a network of synchronic (e.g. reigns, battles in the same year) as well as diachronic events often based on genealogies and local traditions* (Moeller 2001, 250f, cp. also the discussion in chapter 8.3).

The general historicity of the mythical events was rarely questioned, maybe with the exception of Eratosthenes, who classified this time as some form of proto-history (Grafton 1995, 16 and 22).

Due to various reasons – differing assumptions for generational spans, varying local traditions etc. – the derived dates for the mythical periods contained a plethora of inconsistencies. In addition, the mythical names are generally not archaeologically attested. Early Greek chronography is thus

> *'not just a construction based on generation reckoning by means of genealogies […], but a far more complex and comprehensive tradition'* (Mooshammer 1979 in Moeller 2004, 173).

As a consequence, most modern scholars have general doubts around the historicity of the information contained in these documents about Bronze Age Greece – in marked contrast to the general acceptance of the historic substance of the Egyptian dynastic lists for the New Kingdom as they are transmitted from the Hellenistic priest Manetho, where the royal names rendered in Greek transcription can be related to archaeologically attested pharaohs (Verbrugghe and Wickersham 2001; Luban 2017). Accepted chronologies for the Mycenaean age therefore still depend largely on the comparison of pottery styles, interpretation of pictorial representations and synchronisms to Egyptian and Mesopotamian chronologies.

In some instances there may be information attainable on *absolute* dates *e.g.* via tree-ring (dendrochronology) or C14 dating technologies. The precondition for these technologies is the availability of organic material and wood samples (Manning 2010). Due to necessary calibration methods and problems with the exactitude of the results, there are also limitations in carbon dating however.

One ongoing problem for archaeologists and historians alike lies in a seeming discrepancy between relative and absolute dating for some key events in the LBA (Manning 2010). This discrepancy becomes obvious *e.g.* in the discussion around the timing of the eruption of the Thera volcano at the beginning of the LBA. This eruption is often brought into context with the mythical 'Deucalian Flood' and an important historical anchor for the chronology of the Bronze Age in general.

---

5   Sometimes also called 'Parian Chronicle' (Rotstein 2016).

Based on archaeological relative dating, the Thera eruption may have happened around 1540 BCE or slightly after (Schofield 2007, 20). Archaeologists found pottery of the so called 'floral style' of Late Minoan (LM) IA in the excavated ruins of Akrotiri on Thera, but no pottery of the subsequent 'marine style' of LM IB. The conclusion was that the volcanic eruption on Thera must have happened before the beginning of LM IB and thus some years before 1500 BCE. This date is an important point of reference for the so-called *'low chronology'* for Egypt and the Aegean (cp. the chapter 'Introduction: High and Low Chronology' in Bietak and Hoeflmayer 2007).

The a.m. 'Parian Chronicle' equally places the resulting flood (the 'Deucalian Flood') in the year 1529 BCE (Rotstein 2016, 38). Relative dating based on pottery analysis in connection with destruction layers and several deposits of ash and pumice further point at the possibility that the eruption may have happened in three stages with intervals of several years between 1530 and 1450 BCE (Rohl 2007, 202ff).

Absolute dating technologies based on the C14 analysis of an olive branch found in the Bronze Age layers on Thera however indicate an earlier date around 1600 to 1630 BCE and form the base of the *'high chronology'* (Manning 2010). Absolute and relative dating thus seems to lead to a discrepancy in the dating of the Thera eruption of roughly 100 years. Various discussions and theories emerged how to solve this apparent difference, which seemed to split the historians and archaeologists into two camps.[6]

The apparent discrepancy has recently been called into question however by Boaretto, who points at the problems of absolute dating using olive branches in C14 analyses, because of their unusual growth patterns (Roemer 2018, 2). As it stands, the arguments for the earlier date of the Thera eruption based on absolute dating techniques – and the doubts around them – probably cannot outweigh the case in favor of the later dating around 1500 BCE resulting from the various archaeological and historical references.

A still open question is, how much the myths can contribute to solve the conundrum of relative and absolute dating in the Late Bronze Age. For one, myths contain a plethora of genealogical information and synchronisms, which in some instances may be useful for the establishment of relative chronologies. Furthermore, it seems references within the tales, *e.g.* regarding astronomical events, may provide clues even for absolute dating (Mosenkis 2016, 147ff; Gertoux 2016). These topics are further explored in chapter 8.3. There may be further hints to specific events hidden in the mythological language that yet await a proper consideration.

---

6 A controversial theory promoted by James ('Centuries of Darkness', 1991) and Rohl (2007, esp. 367ff) called the *'new chronology'* eliminates the 'Dark Ages' after the end of the LBA of around 300 years and arrives at much lower dates for events in the LBA. This theory is not generally accepted, though.

4

The Historical and Archaeological Framework of Travel and Mobility in the Bronze Age

The following passages contain a compressed 'tour de force' of several millennia of migration, mobility and development of population groups in Europe, the Near East and northern Africa. A concise overview like this can only be done with a broad brush and is probably incomplete on several accounts. Yet, the developments summarized here are important to understand some of the precursors to the Mycenaean journeys described or assumed in the later chapters.

In this context it is important to note that whilst some pre-historic migrations of people are indisputable, it is notoriously difficult to identify true 'migrations', *i.e.* permanent dislocations of groups of people over some distances, vs. 'mobility' being the broader definition not necessarily including permanent dislocations and also vs. local developments only from the material remains (Knapp 2021).

Nevertheless the available fundus of material, textual, genetic and linguistic evidence indicates that people seemed to rarely have lived in complete isolation from each other. Migrations and mobility are part of human history since our early ancestors have left Africa to settle all over the planet. Predecessors of modern humans reached Europe probably around 800.000 BCE and slowly spread over the continent as hunter-gatherers in spite of various periods of extreme cold, which rendered part of their environment uninhabitable.

Neolithic (ca. 10000 – 6000 BCE)[7]

The 'Neolithic package' consisting of the domestication of animals like sheep, goats and pigs, the farming of cereals and a bit later the usage of pottery[8] spread from Asia Minor and the Levant to Europe from ca. 9500 BCE onwards and reached Greece, esp. the Thessalian plain, around 7500 to 6500 BCE (based on archaeological research by Oezdogan 2011 in Drews 2017, 8; cf. also Cunliffe 2011, 96).

We have to assume that humans already ventured out onto the ocean very early in pre-history (see remarks on potential Mesolithic finds on Crete in Knapp 2018, 33 and

---

7   Chronology after Drews (2017).
8   The spread of ceramics during the Neolithic period started around 6500 BCE (Cunliffe 2011, 96).

Knapp 2021, 46). But it seems that only at the beginning of the Neolithic period seafaring changed the function of the ocean for our ancestors from a mere 'provider of resources' into a 'vector for travel' (Broodbank 2006 in Knapp 2018, 33).

There is indirect evidence – for example the settlements of Neolithic peoples on Mediterranean islands like Cyprus and Crete – for maritime exploration already since around 9000 BCE or 7000 BCE for Crete respectively (Tartaron 2013, 108).[9] Cunliffe assumes that already existing maritime networks could have facilitated the movement of farming communities along the European coastal areas (Cunliffe 2011, 95 and 102). Wherever the new farming communities moved they are likely to have encountered scattered groups of hunter-gatherers and will occasionally have come into contact with them.

The subsequent further spread of the 'Neolithic package' from the Aegean over continental Europe is assumed to have taken place via a southern route by ship along the coastline of southern Europe and a northern route along the Danube river basin and its tributaries from around 6000 BCE onwards. Also the transmission of the 'Neolithic package' via the European riverine systems may have happened by using existing Mesolithic networks (Cunliffe 2011, 102ff, 114ff and 124; Sheppard Baird 2007, 6).

Chalcolithic (ca. 6000 – 3000 BCE)

From about 6000 BCE, pure copper was used for the first metal tools in some parts of Eurasia. The respective era, which lasted until ca. 3000 BCE in the eastern Mediterranean and the Near East, is called the '*Chalcolithic*'. Some of the first metallurgical centres in Europe are to be found on the Balkans dating back to approx. 5500 BCE. Copper in this early phase was tied to elite transactions and had a high exclusivity in terms of utilization (Vandkilde 2016, 106). In spite of the initial uses of metal objects, the lifestyle of a majority of the people in this phase was still predominantly Neolithic.

The know-how about copper smelting spread from these early centres and reached Egypt, parts of central Europe, the Iberian Peninsula and the Atlantic fringe. In the Aegean during this period, the islands and mainland coastlines were gradually settled (Tartaron 2013, 108). Some of these processes will have involved the movement of groups of people as well.

Next to copper, other materials were traded over some distances in this period (Wilkinson 2014, 25). Obsidian was a desired material in the late Neolithic as razor sharp objects could be shaped out of the volcanic glass. In the Aegean, Neolithic people sailed to Melos in the Cycladic islands to obtain this material (Gillis 1993, 65).

Early Bronze Age (ca. 3000 – 2100 BCE)[10]

The Bronze Age commenced in Mesopotamia and the Near East shortly before 3000 BCE with transitional stages and considerable regional differences. '*The beginning of the Bronze Age coincides with the formation of early states, writing and the consolidation of urban life from around 3000 BC in Mesopotamia.*' (Kristiansen and Larsson 2005, 108)

---

9   Cunliffe (2011, 94) points to the fact that hunter-gatherers lived on Cyprus as early as 10.500 BCE and could have only gotten there by boat. Drews (2017, 6f) puts the colonization of of Cyprus at ca. 9000 BCE and of Crete at ca. 6600 BCE. Cf. also Sheppard Baird 2007, 3.

10 The Bronze Age chronology given in this chapter follows the eastern Mediterranean dates. The northern, central and western parts of Europe have entered the Bronze Age and its sub-stages later as indicated here (Pare 2000).

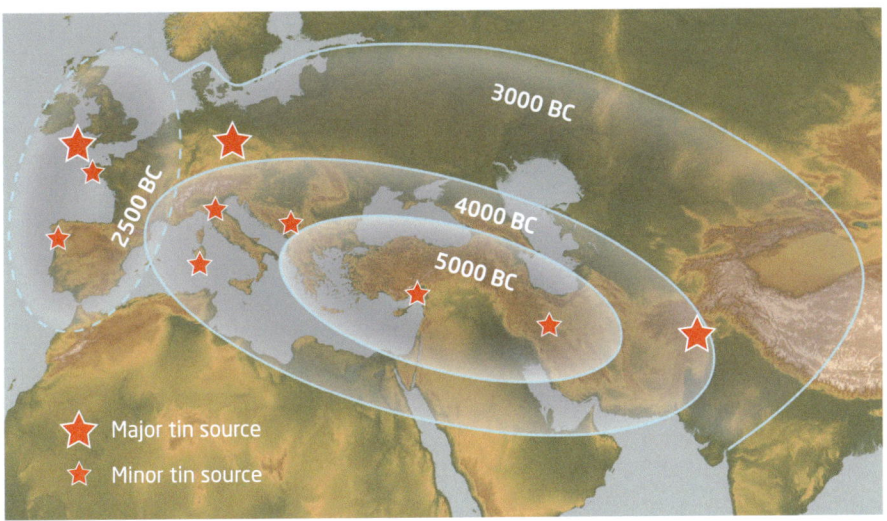

Fig. 1: The spread of metallurgy (map: Olav Odé, after: Vandkilde 2016, 15).

In the *Early Bronze Age* (EBA) mostly arsenic copper[11] has been used for the production of Bronze. Almost in parallel, some areas began to experiment with 'true bronze', *i.e.* an alloy of approx. 90% copper and 10% tin, which improved the quality of the Bronze further.

Early metallurgical locations in the Bronze Age, which were often situated in proximity to tin sources, were quick to adopt the new alloy. *'The earliest copper and tin alloys are dated to c. 3000 and found in Anatolia'* (Kristiansen and Larsson 2005, 110). Tin Bronze technology spread from its origins in Mesopotamia, the Near East and Anatolia to the Aegean, subsequently to all parts of Europe, to Asia and eventually even reached China during the 3rd millennium BCE (Vandkilde 2016, 105; Rahmstorf 2010, 184).[12]

At the beginning of the Early Bronze Age different cultural groups were scattered across Europe and the Near East. Cultural centres – often also centres of copper and bronze metallurgy – emerged in the Balkans, the Caucasus region, in Anatolia and in the southern part of the Iberian Peninsula. Bronze production in these centres remained by and large elite controlled and primarily focused on local demand. Access to metal supplies was a crucial factor for development (Rahmstorf 2010, 683).

In *Egypt*, the first dynasties of pharaohs after the unification of Upper and Lower Egypt built huge pyramids still largely with copper tools. Romer (2012, 282) estimates the copper used in these tools for the construction of the step pyramid in Saqqara for pharaoh Djoser around 2650 BCE amounted to 70 tons. In the course of the 3rd millennium BCE bronze items also reached Egypt.

The city-states of *Mesopotamia* were early cultural centres in the Bronze Age, but the land 'between the rivers' was also a thoroughfare for metals, especially tin, from central

---

11　Copper with more than 1% arsenic added in the smelting process to improve the casting behavior and to harden the final alloy.
12　Regarding the connectivity towards the east, esp. of eastern Anatolia and western central Asia also in terms of metal trade during this period cp. Wilkinson (2014).

Asian sources in Afghanistan traded into the Mediterranean Basin via the Indus region from 2200 BCE onwards (Rahmstorf 2010, 690 and 2015, 198).

In the *Aegean*, settlements on the Cycladic Islands and Crete but as well in Greece (Lerna) and Troy on the western Anatolian coastline have an EBA blooming period between 2550 and 2200 BCE (Rahmstorf 2010, 680). Connections existed between the islands, to the Balkans and to the Carpathian Basin.

On the western end of the Mediterranean, one of the Early Bronze Age metallurgic centres in Europe developed around the *Los Millares* culture in southern Spain, which emerged in a heavily mineralized area since about 3200 BCE and flourished between ca. 3000 and 2600 BCE (Kristiansen 2012, 166). The Los Millares people produced predominantly arsenic bronze. The exploitation of the treasured metallic minerals made heavy fortifications around the Los Millares settlements necessary (Sheppard Baird 2007, 15ff). Semi-urbanized settlements emerged on the Iberian Peninsula (Kristiansen and Larsson 2005, 109). A monumental complex, which hosted up to 1000 inhabitants has been excavated near the modern city of Almeria.

The remains uncovered in southern Iberia from this period also point at a stratified society with an unequal distribution of wealth. Further, there are notable similarities of the architecture of the Los Millares culture to contemporary structures on the Balearic Islands and Sardinia, which may indicate connectivity already at this early date. Also the vast copper, silver and gold mines north of Huelva began to be worked as early as the 3rd millennium BCE (Sheppard Baird 2007, 15). After ca. 2600 BCE this culture collapsed and transformed into smaller centres of the later Maritime Bell Beaker groups (Kristiansen 2012, 166)

The rest of Europe outside the Mediterranean Basin, *i.e.* especially the northern parts developed at a somewhat slower pace and remained in the Neolithic for longer. After 3000 BCE, in an abrupt change the so-called Corded Ware culture spread over northern and parts of eastern Europe largely replacing the earlier Funnel Beaker culture (discussions in Wentink 2020, 32; Drews 2017, 134ff; Vandkilde 2016, 106 and Kristiansen 2012, 167ff).

The assumed movements of groups of people from western Asia into Europe were sometimes being brought into connection with the spread of Indo-European language groups (Anthony 2007, Kristiansen 2012).[13] Recent DNA analysis indeed shows '*evidence of a widespread influx of genetic newcomers*' in this period, who were closely related to populations from the Pontic steppe (Wentink 2020, 32).

Then from about 2750 BCE onward the so-called '*Bell Beaker*' complex begins to spread from western to central Europe probably as a mix of cultural diffusion and migration movements (Olalde et al. 2018). In the 2nd half of the 3rd millennium BCE the Bell Beaker phenomenon is attested for as a new set of material culture '*from Portugal to Poland and from Scotland to Sicily*' (Wentink 2020, 38).

Representatives of this cultural phenomenon, which includes major regional and increasing linguistic differences, seem to have partially a steppe ancestry (with the exception of the Iberian Peninsula, where an influx of Steppe DNA is noticeable only after 2000 BCE; cp. Olalde et al. 2018), but the genetic signature also points at significant intermarriages with the earlier Neolithic local population. The communalities within the Bell Beaker complex could thus signify a cultural link between different groups in a

---

13   It needs to be stated that the alleged movements still await final archaeological substantiation.

period of increasing mobility and exchange of goods over larger distances in major parts of Europe. Wentink (2020, 38 and 236) speaks of a common 'social front' between members of different and distant population groups to explain the communalities. The Bell Beaker phenomenon finally disappears around 1800 BCE.

Middle Bronze Age (2100 – 1600 BCE)

The Middle Bronze Age (MBA) covers the period from around 2100 to 1600 BCE and sees the emergence of some forceful civilizations and dynasties and an increase in long distance economic exchange focused on the procurement of metals.

In *Egypt* the dynasties of the Middle Kingdom (2055 – 1650 BCE) emerged after the First Intermediate Period, which had ended the Old Kingdom. After a period of reunification during the 11th dynasty and a consolidation of power during the 12th, especially pharaoh Senusret I (1971 – 1926 BCE) extended commercial and diplomatic contacts into Canaan as far as Ugarit. Amenemhat III (1860 – 1814 BCE) established semi-permanent mining camps in the Sinai in order to secure the flow of metals into Egypt.

The first major civilization in Europe evolved on *Crete* late in the third millennium BCE and stood in commercial and diplomatic contact with the Egyptian Middle Kingdom. The modern denomination for this civilization is termed '*Minoan*' after the mythical king Minos. The palace-centered society of the Minoans developed a naval based sphere of influence and trade (sometimes called a 'thalassocracy' implying also some form of political hegemony, cp. discussions in Kristiansen and Larsson 2005, 96 and Mull 2017, 73) in the eastern and part of the western Mediterranean including the Cycladic islands and parts of the coastal areas of western Anatolia.

In *Asia Minor*, Assyrian commercial settlements (Assyrian 'karum') like the trading post Kanesh connected Anatolia via the Tigris River to the Mesopotamian cultural centres, esp. Ashur. In Kanesh an extensive commercial documentation has been excavated illustrating the trade links within Anatolia and to Mesopotamia. The area also formed a nucleus for the later Hittite empire.

Around the coastal areas of *southern Spain* the chalcolithic Los Millares culture was followed by the *El Argar* culture around 2200 BCE, whose people were early adopters of the Tin Bronze technology. A regular use of tin bronzes can be attested on the Iberian Peninsula for the time of 1800 to 1700 BCE (Rahmstorf 2015, 187f).

In *central and western Europe*, the Bronze Age began some centuries later than in the Mediterranean Basin. For these parts of the continent *'the earliest appearance of a regular bronze-using economy is to be found in Britain and Ireland in the period 2200 – 2000 BC, after which it spreads eastwards and southwards through Europe, reaching all parts by 1400-1300 BC'* (Cunliffe 2011, 181).

The *Bell Beaker culture* in Western Europe on the *Atlantic fringe* entered the Bronze Age around 2200 BCE. These mobile groups were experts in boatbuilding and mining. They connected the Iberian Peninsula with the western Mediterranean, north Africa, Sicily, coastal France and north western Europe (Kristiansen 2012, 166). Access to tin deposits and Bronze metallurgy brought prosperity to their centres in Britain (esp. the 'Wessex' culture close to Cornwall), Brittany (Armorica), and northern Portugal soon after 2000 BCE (Drews 2017, 136).

With the spread of the Bell Beaker culture from western into central Europe, the respective groups mixed with Corded Ware populations. The Unetice culture based in today's Poland, Czech Republic and Germany as an amalgam of Bell Beaker and Corded Ware elements began to use and trade tin Bronze around the same time. From 2000 to 1600 this 'merged' culture formed an important link in the metal networks that connected southern Europe with Scandinavia, whilst tin was being traded over some considerable distances over the whole of Europe (Ling and Uhner 2014, 25f; Drews 2017, 135; recently Norgaard et al. 2021).

The time from the second half of the third to the second millennium BCE witnessed two crucial developments encompassing many areas of Bronze Age Eurasia: For one, many societies became dependent on copper based metallurgy on a larger scale and for the first time to metal resources procured from distant areas. To participate in this development, it became imperative to trade with outside regions (Vandkilde 2016, 105).

With improved nautical technologies, marine traffic increased. Overall,

> 'exchange networks saw a flood of varied commodities transported over very considerable distances. It was almost as though the natural routeways of Europe had coalesced into one great system of intercommunications.' (Cunliffe 2011, 179)

Cunliffe stresses that these Middle Bronze Age (MBA) economical exchange networks did not come into existence out of the blue:

> 'Networks of exchange had long been in operation. What changed now was the extent of those networks and the sheer volume of materials that flowed through the arteries of Europe. Most important was bronze.' As a consequence of new technologies in shipbuilding, but also for land transport and warfare, '[m]obility begins to break down the earlier cultural isolation' which was characteristic for the Chalcolithic and the EBA (quotations taken from Cunliffe 2011, 181f).

The more widespread use of metal objects started to trickle down the layers of society and stopped to be elitist. Overall from around 2200 BCE we are seeing a breakthrough of bronze metallurgy in Eurasia (Vandkilde 2016, 107, 109).

The second development with far reaching consequences throughout Eurasia starting from around 2100 to 1700 BCE was the invention of the spoked-wheel chariot and improved weaponry like swords, spears and the compound bow. The new weapons shot from chariots as mobile platforms mobilized Indo-European speaking warrior groups from the steppe somewhere between the Ural and the Caucasus mountains (Drews 2017, 90ff). These groups soon afterwards made their presence felt and began to form martial elites in the Carpathian Basin, the Near East, around the eastern Mediterranean and maybe even up to northern Europe.[14] Within these moves they seem to have targeted especially the strategically important early centres of metallurgy.

The disruptions caused by these mobile warrior groups contributed to the end of the Middle Bronze Age. In *Anatolia* the invasion of chariot driven warriors, who superimposed themselves over an indigenous Anatolian population, eventually lead to the foundation of

---

14 Drews (2017) discusses the respective moves of the mobile population groups into the Near East 113f, the Carpathian Basin (140ff), southern Scandinavia (156ff) and Italy (161ff).

the Hittite kingdom around 1800 BCE. The Hittites called themselves 'Neshites', probably after their original settlement centre in the 'karum' Kanesh.

In *Egypt* the so-called 2nd Intermediate Period (ca. 1750 – 1550 BCE) included a time of foreign occupation of northern Egypt by the so-called 'Hyksos' of presumably Canaanite or Levantine origin, maybe also including some Indo-European groups (Rohl 2007, 235; Drews 2017, 119ff). The chariot warriors arrived in Greece around 1650 BCE, formed a military aristocracy in some strategically important centres and are potentially the origins of the so-called 'Achaeans' (further discussed below and in Drews 2017, 122 and 176ff).

Late Bronze Age (LBA) (1600 – 1100 BCE)

The Late Bronze Age commences at around 1600 BCE in the Mediterranean Basin. In terms of bronze production technology, the Late Bronze Age sees the widespread of 'true bronze', an alloy of ca. 90% copper and 10% tin. A wider availability of tin from Mesopotamian sources may have played a role in this development and may also have spurred a more intense copper production, especially on Cyprus (Constantinou 2012, 8f).

The commercial exchange in this period reaches new heights and connects the major cultural centres in the eastern Mediterranean, like the Egyptian New Empire, the Levantine ports, Hittite Anatolia and Mycenaean Greece. Enormous amounts of metal were in circulation and suggest organized forms of directed and long-range transport and trade (Vandkilde 2016, 110).

In *Egypt* after the expulsion of the foreign Hyksos rulers the Late Bronze Age bears witness to the rise of the forceful 18th, 19th and 20th dynasties, which entertained intensive commercial and diplomatic contacts with the other powers in the region. With the territorial conquests of Thutmosis III (1504 – 1450 BCE), Egypt attained its greatest geographical reach ever in the 15th century BCE. The extent of diplomatic contacts with the other powers of the age is documented in the so-called 'Amarna-letters', representing a record of correspondence found in the capital of pharaoh Akhenaten (1379 – 1326 BCE) (Moran 1992).

Almost in parallel the *Hittite* empire reaches the zenith of its power in Anatolia. Hittites and Egyptians as the two dominant military powers in the eastern Mediterranean clash in 1274 BCE in the battle of Kadesh in Syria, which ends inconclusive, even if the young pharaoh Ramses II claims a great victory in a temple inscription. In the subsequent status quo, which was formally sealed in a peace contract, the Hittites remain in control of the important metal producing and distributing centres of Cyprus and Ugarit (Bell 2012, 181).

Minoan Crete as the first European civilization falls into a period of decline after 1600 BCE. One reason assumed for the diminished power of the Minoans may have to do with longer-term effects connected with the eruption of the volcano on Thera/Santorini around 1540 BCE, which is often connected with the mythical Deucalian Flood.[15]

In the *western Mediterranean* the *Nuraghic* culture in Sardinia began to exploit the rich mines for copper and lead on the island from 1800 BCE onwards. The name stems from tower-like structures (nuraghen), which contained one or several inner 'tholos' chambers. Further west on the Iberian Peninsula, the *El Argar culture* seems to have been connected to the Mycenaean trade network after 1450 BCE until its collapse around 1350 BCE (discussed in Shepard Baird 2007, 18f).

---

15 Absolute chronology puts the eruption earlier around 1625 BCE. The date is discussed in Schofield 2007, 66f and Cunliffe 2011, 196.

Date	Egypt	Crete	Cyclades	Mainland Greece	Cyprus
1700 BC			Eruption of Thera (ca. 1625-1540 BC)	Grave Circle B	Late Cypriot
1600 BC	New Kingdom Eighteenth Dynasty (ca.1570 BC)	Late Minoan IA	Late Cycladic	Late Helladic I Grave Circle A	
1550 BC		Late Minoan IB Destruction of Palaces		Late Helladic IIA	Late Cypriot IB
1500 BC					
1450 BC		Late Minoan II Mycenaeans control Crete	Mycenaeans in control	Late Helladic IIB Mycenaean control of Aegean	Late Cypriot IIA
1400 BC		Late Minoan IIIA		Late Helladic IIIA Mycenaean growth in Levant	Late Cypriot IIB
1300 BC	Nineteenth Dynasty	Late Minoan IIIB		Late Helladic IIIB Expansion of Mycenaean Palaces	Late Cypriot IIC
1200 BC	Reign of Ramses III (ca. 1198-116 BC	Late Minoan IIIC		Late Helladic IIIB	Late Cypriot IIIA
1100 BC					Late Cypriot IIB

Fig. 2: Chronology of the Late Bronze Age (LBA) in the eastern Mediterranean (After: McMillan 2016, v).

Late Bronze Age Greece – The 'Mycenaean Age'

The timing and context of the 'coming of the Greeks' to their future homeland in the southern Balkans is still disputed between archaeologists and linguists, many of which assume first Indo-European movements to Greece in waves maybe already around 3100 BCE and later in 2200 BCE at the transition from EH II to EH III.[16] According to one theory, an Indo-European warrior elite (*i.e.* the 'Achaeans') finally migrated into Greece around 1700 to 1650 BCE and established itself in strategically important fortified strongholds, from which they later on extended their influence militarily and via intermarriages over some of the pre-existing kingdoms (Woudhuizen 2013; Kristiansen 2012, 176).[17]

The later dominance of Mycenae has given the modern name to the LBA culture in Greece in total as 'Mycenaean'.[18] Next to the immigrant military stratum, this LBA culture in Greece includes elements of the indigenous pre- or old Indo-European population reckognizable primarily via identifiable linguistic roots, possibly of Thraco-Phrygian origin and sometimes called 'pelasgian' (cp. Haarmann (2017) arguing for pre-Indo-

---

16 A considerable number of archaeologists connect the destruction level in many places of Bronze Age Greece at around 2300 to 2200 BCE, the transition from EH II to EH III, with the 'Arrival of the Greeks'. Cp. Anthony 2007, Rahmstorf 2010, 682 and 692, Robbins 2001, 117ff. Woudhuizen (2013, 6) reckognizes the first Indo-European immigration wave at 3100 BCE and ascribes them to the 'Pelasgians'. The 'second wave' of immigrants according to Woudhuizen were of Thraco-Phrygian origin.

17 *E.g.* Drews 2017, 122; Harding 2005; Other authors date the immigration earlier into the end of the 3rd millennium BCE. Dickinson (2019, 35f) argues for a gradual emergence of elite structures in Mycenaean Greece.

18 Cp. the discussion of the term 'Mycenaean' in its geographical and chronological dimensions in Tartaron (2013, 7).

European origin of the 'Pelasgians'; Woudhuizen (2013, 6) claims an old Indo-European ancestry for this stratum).[19]

The rise of Mycenaean Greece to a regional power in the LBA can be structured into three phases, which correspond to a certain sequence in distinct ceramic styles (Blake 2008, 4ff):

From 1600 to ca. 1450 BCE (phases Late Helladic (LH) I and II A) the Mycenaeans consolidated their power in Greece. In Mycenae, shaft graves were excavated by Heinrich Schliemann in the late 19th century, which date back to 1600 to 1500 BCE. These shaft graves contained rich finds, which marked a break to the previous cultural strata of the Middle Helladic (MH) period. Judging from the artifacts uncovered, the main cultural influence for the Mycenaeans in this period seems to have come from Minoan Crete, whilst Anatolian and Egyptian traces are also visible (Tartaron 2013, 12f).

The Mycenaeans in this early phase seem to have obtained their metals (*i.e.* silver, lead and probably copper) mainly from the Laurion mines in Attica (Schofield 2007, 62). Tin may have come from sources in Asia via Mesopotamia, but likely also from Britain. In the shaft graves amber from the Baltic or British coastline has been found. This amber has been interpreted as a by-product of the tin trade from the 'Wessex culture' in south England, which reached Greece via Gaul and was probably transported on along the coast of Italy towards Greece and other centres in the eastern Mediterranean (Maran 2004; Harding in Drews 2017, 180).

Since it is assumed that the Mycenaeans at this early stage did not engage in a direct trade within the eastern Mediterranean, the gold and luxury goods of Egyptian origin found in the shaft graves may have reached them via Crete (Schofield 2007, 63). The Minoans during this period retained a strong presence in the eastern Mediterranean, whilst Mycenaean trade was not very active in this area in LH I and trended westward, where first contacts in the western Mediterranean were established (Blake 2008; Mee 2008 in Drews 2017, 215). Mycenaean pottery in this phase of LH I appeared in southern Italy, Sicily and the Aeolian islands (Blake 2008 in Tartaron 2013, 22).

From ca. 1450 to about 1200 BCE (phases LH II B, LH III A and LH III B, the 'Palatial Period') a few palace based power centres emerged in Mycenaean Greece probably as the result of consolidation and internal struggles for regional hegemony (Tartaron 2013, 14 and 21; also Woudhuizen 2013). Some archaeologists even argue for a unified Mycenaean kingdom or 'empire' later in this period (Desborough 1972 in Dickinson 2019, 34; also Kelder 2010), others are more cautious and postulate a more decentralized cultural entity.[20] At any rate, Mycenae seems to have been the most important settlement and centre of power, hence the term 'Mycenaean age' for this period, others being Thebes,

---

19 According to the Danaus myth, the Pelasgians of the Peloponnese later changed their name into 'Danaans' (Apollodorus 'The Library of Greek Mythology', II, 1.4: "After he had taken control of the country, Danaos named its inhabitants the Danaans after himself").

20 Dickinson (2019, 42): "..a mosaic of principalities large and small, the leading ones 'palace societies' with a literate administration, others more simply organized but relatively stable 'chiefdoms', others again loose and potentially unstable tribal groupings."

Fig. 3: The Lion Gate of Mycenae (photo: Haris Andronos, stock.adobe.com).

Pylos and Orchomenos.[21] Records in these Mycenaean palaces are being kept in Linear B script, which renders an early stage of the Greek language.

Around 1450 BCE, Mycenaean Greeks seem to have taken over the Minoan palaces in northern Crete[22], inherited the Minoan trading empire in the Mediterranean and taken control of the Aegean Sea (Kristiansen and Suchowska-Ducke 2015, 362). At the beginning of this sub-period, Mycenaeans are for the first time depicted on wall paintings in Egypt, which some researchers take as an indication for first direct contacts of Mycenaeans to the land of the pharaohs (in the tomb of the palace official Rekhmire, Schofield 2007, 71f).

From LH III A onwards, Mycenaean objects (mostly ceramics) with a stylistic centre in the Argolid appear in bigger numbers in the Aegean, Cyprus and the Levant (Manning and Hulin 2005, 8). The Mycenaean world in this time underwent a period of rapid cultural and economic expansion. This is the time of the Mycenaean 'Koine' (area of relatively uniform cultural expressions) and the apex of Mycenaean civilization, which sees a spreading of typical Mycenaean pottery of LH III A and LH III B1 all over the Mediterranean (Kristiansen and Suchowska-Ducke 2015, 362; Tartaron 2013, 17). Mycenaean contacts seem to have extended to the western Mediterranean and – towards the end of the Late Bronze Age – probably also to the Black Sea area.

Factors that are likely to have contributed to the ascent and regional spread of the Mycenaean culture are nautical innovations but also the circumstance that Greece is positioned at a unique

---

21　Dickinson (2019, 43); Thebes may have been on par with Mycenae or even more important prior to its destruction around the end of the 13th century BCE. Also Banyai (2019, 137ff) sees indications that for a period in later LH III B – *i.e.* in the second half of the 13th century BCE – Thebes was the most important palatial centre.

22　According to a theory by Wace discussed in Schofield (2007, 70). Dickinson (2019, 37) offers alternative views to the commonly held belief of a Mycenaean 'conquest' of Knossos.

and strategically beneficial interface of maritime routes between the cultural centres of the eastern and the mineral rich areas of the western Mediterranean as well as the Black Sea and – via riverine and land routes – to central and northern Europe (Kelder 2019).

Around 1200 to 1180 BCE the palatial structures that were characteristic for the LBA come to a relatively abrupt end (recently discussed in Muehlenbruch 2021, 159 – 177). We see a disruption in the archaeological record of many cities in the eastern Mediterranean and also a reduction of Mycenaean pottery exported to the trade centres within this region. This cultural break is sometimes ascribed to the impact of the so-called 'Sea Peoples', which seem to have attacked and destroyed important trading hubs.[23] As described above, also the Mycenaean palace culture collapses around this time. Tartaron (2013, 19) summarizes – importantly for the focus of this book – that *'long-distance exchange in raw materials and exotic finished goods is central to the story of both prosperity and collapse'*.

In the later years between ca. 1200 and 1150 BCE contemporary to or shortly after the collapse of the Mycenaean palace structures, LH III C ceramics are replaced by locally made copies (LH III C1) in many places of the eastern Mediterranean maybe pointing towards migrations of former members of the elite into new territories (contra: Knapp 2021).

The demise of the Mycenaean palace culture on mainland Greece is followed by the so-called 'dark ages' with some significant cultural breaks and migration moves. Recent analysis allude to the fact that the 'dark ages' may not have been as 'dark' in all areas of Greece as previously assumed (cp. Muehlenbruch 2021, 159ff), but we are faced with the likely loss of literacy for some time.[24] Some Mycenaean Greeks resettle on Cyprus and maybe in Cilicia and the Levant. They bring cultural features with them, which became integrated into the local cultures in the transition from the LBA to the Early Iron Age (Knapp 2012, 46).

The 10th and 9th centuries BCE then see the beginning of Greek colonization efforts driven initially by Euboean traders, but soon followed by colonists from various cities in Greece. Dickinson (2006 in Tartaron 2013, 22) clarifies that in the post-palatial world in Greece of the 12th century BCE maritime interaction continued, but with significant changes regarding scale and content. What had disappeared was the *'well-organized and regulated system of diplomatic and commercial exchanges in the Near East.'*

Also the long-distance ties were cut, if not quite as completely as once thought. Knossos and Enkomi for example continued to be vibrant nodes of international trade throughout the Early Iron Age (Kotsonas 2016; Manning and Hulin 2005, 5; Muehlenbruch 2021, 168). It thus appears that the *'thriving interregional relations of the fourteenth and thirteenth centuries were more the product of exceptional circumstances'* (Tartaron 2013, 23). Let us then go a bit deeper in the analysis, what was so exceptional about the trading relationships in the LBA in the following chapters.

---

23 Other theories and a catastrophic combination of various factors have been proposed as alternative explanations for the cultural break (Cline 2014; Knapp and Manning 2016).

24 Regarding literary traditions in Greece from the Mycenaean until the Classical Period, the break during the 'dark ages' and certain continuities in Crete cp. Haarmann (2017, 278ff). Haarmann ascribes a 'bridging function' to Crete in the context of the introduction of an alphabetic script. A different theory is expressed by Lane Fox, who sees the Euboian Greeks during the 10th to 8th centuries as intermediaries, before the alphabetic script is more widely used by Greeks and eventually the Etruscans (cp. Lane Fox 2009, 159). Waal (2018, 119) argues for a continuation of the written tradition by an early adaptation of the Phoenician alphabet during the 'Dark Ages' in Greece.

5

The Economic Background of Bronze Age Long Distance Travel

Amongst the drivers of transcontinental exchanges in the LBA, evidently economic factors played a key role. Next to a state-directed gift exchange between the palatial centres in the eastern Mediterranean – often based on an expected reciprocity (Panagiotopoulos 2006, 396) – also a variety of bigger and smaller scale commercial transactions have taken place.[25]

Archives uncovered in Ugarit bear witness of large scale commercial transactions conducted by professional merchants connected to the palace, but also acting independently (Bell 2012). Commercial exchanges are also captured on wall paintings in tombs of several Egyptian high-ranking officials. Merchants as a distinct group within eastern Mediterranean Bronze Age societies become evident in Ugarit and in Cyprus, but less pronounced in Mycenaean Greece (van Wijngaarden 2012, 68).

Tartaron (2013, 6) stresses the additional importance of smaller scale networks and transactions, which are less well documented. In total, the goods traded will have encompassed luxury items, textiles, oils, salt and many other items, but most importantly metals (Kristiansen 2016, 157f).

In the following paragraphs we will look into the structure of demand and supply for metals in the Bronze Age, the trade routes and forms of exchange and finally the emerging trading networks that came to the fore.

The Demand Structure for Metals

In the emerging markets[26] of the Bronze Age during the LBA the cultural centres around the eastern Mediterranean and the Near East (Egypt, the Hittite empire, Babylon, the Mycenaeans) created a high *demand* for metals, esp. for copper and tin, the components of 'true bronze'. This is especially true after bronze items became geographically and socially widespread, *i.e.* after the 'take off' of the Bronze culture in the MBA from around 2200 BCE, but especially after tin became more widely available ca. 1600 BCE (Constantinou 2012, 8).

Bronze was needed in high quantities for weapons, tools and other household- and luxury items since it was harder than pure copper (Mull 2017, 133ff). Bronze sickles were

---

25 Gillis 1993, 61; Schofield 2007, 102; van Wijngaarden 2012, 62; A sharp distinction between commercial trade for profit and state directed exchanges has sometimes been called into question (cf. van Wijngaarden 2012, 68).
26 A discussion on the existence of early 'markets' can be found in Rahmstorf (2016, 292ff).

used to harvest grain. Bronze tools were needed to build monumental structures from stone (chisels, knives, adzes), but also from wood (*e.g.* ships, houses, see Vandkilde 2016, 107).

During the Bronze Age another important driver of demand for metals were luxury items exchanged between the royal courts. Documented 'gifts' in the Amarna Letters and metal supplies identified at royal palaces in the eastern Mediterranean and Mesopotamia often reach weights of hundreds of kilogramms. (Moran 1992; Earle et al. 2015, 638) .

A further important driver of demand for metals and especially bronze was warfare and aggression as is documented by the quantities of arms and armor found throughout Europe (Cunliffe 2011, 182). Drews (2017) points at a seemingly increasing militarism across Europe during the LBA, for which swords, lances and arrows in new quantities are indicative. Ling et al. (2019) have documented the astonishing number of swords found in central and northern Europe from this period of time.

Whilst in northern Europe and Scandinavia an annual metal demand of 2.5 to 4 tons have been calculated, the aggregate demand in the eastern Meditgerranean must have been a lot higher. The commodity flows of the age fostered an increasing *social stratification* with rich traders attached to royal courts channeling considerable metal volumes into the targeted markets (discussion in Earle et al. 2015, 638 and Bell 2012, 180ff). At the same time, we see a 'democratization' of Bronze, with Bronze tools permeating all layers of the societies.

One factor driving trade networks during the LBA was the fact that the locations of metal supply often were remote to the cultural centrs of high metal demand (Ling et al. 2019, 2). The rising demand for metals led to various forms of *bulk trade*, by caravan and by ship. The 'Uluburun Ship' found in the waters off the Turkish coast with 11 tons of copper and tin on board bears witness to this development. Overall the availability of copper and tin thus became equal in importance for the Late Bronze Age societies as crude oil is for the world economy of today (Bell 2012, 181).

The Supply Structure for Metals and Points of Origin

On the *supply* side of metal ores, we are faced with a differentiated picture in Europe. As stated above, *copper* was relatively abundant and thus accessible in the eastern, central and western Mediterranean Basin (esp. on the southern Iberian Peninsula) as well as in the Alps[27], the Balkans, Anatolia and the Black Sea area. Also in northern and western Europe copper was mined, esp. in Britain (O' Brien 2015).

Oxidized or sulphidic copper minerals were also available for bronze production within the Mediterranean Basin in great quantities *e.g.* in Cyprus, in Sardinia, the southern Iberian Peninsula, probably in Laurion on Attica and in Anatolia (esp. in Ergani Maden, cp. Constantinou 2012, 7). Cyprus developed into one of the main copper suppliers of the later LBA and becomes tangible in textual sources from around 1900 BCE onwards (Knapp 2018, 171).[28] Mari and Babylon imported Cypriot copper from ca. 1950 BCE and 1750 BCE onwards, Minoan Crete from the 16th century BCE followed by Mycenaean Greece and the Hittite empire in the 15th century BCE. Copper exports from Cyprus to Egypt intensified

---

27   In Saint Veran in the western Alps copper mines are estimated to have yielded 71 tons of copper p.a. (Drews 2017, 136).

28   The discovery of copper in Cyprus dates back to the EBA. Textual evidence points at exporting activities from ca. 1900 BCE onwards. Archaeologically this development can as yet only be supported from LBA onwards (Mantzourani et al. 2019, 98ff).

during the Amarna period in the 14th century BCE as documented by the 'Amarna letters' (Constantinou 2012, 7, 9,12).[29]

In terms of output capacities, we have estimates for production volumes that reach from 10 tons p.a. in Austria, 50 tons p.a. overall for Britain and Ireland and up to 200.000 tons over the whole of antiquity in Cyprus suggesting an average copper production of over 100 tons annually on the island (Earle et al. 2015, 638; O'Brien 2015; Constantinou in O'Brien 2015; 61).

Estimating the total copper production in Europe p.a. for the LBA[30], one has to take additional mining centres *e.g.* in Sardinia, southern Iberia, Anatolia, Greece and the Balkans into account. O'Brien lists 47 known copper mines in Europe – albeit with the exclusion of important centres like Cyprus, Anatolia and Scandinavia (O'Brien 2015, 33). With an average annual output of ca. 5 tons of copper per mine (*i.e.* 200 ingots of 25 kg.) based on the average for Britain and Ireland (50 tons p.a. for 8 mines) and Cyprus (100 tons p.a. for 19 mines) one would arrive at a rough estimate of ca. 350 to 400 tons p.a. for the copper production capacity of Europe in total.

One has to assume, though, that traces of some copper mines have not been found yet or have disappeared when copper ores have been mined in the same source in more recent times. If the number of copper mines including the ones not discovered yet has been higher by 20%, the copper capacity would probably be closer to 500 tons p.a. with Cyprus holding around 20% to 25% of this copper capacity.[31]

This rough estimate for the production capacity in total would assume that all mines are working in parallel. However, whilst for each period a few dominant sources can be identified, the importance of certain mines shifted between the periods (Ling et al. 2019). Overall the production volumes may thus have been below the a.m. estimate for the average annual capacity in total.

All over Europe supply and supply chains changed and switched over time. Whilst the Nordic Bronze Age began ca. 2100 BCE with supplies of metal reaching Scandinavia from Austria and Slovakia (copper) via Unetician hubs in central Europe as well as tin from Britain, these supply chains came to a halt from 1600 BCE with the downfall of the Unetice culture (Norgaard et al. 2021). From 1600 to 1500 BCE important copper sources were the Great Orme mine in Wales, Mitterberg in Austria and mines in Slovakia. During this time, metals were transported north via an 'eastern route' with access to the Carpathian Basin. In this period also Baltic amber seems to have been traded down to Mycenaean Greece via this 'eastern route' (Norgaard et al. 2021).

From 1500 BCE onwards the Welsh supply dried out and also the eastern Alps lost in importance as a metal supplier for northern Europe whilst northern Italian copper began to appear in volume and was traded north on a 'western route' utilizing the riverine systems. Only a bit later, first copper supplies via the Atlantic trading networks from the Iberian Peninsula (Huelva, Jaen) gained in importance for northern Europe and at some point maybe also for supplies to the eastern Mediterranean. This Atlantic network emerged as a major trading route finally around 1300 BCE. From this time on Mediterranean ores, esp.

---

29 On the 'Amarna-letters' cp. chapter 4 'The Late Bronze Age' and Moran (1992).
30 This estimate excludes the copper mined in the Ural mountains and the Caucasus.
31 Estimate by the author : 47 mines x 5 tons p.a. = 235 t p.a.. Add Cyprus (100 tons p.a.), Scandinavia and Anatolia.

from Iberia and Sardinia, were the main sources of metal supply for Scandinavia (Ling et al. 2019, 24, 26f and 32; Ling and Uhner 2014; Kristiansen 2016, 166; Norgaard et al 2021).

Also other metals, esp. *tin* as the other component of true Bronze, had to be procured often over considerable distances. Not all tin sources have been identified so far, but it seems that tin was available during the Bronze Age mainly in Britain at Cornwall, in western Iberia, potentially in the Erzgebirge Mountains (Bohemia) and in central Asia (Afghanistan).[32] Central Asian tin has reached Europe since the 24th century BCE, but may have become more important after the only Anatolian tin source in the Taurus Mountains at Kestel Goltepe had been abandoned already about 1840 BCE (discussions on the availability of tin and the trade routes in Earle et al. 2015, 635, 637 and 639, Rahmstorf 2010, 690, 684 and 689f; Mull 2017, 120ff; Schofield 2007, 103; Sheppard Baird 2007; Constantinou 2012, 7).

Tin may have become more widely available with the additional exploitation of alluvial deposits (sediments in flowing rivers and streams) in Nuzi near the Zagros Mountains in Mesopotamia in the LBA after 1600 BCE. The Greek word for tin 'kassiteros' even derived from the Babylonian dynasty of the Kassites, who controlled the production and trade of tin from Mesopotamia (Constantinou 2012, 8f).

Overall, tin had to be supplied over long distances from central Asia, Mesopotamia, the Iberian Peninsula and northern Europe to the cultural centres in the eastern Mediterranean. The distance to the areas of demand made trans-regional directional trade incl. complex and long logistical chains necessary (Vandkilde 2016, 106; Pare 2000, 29ff).

Translated into transport volumes, 350 to 500 tons of copper mined p.a. would translate into 40 to 50 shiploads of the Uluburun type annually, although it needs to be taken into account that some of the metal ores may have been mined and smelted for local use or transported on land routes. One would need to add 40 to 50 tons of tin and probably considerable amounts of recycled metals next to all other produce and luxury items shipped in the LBA.

To supply the quantities of metals needed, distant players in the western Mediterranean like Sardinia and southern Spain for copper, but also northern European regions such as southern England, northern France and Bohemia as well as central Asia for tin became important trade partners.

With the resulting cross-continental trade in metals,

> '[d]uring the Bronze Age emerged a truly international network of metal trade and exchange, making all regions dependent upon each other, despite their different cultural traditions.' (Kristiansen and Larsson 2005, 5; cf. also Pare 2000, 24).

We will now look closer at these trade routes and subsequently at the nature of the international network of metal trade.

Trade Routes

During the LBA, different regions in Europe and the Mediterranean relied on different metal trade routes, the importance of which changed in the course of time depending on the structure of demand and supply. The routes that the metals have been traded on

---

32 Tin ores also existed and exist in the Erzgebirge in central Europe, however there is as of now no evidence of an exploitation of these potential sources during the Bronze Age (Earle et al. 2015, 636).

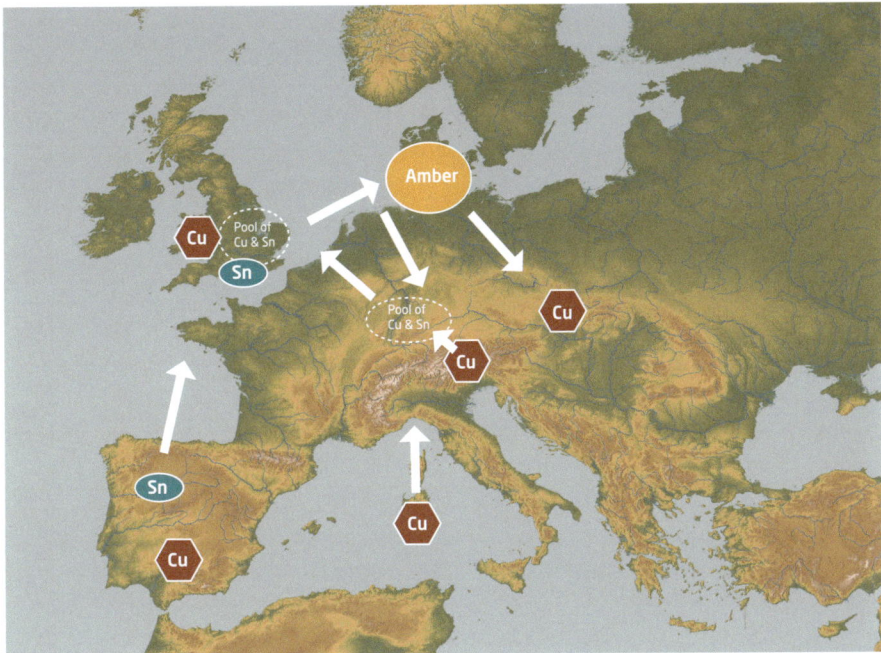

Fig. 4: Sources of copper and tin in early supply chains during the MBA (map: Olav Odé, after: Ling et al. 2019, 30).

during the Bronze Age included land and water transportation. In Asia, donkey caravans from the mining centres to the major ports or points of manufacture were a preferred mode of *land transport*. Also in Europe first primitive trails and built roads can be identified as routes of connectivity (Ling et al. 2019, 1; Bell 2012, 181; Kristiansen and Suchowska-Ducke 2015, 361f).

Within Europe, next to land transport, the *riverine systems* seem to have played an important role as trading highways *e.g.* from England or the Baltic Sea following the Oder, Weser, Elbe, Vistula and Danube via the Carpathian Basin to the shores of the Black Sea and from there to the Mediterranean Sea.[33] Other routes were probably in use as well, like the connection via Rhine and Rhone from the North Sea to the Mediterranean[34], the Elbe and Weser from and to Scandinavia and possibly the Aude and Garonne route from the Mediterranean to the Atlantic Ocean (Earle et al. 2015, 642; Cunliffe 2011, 43; Ling et al. 2019, 27ff; Ling and Uhner 2014, 30). The navigation of the European rivers may have included stretches where the boats would have to be transported over land (portages) to bridge the gap between two river systems (Cunliffe 2011, 45).

In addition to transport via the big European rivers, *maritime routes* were of great importance for metal trade in the Bronze Age. Within the eastern Mediterranean and the Aegean routes were travelled that connected the major cultural centres of Egypt, the

---

[33] The importance of riverine transport in antiquity has already been stressed by Diodorus Siculus ('Library of History', V, 22). On the importance of the Danube for Bronze Age transport cp. Earle et al. (2015, 641), Gerloff (1993 in Pare 2000, 31) and Kristiansen and Larsson (2005, 118).

[34] Suggested by Maran (2004) in connection with the Baltic amber found in the shaft graves of Mycenae.

Levant, Cyprus, Anatolia and Mycenaean Greece incl. Crete. Major ports on the Levantine coastline formed the end point for tin transport on the land routes from inner Asia and had fleets with big freighters to ship these resources often via Cyprus to other points of demand. From these major harbors like Ugarit, Troy or the Cypriot ports, huge freighters took the cargos on to further destinations (Bell 2012, 181).

Also the Black Sea seems to have been connected to these Mediterranean trade routes. In the Pontic Area the northern Anatolian mountains bordering the southern shores of the Black Sea and a region called Colchis near the Caucasus mountains were important metal producing areas (Andreadou 2015). Furthermore the estuary of the Danube formed the link into an important riverine route to northern Europe. The access to the Black Sea trade routes from the Aegean Sea was controlled by the city of Troy, for a long time vassal of the Hittite empire.

Additionally a 'western route' via the Atlantic Ocean connected the copper mines of southern Spain and Sardinia with Brittany, the British Isles and ultimately Scandinavia from about 1300 BCE and maybe slightly earlier (Ling et al. 2019, 32). Cunliffe (2011, 217ff) has stressed the importance of the earlier Bell Beaker cultures developing the Atlantic route, later joined by Scandinavian sailors (cf. Earle et al. 2015, 642).

Frequency, Volume and Forms of Exchange

Regarding the overall volume and frequency with which goods were traded in the LBA, recent research is split into a 'minimalist' and a 'maximalist' position (discussion in Tartaron 2013, 24ff).

Based on the still overall limited number of material finds on record today and converting them into 'shiploads', the *'minimalists'* assume infrequent, sporadic and mostly state-directed trade predominantly in the form of gift exchange (*e.g.* Snodgrass 1991, Parkinson 2010, Manning and Hulin 2005, 2). According to the minimalist theory the predominant form of goods exchange was reciprocal and non-monetary. Complex markets in the modern sense were still absent.

The *'maximalists'* on the contrary assume that trade in the LBA was primarily privately driven, *i.e.* commercially oriented, and took place on relatively complex markets (*e.g.* Cline 1994; van Wijngaarden 2002). Maximalists refer to the likely circulation of perishable goods on a large scale on top of the artifacts found, which have left no trace in the material record.

There are several shipwrecks found in the Mediterranean, which have been instrumental in the interpretation of LBA maritime trade. The cargo on the Uluburun shipwreck is probably indicative of a load of merchandise maybe destined for an Aegean ruler, and could also still be plausibly explained within the framework of a directed and reciprocal gift exchange between the royal courts as described in the Amarna letters (Zukerman 2010, 894; Tartaron 2013, 25f; Kristiansen 2016, 164; Moran 1992). The Gelidonya shipwreck gives a relatively clear indication for a more decentralized commercial goods exchange. Tartaron also points to the fact that the amount of perishable goods traded on top of the artifacts discovered was likely immense (Tartaron 2013, 25 based on Bass 1997). Whilst the exact nature of long-distance commercial trade in the eastern Mediterranean is still highly uncertain, all in all the minimalist position is getting less plausible with a growing body of evidence for long distance and high volume trade (Manning and Hulin 2005, 4).

The Uluburun shipwreck also proves that metals formed an important part of the exchange, were traded over considerable distances and in *bulk*.[35] Bulk trade required adequate modes of transport, *i.e.* caravans on land and larger boats on maritime and riverine routes (see next chapter).

Next to bulk trade also *small volume exchanges* via individuals have to be assumed (Artzy 1997 in Manning and Hulin 2005, 4). These small volume exchanges are more difficult to track, but no doubt existed. Tartaron (2013, 5f) stresses the potentially high importance of regional networks with smaller volumes of exchange.

In spite of their considerable complexity, we are still faced with *pre-monetary* economies in the LBA. However, highly differentiated value-relationships between different types of goods already could be assessed via internationally accepted *standard weights* and weight units and ingot fragments already seem to have served as proto-currencies.[36]

During the Bronze Age, various forms of *standardization* have been put into place. During the central European EBA (2000 to 1700 BCE), metals were transported and exchanged in the form of different items with very similar weights, such as metal rings ('Oesenringe'), ribs ('Spangenbarren') and axe blades between the east Alpine mines and northern Europe (Rahmstorf 2010, 686ff; Vandkilde 2016, 107 and 109, recently Kuijpers and Popa 2021). Kuijpers and Popa (2021) have shown via statistical analysis that the rings and ribs and to some extent also the axe blades follow a standard system of weighing and thus a form of 'commodity money'.

In the LBA, copper and tin were sometimes traded in the form of standardized so called 'ox-hide' ingots. '*The ox-hide ingots (flat, almost rectangular copper ingots weighing ca. 10 – 37 kg) were commonly used for copper exchange in the East Mediterranean, their shape being convenient for shipping*' (Giardino 2000, 99; cf. also Vandkilde 2016, 107). In fact, the weight of most copper ingots circulated closely around 25 kg (20 to 29 kg), a weight unit that was known as a 'talent' in antiquity. In other words, we see a commoditization of copper and tin during this period (Constantinou 2012, 11; Pare 2000, 28; Vandkilde 2016, 107).

Overall the complexity and sheer volume of transactions over long distances and between different cultural centres in a pre-monetary world required a) a standardization of transactions and b) an institutional framework to protect merchants and to ensure that deals were being kept.

Economic Networks

Some authors define Bronze Age interregional networks as instrumental for the cultural and economic exchange in this period (*e.g.* Kristiansen and Suchowska-Ducke 2015, 362; Kristiansen 2016, 156). Two basic forms of economic interaction during the Bronze Age have been identified: a) (sometimes elite-controlled) long-distance networks[37] and b) local processes and smaller-scale interaction. Both forms have existed simultaneously (cf. Earle

---

[35] Knapp (2018, 52) identifies the cargo on the Uluburun ship not as bulk, but as a compound cargo due to the fact that the cargo was composed also of other items. Since the majority of the load (over 10 tons) were standardized ingots of copper and tin, I would argue that the term 'bulk load' would still be applicable to the Uluburun wreck.

[36] Already before the middle of the 3rd millennium BCE silver has been used as proto-money/ value unit in trading (Rahmstorf 2010, 686; Rahmstorf 2016, 295ff; Lane Fox 2009, 94).

[37] Kristiansen (2016, 159f and 165) stresses the role of specialized foreign traders and their family connections within these networks.

et al. 2015, 634; long-distance networks are discussed in Kristiansen and Larsson 2005 and Kristiansen 2016. For smaller scale and local exchanges see Harding in Earle et al. 2015, 634 and Tartaron 2013, 5ff).

As stated above, the complicated processes of exchange in a pre-monetary trading environment suggest the quantities exchanged to be often rather small. The defining and new element of the Bronze Age from about 2200 BCE onwards has been the development of a European large-scale trade in metals and the creation of long supply chains due to the distances between the locations of supply and demand (Earle et al. 2015, 634, 648).[38]

For the large-scale trade in metals over the large distances, again two different models have been put forward. Maran (2004, 5f and 11) suggested a *'system of overlapping networks'* between the micro-regions of the LBA. This model would allow for an *indirect long distance trade* via several intermediaries. Renfrew – referring to the amber trade from the North Sea to the Aegean – speaks in this context about a *'prestige chain' of gift-exchange stretching across Europe* (Renfrew in Drews 2017, 180).

From an economist's point of view this model of indirect exchanges over long distances would likely lead to considerable *transaction costs and risks*[39], when the goods are passed from one intermediary to the other. Transaction costs are defined as:

- Research and information costs involved to find a suitable seller or purchaser,
- the bargaining and decision costs involved in a particular deal and
- policing and enforcement costs to ensure that a deal is kept and that the goods arrive at their destiny.

In the LBA, if you assume a model of indirect exchange via several intermediaries in long-distance trade, the research and information costs would be incurred in the process of finding a buyer or seller at various interfaces to which substantial and regular quantities of *e.g.* copper and tin are being passed on. Bargaining and decision costs would be incurred to identify and agree prices for different cargoes of metal in a pre-monetary world. Against the risk that cargoes of metal do not arrive at all or not in time, policing and enforcement costs would arise to ensure deals are kept.

In a fictitious example let us assume a Mycenaean marine trader who sailed up from the Peloponnese to the Rhone estuary with a demand to purchase 1 ton of Cornwall tin, *i.e.* the same quantity as found on the Uluburun ship off the coast of Turkey. In an indirect exchange model the tin may have changed hands several times, potentially between specialized traders for the cross-channel transport from England to Gaul, others for the land and river transport through northern Gaul and again others for the route along the river Rhone.

Political rivalries, warfare, plunder and natural catastrophes may have interrupted the tin trade on this route at several interfaces. The Mycenaean mariner, who spent several days at sea to reach his destination, would have had to load a cargo for the barter trade (*e.g.* perfumed oils) upfront with the expectation of a certain exchange ratio in a pre-monetary system. He runs the risk of not sufficient tin having reached the Rhone estuary,

---

38   Cf. also Tartaron (2013, 6) on local and micro-regional maritime networks. Manning and Hulin (2005, 9) see the development of region-wide organized commodity exchange developing later in LH III.
39   The concept of transaction costs has been introduced by the economist Ronald H. Coase.

of other traders who have come before him and already bought up the available quantities and of his cargo not being valuable enough to acquire the required amounts.

A transcontinental network of trading entrepots, specialized dealers and some established practices and mechanisms may have helped to reduce some of these transaction costs. Nevertheless, on balance the risks and costs of an indirect exchange network for metals required in some quantity and at a plannable schedule at their destinations will have been substantial.

In view of these risks and costs, Kristiansen and Larsson (2005) point to the manifold indications for a *direct connectivity* between the cultural regions in the Bronze Age over long distances.[40] Also Harding (in Maran 2004, 57) presupposes the possibility of direct contacts between distant trade partners. The assumption of these direct connections is based on an obvious exchange of 'cultural hardware' (*i.e.* culturally important goods) but also 'cultural software' (*i.e.* ideas, beliefs and organizational concepts) between far apart regions (Kristiansen and Larsson 2005; Vandkilde 2016, 112).

This direct exchange would imply the movement of people over long distances, notably of leaders of groups or important craftsmen, an institutional framework and a 'travelling culture' (Kristiansen and Larsson 2005, 39 and 41ff; cp. also Kristiansen and Suchowska-Ducke 2015, 362; Kristiansen 2016, 154). One of the key questions of the analysis put forward here is, which evidence for this kind of long distance journeys we have and who the travellers were. Kristiansen and Larsson (2005) in this context also point at some assumed similarities in the material record between the Mediterranean world and norther Europe. We will later revert to these questions looking at the evidence of long-distance travel of the Mycenaeans and how their experiences found entrance into their 'cultural software' via the myths.

In economic terms, some authors interpret the result of these metal trade activities over long distances as an 'international' *'integrating system of trade that stretched across Europe* [and] *created the comparative advantage of one region over another for export products'* (Earle et al. 2015, 635). Thus one way or the other, as a consequence of the metal trade over long distances,

> *'In the Bronze Age local communities throughout Europe became dependent upon each other to maintain open lines of long-distance exchange in order to secure the distribution of metal from the few dominant source areas.'* (Kristiansen and Larsson 2005, 39).

In other words we are potentially looking at a vast and integrated trading system for metals in Europe esp. during the Late Bronze Age.

Due to the enormous importance of copper and tin within these long-distance trade networks stretching from the Atlantic Ocean over most parts of Eurasia up to China, Vandkilde (2016) terms this development as *'bronzization'*, as a primary precursor of later globalization trends.

However, at the end of the Bronze Age this international trade in metals and luxury goods came to a sudden halt in conjunction with a major cultural break, when the important players in the eastern Mediterranean such as the Hittite empire and the

---

40 These indications pointed out by Kristiansen and Larsson (2005) include some striking similarities in the material record between the eastern Mediterranean and northern Europe.

Mycenaean palace cultures vanished or went into serious decline (Egypt) and important trading entrepots like Ugarit were destroyed.

> *'During the last centuries of the second millennium BC Mediterranean trade faced a major crisis. The general term of 'Sea Peoples' conventionally denotes the complex international events that happened around the 13th and 12th centuries BC, when the appearance of new human groups in the Mediterranean modified the age-old balance of power.'* (Giardino 2000, 102)

There are indications that shortages in metal supply around 1200 BCE – potentially as a consequence of disturbances of the established trade centres and routes – also played a role in the collapse of the palatial systems at the end of the Bronze Age (Chadwick 1994 in Tartaron 2013, 20).

After a hiatus of several hundreds of years, trade and exchange networks in the Mediterranean only became re-established on a lower level in the subsequent Iron Age. The first trade networks and colonization efforts after the end of the Bronze Age were driven by the Phoenicians and the Euboeans (980 to 800 BCE). A key motivation for the establishment of these networks was once again the acquisition of metals (Lane Fox 2009, 65ff). The Euboeans bought the metals possibly against Euboean wine and olive oil. However, *'the underlying trade* [by the Euboeans] *was very much smaller than the big cargoes and quantities of objects which are attested by surviving 'Mycenaean' texts and which we recover from shipwrecks in the age of the 'Mycenaean' kingdoms (c. 1350 – 1180 BC).'* (Lane Fox 2009, 70)

6

Shipbuilding in the Bronze Age

Since the Bronze Age was the first epoch in human history with regular transcontinental exchanges of goods and ideas, the question arises, how did the people and goods move over these huge distances? It is apparent that the high mobility of this era was facilitated by new 'mobility systems', esp. ships. Unfortunately, transmitted visuals and documentation of Bronze Age ships are scarce. Overall fewer than 400 images of ships have survived covering a time span of 2000 years (Tartaron 2013, esp. 37; Vandkilde 2016, 112).

In the chapter above we have seen that the riverine systems in Europe may have played an important role as highways to connect people from Britain to Greece. Also the Mediterranean – the 'wine dark sea' of the Homeric epics -, the Black Sea and the Atlantic Ocean have been crucial as a links between the cultural centres of the time. In order to utilize these riverine and maritime routes, the Bronze Age people needed ocean-going ships.

Some form of ocean-going vessels will have been necessary already in the Neolithic for the post-ice-age settlements on Mediterranean islands like Cyprus or Crete (ca. 9000 – 7000 BCE). The early settlers must have reached these islands on some form of boats, even though we have no remains of their stone-age vessels (Rahmstorf 2010, 676; Guttandin et al. 2014, 12). Dug-out canoes or rafts may have been the first methods of maritime transport, which were also used in the Aegean during the Neolithic and the EBA (Tartaron 2013, 81).

In the Aegean Sea, due to the many islands spread out over the ocean and forming a link between the Greece mainland, Asia Minor and Crete, early seafarers on a clear day would never lose dry land out of sight. This factor will have encouraged Neolithic and later Bronze Age people to utilize the maritime routes with their early boats. Maybe this is why researchers confirm that maritime technology developed considerably earlier in the eastern Mediterranean compared to northern Europe or the regions bordering the Atlantic Ocean (Guttandin et al. 2014, 12; Earle et al. 2015, 644).

Sheppard Baird (2007, 13) sees a first major step in the evolution of tooling also used in shipbuilding techniques after 4000 BCE, potentially helped by the then available first metal tools like saws, which could be produced with the arsenic copper and which were used to cut planks for ships.

Shipbuilding in the EBA

Material and pictorial evidence for early shipbuilding in the *Early Bronze Age* is scant (an overview is given by Knapp 2018, 67 and 167f). Some of the first crude pictorial representations of boats in the Mediterranean go back to the culture on the Cycladic islands and date to 2800 – 2300 BCE (Guttandin et al. 2014, 59).[41] The representations show that *long canoes* with many paddlers were in use probably already in the 4th millennium BCE. These were built from wood planks, but in appearance still resembled the earlier dugout formats. In spite of their primitive looks, the maximum range of paddled longboats already reached 40 to 50 km per day (Broodbank 2000 in Tartaron 2013, 112; Tartaron 2013, 81; Guttandin et al. 2014, 73).

The remains of Egyptian boats from this period show the early development of planked vessels (Rahmstorf 2010, 676). Egypt during the 5th and 6th dynasty stood in maritime contact with Byblos on the Lebanese coast from ca. 2650 BCE onwards to obtain cedar-wood. Natural harbors like Liman Tepe on the Anatolian coast were settled already since the Chalcolithic period and show that Anatolia has been connected via sea-routes to other entrepots (Knapp 2018, 65 and 78). Some clay models of boats have been found on Crete from 2700 – 2200 BCE (Guttandin et al. 2014, 60).

In northern Europe, where the EBA commenced later, cultural centres in Belgium, Brittany and the Loire estuary in northern France, the 'Wessex culture' in southern Britain, the Tagus estuary in Portugal and southern France were also connected from around 2000 BCE, with sewn-plank boats (van de Noort 2009, 161). For travel on the Atlantic Ocean the (Maritime) Bell Beaker peoples had developed sea-worthy vessels already since the 3rd millennium BCE (Earle et al. 2015, 644; Cunliffe 2011, 203ff and 208ff). In parallel the older format of dugout canoes continued to be used for navigating the European river systems and smaller waterways and remained the most common boat in the Bronze Age (Romey 2003, 28).

Shipbuilding in the MBA

The *Middle Bronze Age* sees an increase in evidence for seagoing vessels and indications for an expanding maritime consciousness esp. in the eastern Mediterranean. Maritime trade was expanding in scope, scale and geographic reach during the MBA (Knapp 2018, 81 and 170). Levantine ports like Ugarit, Tell Tweini, Tell Kazel (Sumur) or Byblos were in full development by this time. Overall *'The movement of materials in bulk required more efficient modes of transport'* (Cunliffe 2011, 182).

During the Middle Minoan period (ca. 2100 – 1600 BCE), trade expanded and palaces were built on Crete as centres of power and administration. Improvements in shipbuilding tools allowed for changes in shipbuilding to freighters with higher capacity and smaller crews. A number of renderings of ships on seal stones from the Middle Minoan epoch point at an increase of trade in these days (Guttandin et al. 2014, 61, 93).

The transition from the Middle to the *Late Bronze Age* saw several important innovations in shipbuilding. For one, paddels were replaced by oars, starting in Egypt in the later 3rd millennium BCE. Secondly, the expanded log-boat principle and *the sail* were a further major evolutionary step in shipbuilding during the Middle Bronze Age (the advances in shipbuilding at the transition to the LBA are discussed in Tartaron 2013, 51; Van de Moortel 2015, 268; Broodbank 2000 in Manning and Hulin 2005, 5).

---

41 For the type of ships found on representations in the eastern Mediterranean from the Early, Middle and Late Bronze age, discussions have been published by van de Moortel (2017), who refers back to a classification of these boats suggested by Wedde (2000) and by Guttandin et al. (2014).

These new log-boats with sails seem to have been developed in Egypt, adopted in the Levantine area and *'arrived in the Aegean already by ca. 2500/2400-2200 BC – considerably earlier than previously thought – and were introduced via the East Aegean [...], which allowed the Aegean people to travel the oceans over longer distances* (van de Moortel 2015, 268).[42] The sails on these log-boats were large and square, held fast by upper and lower yards (vertical beams). These bottom-footed sails however limited the maneuverability of the boats almost entirely to downwind travel (Emanuel 2013, 4; Tartaron 2013, 53).

'The adoption of both technologies led to the construction of highly seaworthy ships with rounded hulls that enabled the Minoans [...], and later the Mycenaeans [...] to dominate maritime trade in the southern Aegean for centuries as well as develop close maritime interconnections with the Eastern Mediterranean.' (van de Moortel 2015, 268; cf. Kristiansen 2016, 158)

The new maritime technologies facilitated Minoan overseas contacts *e.g.* to Egypt and contributed to the rise of a complex society and the emergence of elites (Tartaron 2013, 83). They also made a maritime infrastructure necessary, like ports, anchorages and storage capacities (Broodbank 2000 in Manning and Hulin 2005, 5).

Shipbuilding in the LBA

With vastly expanding trade and connectivity in the subsequent *Late Bronze Age*, several different types of ships were in use for specialized purposes in the Aegean and the eastern Mediterranean. In this period 'freighters' were used for bigger cargoes esp. bulk loads of copper and tin. The fleet of Ugarit has included several ocean-going freighters with capacities of up to 450 to 500 t of cargo (Casson 1995 in Kristiansen and Suchowska-Ducke 2015, 363).

Also the previously discussed Uluburun and Cape Gelidonya ships found in the waters of the southeastern coast of modern Turkey have contributed to our knowledge of shipbuilding in the LBA. In addition to the introduction of sails earlier on, sewn-planks began to be replaced by mortar-and-tendon joining techniques by the mid second millennium BCE. This allowed for a more sturdy construction of ships with a higher loading capacity (*i.e.* the a.m. freighters, cf. discussions in Knapp 2018, 157ff; Tartaron 2013, 49; Manning and Hulin 2005, 5).

Detailed pictorial evidence of ocean-going Minoan ships from the 17th century BCE has been found on the famous 'Flotilla Fresco' in Akrotiri on Thera dating to around 1540 BCE (LM I A) (see picture and discussion in Guttandin et al. 2014, 65 and 108ff; also Schofield 2007, 107). The representations on this frieze also form an important base for the discussion of shipbuilding in the LBA. Cyprus seems to have developed into another important centre of shipbuilding in antiquity (Constantinou 2012, 10).

In parallel the first evidence of war ships or galleys are found in the LBA. Wachsmann (1981 in Knapp 2018, 131) points out the parallels in appearance between the Mycenaean galleys (see below) and the 'sea-peoples ships' depicted in the mortuary temple at Medinet Habu. This closeness in appearance has been disputed, though (see discussion by Wachsmann 1997 in Tartaron 2013, 65).

---

42   Guttandin et al. (2014, 103) point at the fact that first pictorial evidence of sails on seals date to 2100 to 2000 BCE. Cp. also Cunliffe (2011, 182) and Kristiansen (2016, 158).

What Types of Ships did the Mycenaeans Use?

Mycenaean ships are attested in a few representations from the beginning of the Mycenaean period.[43] The earliest pictorials date to the later 14th century (LH III A2), possibly around 1320 BCE, the period during which Mycenaean contacts in the eastern Mediterranean greatly expanded (Tartaron 2013, 41).

Schofield (2007, 106) postulates four identifiable different types of Mycenaean ships according to their respective functions, *i.e.* ceremonial, war, trade and fishing. Wedde (2001 in Tartaron 2013, 57) characterizes the basic functional types of ships used by Mycenaeans in the LBA as the 'merchantman' and the 'galley'.[44] The existence of merchantman type ships designed for trade with a larger cargo capacity and propelled by wind power is deducted from indirect evidence, since it is not reflected in its pure form in the pictorial record. There may have been different types of hybrid forms with multifunctional hulls ('cargo galley', 'merchant galley', see analyses in Tartaron 2013, 57f).

A revolutionary new type towards the end of the LBA was the *Helladic oared galley*, a long, narrow and light vessel, which was primarily propelled by rowers with a rudder in the back and designed for speed. The rowers would be placed in an open gallery with vertical stanchions to demark the respective rowing station (the Helladic oared galley is discussed esp. by Emanuel 2013/14, 3 and 2015, 200).

The Mycenaeans may have invented this new ship type sometime after 1400 BCE in line with Mycenaean expansion in the Mediterranean. Emanuel suspects that the ascendancy of the Mycenaeans in the 14th and 13th century BCE was to some extent even driven by the introduction of the new galleys. This assumption is backed by Tartaron (2013, 68), who reckons that extended ranges for maritime journeys to obtain raw materials and for trade contacts may have necessitated the invention of the galley design.

The first depictions of this type of galley appear only late in LH III B (*i.e.* around 1250 BCE). Before its introduction, types closer to the ones represented on the a.m. 'Flotilla Fresco' in Akrotiri may have been in use and would fill the chronological gap. A fascinating replica or model of a seemingly Mycenaean galley has been discovered in Gurob, Egypt, a site, where the Sherden (one of the 'Sea Peoples', which collectively are sometimes made responsible for the end of the LBA) are known to have lived in the 12th century BCE.[45]

Its shape with a lightweight and slender hull made the Mycenaean galley easy to beach and ideal for rapid attacks by infantry soldiers albeit at the cost of cargo capacity. Wedde (2000 in Emanuel 2013, 3) terms the Mycenaean galley *'the single most significant advance in the weaponry of the Bronze Age Eastern Mediterranean'*. However, in case the attack force included chariotry, the horses and chariots must have been carried by other types of ships with bigger hulls.[46] Also the lack of cargo capacity rendered the Mycenaean galley not ideal as a merchant vessel.

---

43 As in the Dramesi tomb, often identified with Homeric Hyria (Drews 2017, 203).
44 The Uluburun ship with approx.. 20 ton cargo capacity may be a representative type for the 'merchantman ship', albeit of probably Canaanite origin (Wedde 2001 in Tartaron 2013, 57f). In addition, Tartaron (2013, 71ff) stresses the likely existence of various smaller crafts for local requirements serving micro-regional maritime networks.
45 Emanuel (2013/14) refers to the publication of Wachsmann (2013) 'The Gurob Ship-Cart Model and Its Mediterranean Context'.
46 In the Classical Period of Greece, specialized horse transporters (hippagogoi) were in use (Drews 2017, 203f).

Fig. 5: Mythical ship Argo, replica, Volos city, Greece (photo: Wirestock, stock.adobe.com).

Another innovation on those galleys was the loose-footed sail, which enabled the ships – with the addition of brails and the removal of the lower beam – to cruise sideways against the wind. In times of rapidly growing commerce, fast ships were also necessary to reach distant destinations in a reasonable time even if the swift ships could not carry bigger loads.

Also the Greek myths mention this new type of fast ocean-going 'black' (war) ships. They were called 'black ships', because they were made watertight with tar. The mythical 'Argo', the ship of the Argonauts, may have been one of the prototypes for this galley. The Achaeans and Danaans at Troy probably used different types and sizes of these new warships, the standard size being the 'pentecontor' for 50 rowers, 25 on each side, which reached a length of about 30 meters. The Iliad mentions ships with an even bigger capacity of even 120 crewmembers for the Boeotian contingent (Homer 'The Iliad', II, 510 (Catalogue of ships)). Smaller 'triaconters' with a crew of 30 may also have been in use (Emanuel 2015, 203).

How Fast and how Far Could Mycenaean Galleys Travel?

The question about the speed and reach of Mycenaean ships is important for the judgment as to how far the Mycenaeans could travel. The assumption is that long distance travel would have been conducted with galleys that could be rowed or sailed. The estimates for the duration of long distance journeys depend on the average number of kilometers a galley could travel per day to which one would need to add days of bad weather, resupplying fresh water and food etc..

Sheppard Baird (2007, 12) estimates that wood-planked 'pentecontors' ('50-rowers') could reach and average speed of 8 km/h. He then calculates based on a total crew of 100 mariners, who work in shifts, that a day's journey of 192 km could be possible. The distance from Crete to the southern Iberian Peninsula of about 2400 km according to this calculation could thus be covered in as little as 12,5 days.

Sheppard Baird's assumption appears to be supported by a quote in Diodorus Siculus, who mentions that a merchant vessel during his time (*i.e.* in the 1st century BCE) could travel from the Sea of Azov (Lake Maiotis) to Rhodes in 10 days and on to Alexandria in additional 4 days, if the journey is made without a break and is 'supported by favorable winds' (!). We obviously have a best-case scenario given here by Diodorus Siculus. With a distance covered of in total approx. 3.400 km between the Sea of Azov and Alexandria, this would equate to an average of 200 km per day (Diodorus Siculus 'Library of History', III, 34.7; cf. Drews 2017, 204).

In the Trojan Epic Cycle it is mentioned that the distance from Troy to Euboea (ca. 300 km) can be covered in a day and a night. Odysseus gives an estimate of 4 days plus for the trip from the Aegean to Egypt (ca. 800 km, cp. Homer 'The Odyssey, XIV, 252; cf. Tartaron 2013, 111). With a travelling speed of this magnitude, Minoan sailing ships may have been able reach Egypt in 4 days. By and large these quotes would result in a distance of way over 100 km and with the support of 'favorable winds' maybe even 200 km covered in a day. Also Tartaron (2013, 82f) calculates that a sailed Mycenaean galley pushed ahead by tailwinds would be able to cover this per diem distance.

Similar estimates from other areas are supportive of the magnitudes given above. Earle et al. (2015, 645) assume that Scandinavians have participated in long distance maritime travels during the Bronze Age. The boats they have been using are assumed to be represented in rock-carvings, which were found in southern Sweden and look similar in build to the Mycenaean galleys. The authors estimate rowing distances per day for these Scandinavian boats as 100 km with 22 experienced rowers and a cargo of 700 kg.

It would seem that some if not all of the above calculations are maybe a bit too optimistic, especially when considered for long-distance journeys. In Sheppard Baird's estimate it would require the crew to row by day and night without pause and hardly allow for provisioning days and bad weather. Also Diodorus Siculus presents his estimate as a best-case scenario.

An average distance per rowing/ sailing day (excluding 'night shifts') of 50 to 80 km for longer distances seems still ambitious and a more reasonable assumption. Crew fatigue on long journeys must have been a limiting factor (cp. Tartaron 2013, 63). Including rest days for taking on fresh water and supplies and the odd bad weather day the journey from the Aegean to southern Spain of about 2.400 km would then need as a minimum one, more likely towards two months or more depending on weather conditions. Considering the Mediterranean had a summer sailing season due to difficult weather during winter, a trip to the southern Iberian Peninsula would then have been a one-time affair per season.

If the Mycenaeans had the nautical know-how and the ships to undertake long-distance journeys, which evidence do we have that they really made use of these capabilities? How far did they go? This is the topic, which will be looked at in the next chapters.

7

Evidence for Mycenaean Long Distance Journeys in the LBA

Archaeological Evidence

Mycenaean Greece was positioned at a unique interface between the eastern and western Mediterranean, continental Europe as well as the Pontic area. Mycenaean commercial activities at different times during the LBA seem to have included the entire Mediterranean Basin and were connected to central and northern Europe and eventually the Black Sea. This chapter provides a first overview about the traces Mycenaeans left in the respective areas. A more detailed insight for every region is given in each chapter of the later part of the analysis.

McMillan (2016) summarizes the different kingdoms and regions, which apparently stood in contact with the Mycenaeans during the LBA. Mycenaean material remains found in the various destination areas in the central and western Mediterranean can be classified in various ways. Next to the respective areas where they have been found, one can structure them *e.g.* according to the type of product, the social context in the destination areas, the transfer modalities (*e.g.* direct vs. indirect trade) and/or the places where they have been produced.

Regarding the *destination areas*, traces of Bronze Age Mycenaean products, especially their typical ceramics, can be found in Cyprus, Anatolia, Cilicia, the Levantine coast and Egypt in the eastern and Italy, Sicily, Sardinia and the Iberian Peninsula in the western Mediterranean. Some traces of Mycenaean ceramics were even found in northern Europe (Germany).

The extent of Mycenaean Bronze Age trade networks becomes apparent already at an early stage of Mycenaean development in the connection with the metal trade. The amber found by Schliemann in the Mycenaean shaft-graves from the 16th century BCE points to early contacts as far as the Baltic Sea coast and southern England and is often interpreted as a by-product of tin trade (*e.g.* by Maran 2004; Harding in Drews 2017, 180).

'Evidence of contacts between Greece and the Levant and the rest of the Near East is abundantly attested for the Late Bronze Age. Greece formed part of an international network of trade and entertained diplomatic contacts with Egypt, Hittite Anatolia and the Levant. (Waal 2018, 109)

Fig. 6: Mycenaean pottery finds in the Mediterranean and Black Sea area (map: Olav Odé, after: 'Mykene – Die sagenhafte Welt des Agamemnon', Ausstellungskatalog, Badisches Landesmuseum, Schloss Karlsruhe, 2018/2019, Inside Cover).

There are several central and western Mediterranean Bronze Age cultures, with which the Aegean peoples like the Minoans and later the Mycenaeans potentially stood in some form of contact. In case of the Minoans, these may have included already the Los Millares culture in southern Spain, where arsenic copper was smelted as early as 3200 BCE (assumption by Sheppard Baird 2007, but not generally accepted). The Los Millares culture was followed by the El Argar culture, which flourished on the southeastern coast of the Iberian Peninsula from 2200 to 1350 BCE and where the contacts with the Aegean world are somewhat more apparent. The archaeological evidence for an exchange of goods and ideas is nevertheless very limited.

In Sardinia the Nuraghic culture developed from 18th century BCE up to the 2nd century CE and became an important centre for metallurgy, esp. copper. With traces of Mycenaean ceramic and ingots of Cypriot origin found on the island one can assume direct contacts with Cyprus, but maybe also the Mycenaean world. In addition, some finds in southern Italy and Sicily point not at trade, but even towards Mycenaean settlers.

However, some authors inject that the existence of Mycenaean goods in a distant location may not automatically prove *direct* contacts or the presence of Mycenaeans (Cunliffe 2011, 198; Dickinson 2019, 33; Blake 2008, 3). Middleton (2015, 51f) and Gillis (1993, 61) caution to interpret Mycenaean or Aegean style pottery finds always as indications for Mycenaeans having been present in those areas, since the pottery could be indirect imports via middlemen or local copies and an expression of exotic status markers of local elites. Often it remains a possibility that the goods have been transported there on ships of intermediaries or via local trading networks.

Gillis (1993, 62) assumes that long-distance trade for the Mycenaean palatial centres was actually conducted by commercial, professional middlemen and that the Mycenaeans may not have had a commercial fleet at all. Tartaron and others discuss the possibility of Cypriot merchants as primary intermediaries for Mycenaean trade with Egypt and the Levantine coast (Tartaron 2013, 29; Zukerman 2010, 887).[47] Alternatively, Canaanite traders could also have been important intermediaries for Aegean exchange, since the Uluburun ship is assumed to have had a Canaanite port of origin (Gillis 1993, 70). And finally there are hypotheses that Mycenaean trade with Egypt may have been mainly conducted via Crete and Minoan merchants rather than directly.[48]

Recent discoveries have increased the likelihood that Mycenaeans themselves were present in Ugarit, so the participation of Mycenaeans in long distance trade in some form or other seems plausible (Tartaron 2013, 29; Zukerman 2010, 888ff, cf. also section 9.2.1.). A final – and likely – possibility is simply 'all of the above', *i.e.* a differentiated world of maritime transport in which many players took part. One question taken up in the following chapters is whether the Greek myths contain information that helps to provide answers to this still open issue.

Regarding the *type of products* exported from Mycenaean Greece, next to different shapes of pottery, also ceramic figurines, textiles, copper oxhide ingots (potentially of Cypriot origin) and luxury items are indicative of direct or indirect trade, in which Mycenaeans were involved (Vianello 2008, 7; Schofield 2007, 104).

---

47   Zukerman (2010) provides an overview of the scholarly opinions in this regard.
48   This is presumed at least for the shaft grave era and more uncertain for later periods (cp. Schofield 2007, 63 and 109).

A considerable part of the Mycenaean pottery found is supposed to have contained (perfumed) oils, unguents and wine (Jung 2018, 280). An important export item from Mycenaean Greece seems to have been olive oil in scented and non-scented varieties, for which certain types of flasks and jars are indicative (Kelder 2009, 342 and 2010, 134ff).

Regarding the *social context* of Mycenaean goods in the destination areas, Jung (2018, 280) points out that the social character of the goods as well as their quantities in certain contexts generally point at an uneven distribution amongst different social groups. *I.e.* the Mycenaean imports were by and large precious exotica, at least before the 13th century BCE. In the course of the 13th and the 12th century BCE – and especially during the convulsions and migrations at the end of the LBA – these exotic imports became gradually integrated into local practices and the everyday life of the people of the eastern Mediterranean, a process sometimes called 'hybridization' (Knapp 2012, 34ff).

Textual and Epigraphic Evidence

Overall, there are relatively few *textual references* to Mycenaean activities either in the records of the Mycenaens themselves or in those of the other cultural centres around the Mediterranean (an overview of the existing material is given by Tartaron 2013, 35ff; cf. Schofield 2007, 106). The Mycenaeans may appear in Egyptian records as 'Tanaju' (maybe related to the Greek word 'Danaan') and in Canaanite and Hittite texts as 'Ahhiyawa' (assumed to correspond to 'Achaean' in Greek language, see discussion by Cline 2009 in Tartaron 2013, 36).

Diplomatic correspondence found in Hittite archives in the capital Hattusha bears witness of a relationship, which may have been generally friendly and on 'eye level', but seems over the course of two centuries to have turned increasingly sour, probably in the context of an expansion of the Mycenaean sphere of influence towards Asia Minor (Waal 2019, 26; Schofield 2007, 65; Mull 2017, 158f).

The *'Maduwatta-indictment'* transmitted as part of a correspondence probably written by the Hittite king Arnuwanda I (1400 – 1375 BCE) contains Hittite complaints about 'Ahhiyawan' support for a rebel in Asia Minor and Cyprus during a time when the Mycenaeans still retained Miletos as a base and stronghold on the Anatolian western coast (Tartaron 2013, 36; Mantzourani et al. 2019, 108).

The so-called *'Tawagalawa-letter'* probably written by king Hattusilis (1265 – 1240 BCE) directed to a Mycenaean king – maybe the Theban king Eteocles – can be interpreted as an indication of growing tensions over the Sporades. The letter contains a complaint by the Hittite king about Mycenaean protection of a 'rebel', who disrupts the order in Hittite territories on the coast of Anatolia and the islands to the west (Tartaron 2013, 36; Strauss 2006, 19, 196).

Slightly later the *'Sausgamuwa-letter'* by king Tudhaliya IV (1237 – 1209 BCE) directed towards a Canaanite king named Sausgamuwa apparently mentions a trade embargo imposed by the Assyrian king Tukulti Ninurta I against Mycenaean ships (Schofield 2007, 114; Tartaron 2013, 29).

Finally there are textual references in Ugaritic archives, which seem to refer to Mycenaeans based on the Levantine coast.

Regarding the *epigraphic evidence,* Zukerman (2010, 889) points out that the Linear B tablets found so far do not deal with international trade. However, some Linear B inscriptions on tablets seem to reflect toponyms in the Mediterranean and Black Sea area.

The respective body of evidence is summarized by Woudhuizen (2010). The inscriptions belong to the period 1350 to 1200 BCE. The regional distribution of the toponyms found on the tablets focuses on the north-eastern Mediterranean and the Black Sea area up to Colchis at the foot of the Caucasus mountain range. According to Woudhuizen (2010, 6) they may reflect an economic or commercial interest of Mycenaeans in this region with respect to raw materials, esp. metals (tin).

In addition to the Linear B tablets, an important list of Mycenaean and Minoan centres dating around 1400 BCE inscribed on the base of a pillar in *Kom El Hetan* in Egypt is proof that the Egyptians were aware of their Mediterranean neighbors and maybe stood in direct contact with them.

Pictorial Evidence

Next to cultural 'hardware' – *i.e.* trading goods – and some textual references, a few pictorial renderings have been found in the Mediterranean area, which are assumed to represent Mycenaeans and which add to the picture painted by the material remains as discussed above.

In the eastern Mediterranean various pictorial representations have been uncovered, such as those in graves of high-ranking officials in Egypt, where Minoans and Mycenaeans may be portrayed bringing offerings and/or trading goods to Egypt. A papyrus found in Tell el-Amarna (ancient Akhetaten) depicts what may be Mycenaean mercenaries in the Egyptian army (Schofield 2007, 71 and 125). There may also be pictorial renderings of supposedly Mycenaean warriors on Egyptian temple walls such as part of the representations of the so-called 'Sea Peoples' on the walls of the mortuary temple of Ramses III, but the origin of these groups is still disputed (see discussion above by Wachsmann 1981 in Knapp 2018, 131).

Our understanding of Mycenaean trade also has to include the ships they have been using (see chapter 6). For some of the ship-types we have various pictures in different qualities as well. Tartaron (2013, 37ff) has provided a comprehensive overview about the pictorial material available.

The overall perspective gained on Mycenaean trade and travel in the LBA from material finds and from pictorial renderings still leaves many details and gaps to be filled. Some authors are therefore very cautious about assumptions regarding the frequency and volume of Mycenaean long distance journeys.

Questions on the Frequency and Volume of Mycenaean Long Distance Trade

Mycenaean material finds in the eastern and western Mediterranean are being interpreted very differently regarding the frequency of contacts with the respective destinations and the volume of goods exchanged.

Some authors argue in line with the minimalist position outlined above and based on the overall number of Mycenaean items found around the Mediterranean for fewer than 10 contacts per decade overall and thus a very extensive trade (*e.g.* Parkinson 2010 and Cherry 2009). Tartaron (2013, 28) adds to this his view that evidence for Mycenaean long distance trade is still mostly circumstantial and that no indisputable evidence exists that Mycenaean ships ever visited Egypt or the farthest reaches of the Levantine coast.

Cline (1994) and van Wijngaarden (2002) (among others) to the contrary emphasize the thousands of Mycenaean items found so far on distant shores and interpret them as only the tip of an iceberg, the overwhelming majority consisting of perishable goods. They thus take up a maximalist position on this difficult question.

Tartaron (2013, 130) concludes that

'it is uncertain how extensively Mycenaean ships traveled around the Mediterranean in pursuit of trade and diplomatic missions'.

Let us therefore analyze now and at some length how these disparate positions hold up against the body of mythological evidence for Mycenaean long distance journeys.

8

Reflections of Mycenaean Long Distance Travel in the Mythological Record

8.1 Definitions, Structures and Functions of Myth

In the previous chapters, the Greek myths have been mentioned as a potential further reference point for the long distance journeys of Mycenaeans in the LBA. The underlying assumption is that myths of travelling heroes were a way in which Mycenaean Greeks embedded the experiences of long distance journeys into their cultural heritage.

The definition and interpretation of myth is an immensely complex and multi-layered endeavor.[49] For the purpose of this analysis, the *historicity* of myth, *i.e.* the question to what extent historical events such as the long distance journeys of the Mycenaean Greeks are reflected in myths, is of key importance. Regarding the definition of and the historical references contained in myths, the works of Martin Persson Nilsson (1932), Moses Finley (1975), Walter Burkert (1979), of Carlo Brillante (1991) still provide an essential framework.

Burkert (1979, 2 and 22f) defines myth essentially as *'a traditional tale, i.e. a tale which is transmitted and thus preserved albeit with distortions and re-elaborations'*. These traditional tales are often about origins, things that happened in the remote past and they contain *'partial references to something of collective importance'*.

By comparing elements and the composition of different myths[50], Burkert finds references to ancient ritualistic behavior as well as parallels to equally ancient precursors from either Aegean (*i.e.* pre-Greek/Pelasgian)[51], Indo-European[52] or oriental[53] (*e.g.* Hittite,

---

49 Cp. Edmunds (1991). Other approaches (*e.g.* semantic) to the interpretation of myth are consciously omitted here.
50 Burkert (1979, 5) refers to *'systems of definable relations between parts or elements of a whole which admit predictable transformations'*, a method called the 'structuralist approach'.
51 Cp. Brillante (1991, 110) and Haarmann (2017). The term 'Pelasgians' denotes the autochtonous and probably earlier or pre-Indo-European stratum in Greece. It is possible that the Pelasgians, who after being partially pushed out of the Balkans by the immigrating Achaeans, settled also on Crete and on the coast of Asia Minor, are identical with the Peleset or Philistines, who formed part of the mysterious 'Sea Peoples', which attacked the civilization centres in the eastern Mediterranean at the end of the LBA. In the Greek myths, the Pelasgians trace their ancestry back to a legendary Pelasgos, who united the Arcadians on the Peloponnese. In fact, the Peloponnese may have been called 'Pelasgiotis' prior to the invasion from Anatolia led by mythical Pelops. In the Danaus myth it is said that the Pelasgians have changed their name into 'Danaans' after Danaus took over the reign in Argos. 'Danaans' is also one of the probably historically attested names of the Greeks in the Homeric myths.
52 Von Ranke-Graves (1986, 131) stresses the parallels between the Prometheus myth (in which his brother is Epimetheus) with vedic Indian sources in the Bhagavata Purana, in which the brothers Promanthu and Manthu play a role. Cp. also Puhvel (1993) and Dihle (1994).
53 Lane Fox (2009).

Levantine, Mesopotamian) provenance. The respective elements are often structured in a way to bring out contrasts or symmetry in order to enhance the effect of the story (Burkert 1979, 18). The fact that comparable structures and elements are identifiable between different myths should caution us already vs. a too literal interpretation and point to the requirement of further contextualization.

Next to their unique content and structure, myths are also clad in a particular form of language. Metaphors are frequently used as a *'basic trick of language to cover the unfamiliar with familiar words on account of partial similarity'* (Burkert 1979, 28). Also due to this particular way of expressing their content, myths overall do thus not purely represent historical facts or recollections.

One of the reasons for myths to be composed in this form has to do with the *function of myth* in antiquity.

> *'Myth carried out much more important and complex functions in Greek society than the transmission of more or less reliable memories of the distant past.'* (Brillante 1991, 101) For Greeks in antiquity *'adaptations of traditional tales is the only or the main method of general speculation and communication in order to verbalize phenomena, to give them coherence and sense'*. (Burkert 1979, 24)

Myths therefore also serve to provide a collective sense and purpose for the community they are told in, whereas 'history' at least aspires to be factual and rationalizing (cp. Finley 1975, 13).

In order to understand myths, their structure, their metaphors, but also their historical reference points, a similar knowledge of historical levels is thus required. Furthermore, to analyze the relationship between the historical and archaeological record of myths in general and in particular regarding ancient Mycenaean long distance travel and its reflection in those myths, one needs to dig deeper into the process of their origin and the transmission process.

8.2 Myth and History

8.2.1 Approaches to the Historicity and the Origins of Myths

When we use the word 'myth' today in everyday language, the connotation is that of a story that is essentially untrue or fabricated. This was not however how the Greeks in antiquity understood their myths, which for them formed part of their ancient history.

The discussion around the relationship between history and myth has started already in antiquity (see discussion in Brillante 1991, 93). In the recent academic discussion, the question, whether the Greek myths contain historical information and if so, to what extent, is hotly debated between different schools of thought:

Representatives of the *Euhemerist School* (after the Greek mythographer Euhemeros, 4th century BCE) assume that mythological accounts originate from real historical events or personages (already Persson Nilson 1932, 2). Euhemerists also tend to accept mythical genealogies and chronologies. Today also the term *'Positivist'* is in use to denote researches, for which myths try to reflect nuclei of historical events, but use a different and distinct language.

The *Historical School* developed out of the Euhemerist School of mythological thinking. Its proponents also believe in some ancient historic nuclei in myths, but assume a fundamental re-shaping and sometimes creation of myth via the agency of mythic poetry.

The *Comparative School* (*e.g.* Puhvel 1993) traces key contents of Greek myths back to very ancient Indo-European roots, parallels to which can be also found in other Indo-European civilizations like Vedic India or Celtic Europe. The Historicity of the Greek myths in this school of thought is either denied or pushed back to very ancient roots.

Then, of course, there are also the so-called '*Skepticists*', for who myths are essentially invented stories without a historical background.

As a starting point for an analysis, which assumes some historical roots of the Greek myths[54], it needs to be reiterated that from the perspective of the ancient Greeks their myths were clearly not fabricated or fantasy (a belief shared by *e.g.* Finley 1975 and Schofield 2007, 11f).

> '*In their myths, the Greeks recognized events that actually happened*'. They '*imagined their heroes as men who had actually lived, inhabiting the same cities and regions in which they themselves, several centuries later, continued to reside*'. (Brillante 1991, 93f and 101)

For the ancient Greeks, a clear differentiation and separation between historical and mythological tradition would therefore have been difficult to comprehend.

In terms of the content of the stories told as 'mythoi', they often seem to refer back to a glorified Late Bronze Age past (broadly 1600 to 1100 BCE). Most authors would thus accept that there probably were some historical experiences dating back to the LBA, which form the nuclei of some of the myths.

An example based on this assumption would be the homecoming of the Mycenaean heroes after the sack of Troy. The difficulties they face in their hometowns and their subsequent journeys to Italy, Cyprus, Cilicia and the Levant as described in the 'Nostoi' would be reminiscent of the breakdown of the Mycenaean palace culture at the end of the Bronze Age and the subsequent migrations of the former elite to new places in the Mediterranean Basin. Hornblower (1994, 8) for instance clearly assumes that these foundation legends reflect historical processes.

After a period of widespread skepticism, recently a growing number of authors are willing to accept a Mycenaean origin of many the Greek myths to some degree (see Schofield 2007, 188f; Woudhuizen 2013).[55] However, often we are faced with a confusing variety of the same myth by different authors from different times. Considering the origin of a particular myth, Burkert (1979, 3) cautions against the expectation that there are initial versions, which are historically 'accurate'. He states that '*It would be naïve to assume that any traditional tale captured as myth would arise directly from facts*'. Burkert postulates that myths were probably from the start clad in a particular language of metaphors and references. His position is that it is thus often futile to search for the 'original version' of a myth, which is closest to or represents the historical reality.

---

54 An assumption not shared by all of the a.m. schools of thought on the historicity of myths.
55 More skeptical views are expressed by *e.g.* Dickinson (2019, 32), who states that the Mycenaean interpretation of Homer has been increasingly questioned in recent years.

Yet even Burkert (1979, 28f) allows for a certain historicity of myths stating that there are indeed indications embedded in the tales

> 'which, if used with due caution, allow one to get an idea of the historical dimensions in which a myth has come to be'. 'There are clues pointing to definite epochs'[...]'and certain features are intimately connected with identifiable cultural strata.'

These remarks contain an essential conclusion and form part of the vantage point from which this analysis is written.

The task is thus to analyze further the Late Bronze Age context in which the myths have been composed, as well as some of the various mechanisms at work in the transmission process in order to understand the later distortions. In the words of Brelich (in Brillante 1991, 110)

> 'in the order to understand a myth, it is indispensable to establish from which stratum – or in the frequent cases of successive re-elaborations, from which strata – it draws its origin'.

8.2.2 The Transmission Processes During the 'Dark Ages'

If we accept a *Bronze Age origin* for some of the content of the Greek heroic myths, the next question to be asked is how and when these nuclei of historical information were wrapped into the stories we know and which got transmitted to us today. After the end of the LBA and during the subsequent so-called 'Dark Ages' of Greece (ca. 1100 – 800 BCE) concerning the transmission of myths several processes were at work in parallel, which are summarized here and further detailed in the following chapters.

The assumption of a LBA origin of mythical-historical content would imply several centuries of relatively exact and consistent transmission during the so-called 'Dark Ages', during which the Greeks are assumed to have lost their writing abilities (Schofield 2007, 186). In fact, due to the perishability of some of the materials on which the Mycenaean scribes may have written, it is uncertain, when exactly the Linear B script eventually ceased to be used (discussed by Tandy 1997, 201). Since mostly tablets from palatial archives have been found, the demise of the palatial structures at the end of the LBA is thought to have reduced the necessity to use Linear B considerably.

During the 'Dark Ages' also some significant migrations took place, initially from Greece to Asia Minor and to Cyprus. Proponents of the 'Historical School' of mythological thinking assume a deep going reshaping of myths in the course of these migrations sometimes to an extent that the myths actually describe an 9th or 8th century BCE milieu (Tandy 1997, 8ff; cp. also section 8.2.3).

Kristiansen and Larsson (2005, 22) on the other hand are confident that oral tradition was able to bridge this gap of a few hundred years and deliver mythical content relatively unchanged.

> '[...] oral tradition was persistent and able to transmit songs and myths over half a millennium or more without major changes, but rather adding detail from later periods to make the songs comprehensible. Oral tradition is often more persistent than literary tradition and puts very high demands on the correctness.'

A metric verse[56] and some 'pre-packaged' phrases may have helped bards and singers to preserve various competing versions of the stories from the past in oral form, which were finally codified in writing into 'standard versions' as we find them in the Homeric epics and the Epic cycle from about 700 BCE onwards (discussed in Mull 2017, 209ff; cp. also section 8.2.4).[57] A frequently debated question is, what kind of literary or oral poetic forms may have supported this long tradition.

Regarding the typical metrical format, in which the Homeric epics are captured, the Hexameter, Hajnal (2003) has shown that the process to shape this epic language may have begun during Mycenaean times, but the final form and the Hexameter itself are likely to be of a post-Mycenaean origin. This insight does not exclude that the roots of the epics lie in Mycenaean times, but it stipulates that the process of canonization will have taken a considerable amount of time into the post-Mycenaean period.

It is also uncertain, when exactly the Greeks started to use their later alphabet, which seems to have come into use after the first Greek traders and colonists from Euboea came into contact with Phoenician merchants and their northern Semitic alphabet in ports like Al Mina in northern Syria, in Italy and Cyprus (a process described by Lane Fox 2009 and Tandy 1997, 201).

Waal (2018, 117ff) argues on the contrary for Homer's poems being the product of an almost continuous and mixed oral-written tradition, which would presuppose an early (11th century BCE) adaptation of the Phoenician alphabet during the so-called 'Dark Ages'.[58] She concludes that the Iliad was composed over a longer period of time also in written form and that the poet [...] made expansions in what he had already taken down. In this scenario *the Iliad and the Odyssey may have their origins in various shorter poems (in this case about the Trojan War), which were at a certain moment reworked to create a unified composition.*'

Waal (2018, 119) stresses that there may have been different and competing versions of many myths and also different forms of presenting them. One source of the multiplicity of versions are alternative local variants of the same myth. Another may have been the creation of differing versions depending on a variation of ways to present the myth to an audience. We can assume a *'parallelism of sources* [...] *between poetic and oral non-poetic transmission',* which adds to a variety of expressive forms.

8.2.3 Transposition and Re-Interpretation of Myth during the Archaic Age of Greek Colonial Expansion

There are various authors (*e.g.* Shrimpton 1997; Tandy 1997; Lane Fox 2009; Dickinson 2019, 32), who acknowledge some ancient and very likely Bronze Age roots of the travelling myths as they were captured in writing at the beginning of the Archaic Period of Greece (8th century BCE to 480 BCE), *i.e.* around 800 to 700 BCE, but attribute major contents and interpretations to the experiences of travellers during *migrations* to Asia Minor and Cyprus and the Euboean-led first wave of *Iron Age colonization* of parts of the eastern and western Mediterranean around 980 to 800 BCE connected with a resumption of trade and travel.

---

56 Though probably not the Hexameter in its final epic form yet (Hajnal 2003, 90f).
57 This assumption reflects the so-called 'Oralist' theory of Milman Parry and Albert Lord (Waal 2018, 113).
58 This assumption would presuppose a continuation of literacy in Greece.

During this period of Greek colonization (normally dated at 750 – 550 BCE with the a.m. earlier Euboean antecedents) long distance journeys were undertaken in an organized manner to found new establishments abroad. New settlements were founded in the Mediterranean (south Italy, Ionia, Thrace, southern Gaul, Iberia) and the Black Sea coast, initially driven by the Euboeans in the 8th century BCE and followed by major cities like Corinth, Milet, Megara and Phocaea.

The first indications that Greeks became interested in foreign peoples because of the differences to their known environment stem from this Archaic period of Iron Age colonization (cp. Dihle 1994, 17f). In this phase some myths were 'borrowed' or adapted esp. from Near Eastern sources. Other mythical figures were partially given new homes abroad because of the *misunderstandings and inferences* of the travelling Greeks. With the changing regional focus of Greek colonization efforts from east to west, also the myths at times underwent a process of *geographical transposition*. When faced with the new territories, the myths were re-interpreted in the new environment, whereby *'guesses, inventions or distorting bias are always possibilities'* (Lane Fox 2009, 46 and 218).

The founding myths of various Italian, Iberian or Cilician cities, which often trace their origins back to Homeric heroes that emigrated there after the Trojan War, would thus become ex-post fictional additions enriched with contemporary experiences. One author went so far to identify the Odyssey as merely an Euboean creation of this period, but this view has not been generally accepted (Lane Fox 2009, 138).

Whilst Near Eastern influences and adaptations of older stories dating probably to the 'Dark Ages' especially on the Greek 'divine' myths are undeniable (*e.g.* regarding the Aphrodite myth), other heroic myths are clearly of a Bronze Age origin. If allowing for some degree of later misinterpretations and transpositions, this still leaves the question, how to distill the Bronze Age roots of the myths out of the later distortions. Because even with a historical background knowledge, which is essential for the understanding of myth, the interpretation is complicated by the innumerable changes – and variants – wrought in the course of tradition (see Burkert 1979, 28).

8.2.4 Epic Poetry, Canonization and Local Variants

As stated above, Mycenaean contacts with other peoples via long distance trade and commerce were very likely captured already at an early stage – *i.e.* during the Late Bronze Age – in the form of myths and in a special form and language. Irrespective of the prevailing uncertainties of the transmission process during the 'Dark Ages', a major development took place at the beginning of the Archaic period (ca. 750 to 480 BCE) at around 700 BCE, when some myths were finally written down in a poetic form.

There are ongoing discussions as to whether Homer as the assumed author of 'The Iliad' and 'The Odyssey' has been a historic figure or whether we have to assume several different sources and authors for these epics. This investigation assumes an historical author of the epics, maybe called Homer, but different views are possible (contra Graziosi 2002). As Waal (2018, 113) stresses, the historical figure of Homer is still difficult to capture. *'There has been and still is much controversy about the date of Homer as well as the genesis and transmission of his poems.'* Yet, the long poems we call 'Homer's epics' have survived a long time and do not only stand out because of their poetic quality.

Hesiod's 'Theogony' (ca. 700 BCE) contains the tales about the cosmic order and the genealogies of the gods. Linear B records indicate that the Olympic deities have been

Fig. 7: Homer (photo: Ded Pixto, stock.adobe.com).

worshipped already by the Mycenaeans in Bronze Age times (demonstrated by Schofield 2007, 160). Their respective mythology is called '*divine*' mythology by Persson Nilsson (1932, 2). In addition to Bronze Age roots, various parallels in these myths to Near Eastern and Mesopotamian cosmogonies have been pointed out (Mondi 1991, 142ff).[59]

Hesiod in his works 'Theogony' and 'Works and Days (106 – 173)' also differentiates between different 'ages' that the tales referred to. The first in order was the time of the gods and the origin of the universe and ending with the reign of Zeus. Next in line was the 'age of heroes' or demigods, perceived to be different from the later line of mere mortals. Its protagonists were considered *historic* people but of a more powerful and nobler sort, who were related to and interacted with the gods (cp. Edmunds 1991, 3). The heroic age ended according to Hesiod with the Theban and Trojan wars during which many epic heroes vanished (Hesiod 'Works and Days', 156). With the demise of this heroic race starts the age of the mortals, more or less coincidental with the subsequent Iron Age.

The '*heroic age*' as portrayed by Hesiod seems to fall together broadly with the LBA and constitutes the perceived 'ancient history' for the Greeks in the later periods. According to Persson Nilsson (1932, 2 and 18) it is important to distinguish between the a.m. divine and these heroic myths, which have different origins and sources. The heroic myths according to Persson Nilsson are accessible regarding (pre-)historic analysis.

---

59   The historicity of Greek myths also needs to be interpreted in the context of the broader Near Eastern Bronze Age historiography. Kitchen (2006, 45ff) cites the various annals and daybooks already in existence in Canaan during this period. However – as with the Greek myths – these historical annotations have been used to express religious beliefs and thoughts as well. Kitchen (2006, 49) references to the Old Testament as an analogy: '*As in the Near Eastern chronicles, the writers of Kings (and Chronicles) had no need to invent history; they merely interpreted it in terms of the beliefs they sought to express.*'.

The focus of this analysis on the historicity of Mycenaean travel myths lies on the heroic age with the stories ranging from Io and Perseus to the Mycenaean heroes in the Trojan War and its aftermath as written down potentially by *Homer*[60] in 'The Iliad' and 'The Odyssey' and made known to – or continued to be remembered by – a wider, literate society.

These massive epic poems also contain various references to older myths, which already were in existence and known to a broader audience by the time they were written down. The Iliad and the Odyssey refer back to the myths of Daidalos, of Bellerophontes, to the Argonauts, to the Theban Wars and to the Heracles cycle. Already Herodotus commented that Homer and Hesiod in essence managed to *'establish a canonical Greek mythology consisting of these stories and genealogies'* (quoted in Edmunds 1991, 4).

In spite of this quasi-encyclopedic character of Homer's epics it needs to be reiterated that not all myths transmitted to us today have been captured in this work. Some older myths may not have survived the test of time because they went out of fashion. Some others lived on in oral prose rather than poetry (Persson Nilsson 1932, 15 and 108).

Furthermore, in parallel to the canonized versions of the epics by Hesiod and Homer, multiple and sometimes divergent versions of the 'same story' continued to be handed down. Edmunds (1991, 5) thus concedes that

> *'The existence of these local traditions necessarily means that there will be differing versions of the same myths, variations between local and canonic and between local and local.'*

Even the evolving historical thought during the Classical Period as well as the growing geographical knowledge could not eradicate the multiplicity of traditions. *'Although Dionysius speaks of the local traditions as written [...], they were still alive in oral form for Pausanias (second century A.D.) to hear long after the time of Dionysius.'* (Edmunds 1991, 5) This variety of local traditions led to confusion and frustration already during the Classical Period of Greece. Hecataeus complained in the introduction to his work that *'Greek traditions are numerous and ridiculous'.* (Brillante 1991, 95)

8.2.5 Early Geography and the 'Historization of Myth' in the Archaic, Classical and Hellenistic Periods

Various authors from the Archaic (8th century BCE – 480 BCE), the Classical (480 – 323 BCE), from the Hellenistic (323 – 31 BCE) and from the subsequent Roman period of Greece acted as intermediaries for the transmission of mythical long distance journeys dating back to the Bronze Age as well as for the geographical knowledge available in the respective periods.

In their works, mythical, historical and geographical knowledge is often lumped together so that some authors today are called *'historiographers'* or *'mythographers'*. Sometimes older versions of travelling journeys are quoted or 'recycled'. The historiographers built on the various traditions of myths with canonized versions, local variants and 'colonial transpositions'. The narratives they composed thus became a literary genre in its own right, with its own reference points, traditions and at times closer to storytelling than science (cp. Romm 1992, 3 and 5).

---

60   See remarks above as to the historicity of 'Homer'.

Next to mythological and historical information, the classical authors conveyed an ever growing fundus of information on the *geography* of the then known world.

'history appeared very close to – and at first practically inseperable from – geographic and ethnographic research, as is clearly the case in the works of Hecataeus and Herodotus.' (Brillante 1991, 97)

The term '*geography*' seems to be a surprisingly late name for the science of map-making and the description of foreign countries in the Classical Greek Period (Geus 2018, 402). It seems to be first used by Eratosthenes (276 – 194 BCE) maybe inspired by a word play of Herodotus ('The Histories', IV, 36). What we call 'geography' today was initially termed '*peirata gaies*' by the early authors, the 'boundaries of the earth'. The term refers to imaginary boundaries around the known world, which is surrounded by the boundless ('apeiron') Ocean. The first known use of the term 'peirata gaies' is a work by Anaximander, however the term itself due to its metric form probably has its origin in older epic poetry (Romm 1992, 10ff and 26f).

Other terms in use (amongst others by Hecataeus of Milet) were 'periodos ges', *i.e.* the 'encirclement of the earth' or 'travelling along the edges of the world', 'periploi', which were in essence descriptions of 'round trips' or coastal voyages and 'periegesis', which could be translated as 'world tour' (*e.g.* by Dionysius).

During the Archaic age in the process of colonization, many areas around the Mediterranean and Black Sea coastline, which were formerly only known through mythical transmission, became 'terrae cognitae' to the Greeks. Later on during the Classical Period of Greece, especially the western Mediterranean and the Atlantic coastline of Europe became less and less familiar to them after the Carthaginians enforced their trade monopoly there from about 500 BCE onwards.

The following list of historiographers does not attempt to be complete, but is selective regarding references in the later content of this paper.

Historiographers in the Archaic Period

The starting point for an overview of mythical and geographical references in antiquity is the mythographical corpus of Hesiod and especially Homer. For the ancient Greeks, *Homer* was authoritative regarding the 'historical' and also the geographical content of his works. Homer as in many other disciplines was regarded as the '*proteus heuretes*' (*i.e.* 'first inventor') of many disciplines including the geographical information contained in his works (Strabo 'The Geography', I, 1; 2; cp. Geus 2018, 402).

The overall picture that Homer had of the world in total was that of a disc (like a shield) surrounded by the great river Okeanos as the ultimate boundary, a view taken over by his near contemporary Hesiod with possible Near Eastern precedents. In the middle of this disc lies the Aegean with its surrounding familiar landscapes of Greece and the Ionic Isles, further north the Danube and Thrace, Crete in the south, Asia Minor and the Black Sea in the east. There are references to Italy and Sicily further west and Egypt in the far south as well (Homer 'The Iliad', XIV, 245f; XVIII, 607; XX, 7; Homer 'The Odyssey', XI, 157; discussed in Geus 2018, 403; Nesselrath 2005, 153; Romm 1992, 13, 26).

Overall, Homer's work shows an astonishing familiarity with the geography of the Mediterranean, still admired by Strabo ('The Geography', I, 1; 10f). Some of the detailed geographical knowledge embedded in the Iliad and the Odyssey clearly transports a degree of Bronze Age content transmitted over centuries.[61] A considerable part of the reverence of the ancient Greeks toward Homer and his often more detailed geographical descriptions is thus indeed borne out by modern analysis. Visser (1997, 149 [translation by the author]) attests that

> *'in summary it can be stated that mythical tradition, as captured in the Iliad and the Odyssey, also always contains specific and detailed geographical knowledge.'* (cp. also Rausch 2013, 19)

After the archaic 'mythographers' Homer and Hesiod, the first historian and geographer to be mentioned is *Aristeas from Proconnessus* (7th century BCE[62]), whose descriptions form a pre-stage to a scientific ethnography and geography, but also include strong elements of the mythical tradition (cp. Dihle 1994, 20).

Sixth century Ionia was the birthplace not only the first structured or 'scientific' geographical approaches, but also of historical reflection on the transmitted body of myths. Part of the rationalization process and myth criticism became the exclusion of the marvelous and tendency to reject divine intervention. As a consequence, over time the differentiation between myth and history became inevitable (Rausch 2013, 18; Brillante 1991, 94ff).

Amongst the early Ionian philosophers and scientists, *Anaximander* (ca. 610 – 546 BCE) drew what is likely to be the first map of the world, which he pictured as a drum in the middle of the '*kosmos*' (Geus 2018, 404; Rausch 2013; 20).[63] He is credited with a work called '*peirata gaies*', *i.e.* the 'boundaries of the world' (Romm 1992, 27). His student *Anaximenes* (585 – 525 BCE) saw the earth as a disc hovering in the air. He also placed on it the "Rhipaean mountains" as a great mountain range in the north.[64]

The mythical tradition continued with *Pindaros of Thebes* (518 – 438 BCE), a lyric poet from Thebes who composed several long 'Odes' (poems) with mythical content. His odes acquired acclaimed status in antiquity. The 'Pythian Ode' includes a visit of Perseus to the northern countries of the 'Hyperboreans' (Pindaros 'Pythian Ode', X, 30 – 49).

An important next step in the development of early geography was the distribution of the surface of the earth into 5 zones depending on their inhabitability ('*klimata*'). This was done by *Parmenides* (born ca. 515 BCE with an unknown date of death), one of the founders of the Eleatic school of thinkers in Elea (part of Magna Graecia in southern Italy). The new term coined by him was the '*oikoumene*' describing the inhabitable part of the earth, a concept that persisted until Claudius Ptolemy's monumental work in Roman times (Geus 2018, 405; Romm 1992, 129).

---

61 *E.g.* the 'Catalogue of Ships' (Homer 'The Iliad' II, 494 – 759), which lists the contingents of Mycenaean Greeks sailing towards Troy and their respective leaders. The catalogue contains information about locations and settlements that did not exist anymore when Homer captured the Iliad in writing (Visser 1997).
62 Some authors consider Aristeas to have lived in the beginning of the sixth century BCE (cp. Romm 1992, 71).
63 Rausch (2013, 20) points out that it cannot be excluded that some form of cartography already existed during the time of Homer.
64 The concept of the Rhipaean mountains is referred to in the later text in section 12.2 in the context of the 'Hyperboreans' in the far north.

Fig. 8: The world according to Hecataeus of Milet (Bibi Saint-Pol).

Historiographers during the Classical Period

Amongst the first historians and mythographers, *Hecataeus of Milet* (550 – 476 BCE) contributed a major description of the then known coastlines in the world (periegesis) and the peoples that lived on and beyond them including their history. He relied on a category of mostly Greek and Phoenician travel literature called the *'periploi'*, which in essence reflect descriptions of sea journeys. Hecataeus was considered to be the first real geographer by Eratosthenes. He also drew a world map, where the world was still assumed to be a disc surrounded by the Okeanos. His scripts have strongly influenced later historians like Herodotus (Geus 2018, 405f; Romm 1992, 129; Dihle 1994, 26ff). In addition to the periegesis, Hecataeus wrote a work of genealogy or mythography, which survived only in fragments (cp. Hornblower 1994, 13).

Herodotus of Halicarnassus (484 – 425 BCE), the 'father of history' travelled extensively in the eastern Mediterranean. His ambition or motive was to explain the victory of the Greek poleis against the Persians. His work *'The Histories'* contains comments on many ethnicities in the eastern Mediterranean and their reported histories and mythical origins.

In terms of his geographical approach, Herodotus ('The Histories' IV, 36) challenged the mythic traditions (*'peirata gaies'*, *i.e.* of the 'boundaries of earth') and was the first to dismiss the concept that earth is surrounded completely by the primeval ocean. His geographical work was thus not based on theoretical and geometrical concepts but on his own journeys, reliable informants and an increasing body of traveller's reports. In his works Herodotus separated the 'known world' ('*oikoumene*') from very distant territories ('*eschatiai*') nearly empty and void of men ('*eremoi*'). Overall, through Herodotus, '*the myth-based worldview of the archaic era yielded to a more empirical and exacting mode of geographic inquiry*' (Romm 1992, 32 and 36f).

Thukydides (460 – 400 BCE) was called the 'father of scientific history' due to his perceived impartiality and his meticulous gathering of evidence. His '*History of the Peloponnesian War*' opens with a comparison and discussion of the current conflict in comparison to the Trojan War. He clearly accepts the conflict about Troy as an historic fact together with its protagonists (see comments of Schofield 2007, 11).

A few years later *Ephorus of Cyme* (405 – 330 BCE) composed a comprehensive compendium of Greek history ('*Historiai*') in 30 volumes starting from the mythical Heraclids to 340 BCE. Ephorus focused on Greece and included genealogical information in his work.

In his geographical approach, Ephorus structured the world's surface into a rectangle. Greece considered to be the centre of civilization was placed in the middle with foreign peoples around them The Hyperboreans and Skythians were placed in the north, the Hesperides and Erytheia in the west, the Aithiopians in the south and India in the east. All of these locations will be discussed later with reference to their relevance to Bronze Age Mycenaeans.

In terms of the geographical information contained, Ephorus did not travel himself, but used various existing secondary sources. He was quoted and used as a reference by later writers like Diodorus Siculus and Strabo (cp. Hornblower 1994, 36).

Historiographers during the Hellenistic Period

During the subsequent Hellenistic Period (323 – 31 BCE) the conquests of Alexander the Great had a profound impact on the geographic knowledge of the Greeks especially with respect to the regions towards the east and the former Persian empire (Rausch 2013, 7). One of the first and maybe most important geographers of the period was *Eratosthenes of Cyrene* (276 to 194 BCE) who wrote a treatise ('*periodos ges*') including longer paragraphs about India (discussed in Romm 1992, 31). He also devoted an entire section of his work to the examination of Homer. As librarian in Alexandria, Eratosthenes managed to calculate the circumference of the earth with some degree of exactitude (his approach is described in Geus 2018, 409). From his works onwards the discipline of geography became known by this name. Interestingly, he also re-introduced the concept of the world-surrounding Ocean, which had earlier been rejected by Herodotus. Eratosthenes in this approach thus in some aspects moved back closer to mythical thinking (see comments of Romm 1992, 9, 42f).

Further 'periploi' and 'periodoi' were added during the Hellenistic period by authors like *Scymnus of Chios* and *Apollonius of Rhodes* (295 – 215 BCE), the latter being another librarian of Alexandria, who also preserved the fullest account of the voyage of the Argonauts (Romm 1992, 31).

In the early 3rd century BCE an Egyptian priest called *Manetho,* born in Sebennytos[65] and serving in the temples of Heliopolis, transmitted a chronology of Egyptian pharaohs

---

65 An ancient Egyptian city called 'Tb-n Tr' in the local language (Luban 2017, 7).

in his work *'Aigyptiaca'*, which contains cross references to Greek mythological events incl. a remark which puts the end of the Trojan War into the reign of the female pharaoh Twosret (Verbrugghe and Wickersham 2001, 108). Manetho's scripts are only indirectly transmitted via quotations by the Jewish historian Flavius Josephus in the 1st century CE and later epitomes by Sextus Julius Africanus and Eusebius. What is transmitted indirectly of Manetho and also the later epitomes include transcriptions, changes and distortions, which make it difficult at times to relate the original chronologies with archaeological findings, but overall still provide a surprisingly solid base of reference (Luban 2017, 8ff).

Historiographers during the Roman Period of Greece

In the later Roman era, *Diodorus Siculus* (ca. 90 – 30 BCE) compiled a comprehensive account of mythical and historical knowledge of his time in his *'Library of History'* in 40 books, of which more than half have reached present times in full. One of his important sources was the work of Ephoros (see above), but we also know of the works of other important authors through Diodorus (cp. Hornblower 1994, 49). *Hyginus* (64 BCE – 17 CE) has transmitted a further overview of mythical accounts in his work *'Fabulae'*.

Strabo (64 BCE – 24 CE) extensively travelled the Mediterranean and summarized his experiences in his monumental work called *'Geographica'*. Strabo wrote in Greek, but was Roman in outlook and perspective. In this compendium – influenced amongst others by the writings of Eratosthenes – Strabo refers back to Homeric thought and concurs that the earth essentially is an island surrounded by the Ocean (discussed in Romm 1992, 43 and 122). Strabo also wrote a historical work, which unfortunately does not survive.

Another mysterious author called *(Pseudo-) Apollodorus*, who gained the attribute 'Pseudo', because he was mixed up, but is not identical with Apollodorus of Athens and has probably lived in the 1st or 2nd century CE, collected a very comprehensive compendium of myths in his *'Library of Greek Mythology'*, one of the most important bodies of myth transmitted to us today.

Pausanias (ca. 110 – 180 CE), a Greek from Asia Minor, travelled around Greece and captured its geography and history in 10 books called *'Hellados Periegesis' or 'Description of Greece'*. He collected information – and speculation – on various Homeric places and traditions. Pausanias' work refers frequently to the Greek myths, especially the Trojan War, which he believed to be historical (see comment of Schofield 2007, 12). His description of the Greek landscapes also included various related local myths and oral traditions, which were still very much alive during his time.

Avienus (4th century CE) quotes contacts between the southern Iberian Peninsula and Britain during the Early Iron Age in his extensive geographical poem *'Ora Maritima'*. In this composition Avienus draws on the much earlier journey of the Carthaginian Himilco, who travelled along the northern route along the Atlantic coastline around 500 BCE (Nesselrath 2005, 160; Romm 1992, 20f).

Only with the landmark *'Geography'* of *Claudius Ptolemy* (90 – 168 CE) in the 2nd century CE did the term 'geography' take on the meaning that it has today with objective and scientific descriptions of the earth's surface. All previous authors and historiographers clad their geographic knowledge in narratives.

Not to be underestimated is the important role *libraries* played for the transmission process of myths in antiquity, which covered several centuries. There were several important collections of books and scrolls *e.g.* in Pergamon, Tauromenium and Athens next to the probably most renowned one in Alexandria (on historical libraries see Polastron 2007, esp. 10ff, 16ff and 23ff). Some of the outstanding historiographers and mythographers like Eratosthenes and Apollonius Rhodius, the author of the 'Argonautica', in fact were also librarians in Alexandria and had access to the accumulated knowledge of previous generations.

The purpose of this overview was to demonstrate that there has been a quasi-continuous chain of transmission of mythological cum historical information throughout Greek and Roman antiquity, combined with a growing fundus of geographical knowledge elaborated on often by the same authors (on the intertextuality of ancient Greek histographers and geographers see Hornblower 1994, 54ff). On the whole, mythical thinking together with different forms of oral transmission remained important throughout the Classical, Hellenistic and later Roman Periods of Greece, in spite of the establishment of structured historical thinking and continuous progress in geographical knowledge. It is important to note that the *'rationalistic' criticism of myth did not presuppose complete abandonment of the traditional story'* (Brillante 1991, 97; cp. Finley 1975, 12).

Again, myth and history fulfilled different and complementary purposes. History served to understand the causes of human events, myth interpreted them in the light of the remote past and delivered a coherent plot with a single purpose. As a consequence the ancient Greeks did not feel a contradiction between history and myth as we may be tempted to believe (cp. Brillante 1991, 97, 102 and 105).

8.3 Genealogies – Mythical Timekeeping

Greek heroic myths[66] contain a considerable amount of genealogical information. The classical myths comprise hundreds of names and describe the ancestral relationships between the demigods and heroes of the period in great detail. We thus have to assume that this aspect of the myths has been hugely important for the people who transmitted these stories.

The names contained in these genealogies describe the relationships between the Mycenaean (in Homeric terms 'Achaean' and 'Danaan'), aristocracy during the Late Bronze Age, but by far not only. A considerable amount of the ancestral information inside the myths extends to the pre-Mycenaean (*i.e.* 'Pelasgian') inhabitants of Greece as well as neighboring peoples. Many of the names in the myths are of Phoenician (*e.g.* Cadmos, Agenor), Anatolian (*e.g.* Laomedon,..), Thracian (Dionysos) and Egyptian (Danaos, Aigyptos) origin brought into a Greek transcription and thus also describe relationships of the Mycenaeans beyond the Greek borders. These foreign relationships in some cases can be traced back to migrations and/or long distance travels.

It has been stated in chapter 3 that ancient historians created a network of synchronic and diachronic events, which allowed them to provide dates for the mythical age, which probably coincides roughly with the Late Bronze Age. The diachronic process was often based on genealogical counting (cp. Moeller 2001, 250ff). Varying local traditions, in which these events were embedded, however led to frequent inconsistencies in this process.

Yet this is only one of the reasons that Vansina classified genealogies as the *'most complex sources in existence'* (Vansina 1985, 182 in Hornblower 1994, 14). When we attempt to analyze, to which extent these genealogical information may contribute to understand

---

66   Persson Nilsson's differentiation between 'divine' and 'heroic' myth is maintained here.

the chronology and interpret Mycenaean relationships to geographically distant peoples, a few important caveats need to be mentioned upfront:

Firstly, in spite of their obvious importance, the objective of the genealogies contained in the myths has often not been to transmit 'family trees' in the most objective manner. Sometimes family relationships seem to have been constructed or modified to legitimize the claim of a clan or family to a certain territory or throne (cp. Brillante 1991, 98). On the other hand Woudhuizen observes that at least for the genealogical information contained in the Homeric epics there are only little 'political motives or purposes' to distort information to be expected (Woudhuizen 2013, 6).

Moreover, frequently the objective seems to have been to ensure a divine ancestry to important peoples, *i.e.* demigods or heroes. This element of deification within the body of 'heroic myths' is likely to reflect common Bronze Age ideas and is found also in the Bronze Age myths of India, Anatolia and Mesopotamia. To declare someone a demigod probably was a common expression of respect to the noble, great and powerful (discussed in Mull 2017, 215f). Next to prowess in battle and war, this status of semi-divination could be obtained also via long-distance travel (Kristiansen and Larsson 2005, 39). For the later peoples that received the myths as stories transmitted over long periods of time, semi-divination was also an instrument to put the stories into an overarching moral structure and to portray the past as a glorious age of a better race of men.

As stated above, there are also local deviations and sometimes contradictions between different variants of genealogies. In addition, the focus of orally transmitted genealogies tends to be on the very remote and often mythical origins on the one hand and – with some accuracy – on the most recent past on the other, whilst the 'middle section' is gappy and often constructed. This phenomenon as part of the transmitted collective memory has been called the 'floating gap' (Thomas 2001, 198).

The mythical chronologies transmitted to us to some extent are the products of the attempts at rationalization and systemization of later historiographers in the attempt to get rid of the a.m. discrepancies. Some of the historiographers tried to bring several different myths into a '(pseudo-) historical' system by the means of genealogies. Hekataios of Milet and Pherekydes, for instance, tried to reconcile seeming contradictions between different myths via genealogical structures (Hornblower 1994, 11; Dihle 1994, 28; Persson Nilsson 1932, 3, 69).

The lack of exact dates, a coherent dating scheme and a reliable chronology within the myths and epic poetry has brought Finley (1975, 15) to the conclusion that within epic poetry '*the account is fundamentally timeless*'. Yet also Finley din not deny that the epics of Homer may contain kernels of historical fact (cp. Hornblower 1994, 8).

At the same token, it needs to be noted that with the roughly 14 to 15 generations covered in the genealogies of the classical myths counting back from the Trojan War (assumed at 1186 BCE; cp. Mull 2017, 276) to the distant ancestries of the heroes, and allowing for 30 years for the average generation, one would arrive at a time span covered of about 400 years plus that takes us back to about 1500 to 1600 BCE, which quite nicely coincides with the start of the LBA and the beginning of the Mycenaean period. This fact is easily forgotten and quite remarkable. So the overall framework of genealogical chronology seems to be plausible and broadly consistent with archaeological dating.

Additionally, Brillante (1991, 102) has pointed to systematic examinations which revealed that the supposed contradictions in the heroic genealogies are in fact less numerous than previously thought. Also Persson Nilsson (1932, 48) states that in some instances his analysis on the Mycenaean origin of Greek mythology is *'corroborated by genealogies which do not seem idle inventions'*. In other words, there is some consistency also in detail.

Furthermore, there are various references contained in the transmitted stories, for which in some cases we can find historical equivalents ('synchronisms'). In the Dionysos and Io tales, for example, an Egyptian king with the name of Epaphos is mentioned, who with some likelihood can be equated to the Hyksos pharaoh Auserre Apophis. References like this allow us to put certain Greek myths in a general historical context.

Finally, there is a strand of mythological-historical thought, which identifies celestial phenomena described in the myths and relates them to astronomical constellations during the Late Bronze Age. For the date of the return of Odysseus to Ithaca, the Odyssey (XX, 350) mentions an eclipse of the sun in the so-called 'prophecy of Theoclymenos', and cites constellations of the planets (Venus) and stars (Plejads, Boiotes). The scientists Schoch/Neugebauer and most recently Baikouzis and Magnasco (2008) managed to date this particular eclipse to the 16.04.1178 BCE. Also for the destruction of Ugarit presumably by attacking forces from the sea a precise date has been fixed via a similar approach based on astronomical observations by Dietrich and Loretz (2002).

Rohl (2007, 295) takes an decidedly euhemeristic position when he writes:

'What I think we can take from this is that the personalities in the tales are probably based on real characters and events (after all, these stories can be classified as legends rather than myths) and that their legendary relationships to each other and to their ancestors and descendants are reasonably accurate. In other words the genealogies and wars between the city states are historical [...].'

In spite of Rohl's optimism, the a.m. caveats would caution us not to take all aspects and details of the genealogies literally. On the other hand – just like in the case of geographical information contained in the myths – there seem to be nuclei of historical information embedded in the genealogies. One question to be dealt with in the subsequent chapters will thus be to identify to which extent a decoding of this information is possible. Another way of looking at this question is to which extent the 'genealogical storyline' generated by the historiographers is consistent and plausible.

8.4 The Content and Narrative Style of Greek Travel Myths – Quests and Journeys in the LBA

Burkert (1979, 15) pointed out the fact that many myths of the heroic age in terms of content involve a 'quest' of some sort. In the Greek myths, the heroes often travel long distances and thus gain fortune and fame:

'From the beginning of our extant source material, myths, legends and sagas were used to articulate themes of exploration, geographical expansion and contacts with non-Greek peoples. Greek superheroes such as Jason and the Argonauts, and Heracles were leading personages in creating a Greek mythical past, as they were said to have gone into far-away lands to explore and pave the way for a more lasting Greek presence in the form of colonization.' (Bridgman 2010, 157)

The travellers brought back trophies, exotic goods and stories about the world they encountered. Helms (1988, esp. 114f and 119f), van de Noort (2009, 160) and Kristiansen and Larsson (2005) stress the association of geographical distance with the perceived value attributed to the ideas and goods brought along by the heroes. At the same token to obtain knowledge about remote countries in this process may have been the job of specialists, *i.e.* heroic adventurers of some social status who were daring enough to venture into the unknown, and a contributor to the establishment of elites and the stratification of early societies (again Helms 1988, 11 and 49; cp. Cunliffe 2011, 182; Tartaron 2013, 124).

The key insight of recent research in the area of the symbolic construction of geographical space and the political significance of long distance contacts was first outlined by Helms (1988) and summarized by Kristiansen and Larsson (2005,39):

'Magical powers and heroic fame were gained through participating in distant travels and expeditions, where chiefs would meet and compete about their skills, mythical stories and heroic deeds, and return with knowledge, skills and fame, and with esoteric goods to symbolize their social and ritual standing.'

The geographical setting of the Greek travel myths is not confined to the area of today's Greece and the neighboring islands. The stories contain information about the entire eastern Mediterranean world, including Crete, the Levantine coast line, Cyprus, Asia Minor and Egypt, all of which seem to have been relatively well known to the Mycenaean Greeks.

Beyond the eastern Mediterranean, the geographical references and terminology in the myths becomes a bit less specific and sometimes full of mystery. Yet, some information and knowledge is present also about the 'distant west', *i.e.* the Hesperides (probably to be located on the southern Iberian Peninsula, see below), 'the East', *i.e.* the Black Sea (Pontos Euxeinos, Colchis), the 'far North' (Hyperborea), the 'far East' (Erythraean Sea, India), and 'the South' (Arabia, Erembians; Africa, Ethiopians). Tartaron (2013, 135) remarks with respect to Homer's Odyssey that the geographical information in the myths shifts from the 'real and identifiable' to the 'world of monsters, goddesses and the realm of the dead' once the familiar environment of the eastern Mediterranean is left behind.

Still, the geographical information contained in the myths is never arbitrary of fabricated. This point is stressed by Lane Fox (2009, 46) who notes:

'Homer is frequently very precise about places or points in a real landscape [...]. Whatever its ultimate origin, there is detail here of places known to Greeks. [...]. They even cohere in a typical pattern.'

According to Tartaron (2013, 135 and 137) it is even conceivable that the myths contain Bronze Age elements of 'phenomenological itineraries', *i.e.* sailing directions in the form of mind maps. Taken together these may have formed a vital body of 'mnemonic devices' for recalling details of long voyages told in metaphorical and possibly in encoded terms.

The exotic foreign products that reached Mycenaean Greece become tangible especially in graves in Late Bronze Age archaeological contexts from the palatial period (van Wijngaarden 2012, 66). The goods must have reached Greece via trade with other peoples or have been brought back by Mycenaean travellers. The problem today is that individual journeys often leave little traces in the archaeological record. There are also no historical references to individual journeys, which would reflect the experiences of early Mycenaean travellers. That leaves the myths potentially as a unique source of additional information and requires further investigation into the relationship of myth and history.

The Greek epics thus may reflect various travelling experiences during the Late Bronze Age and the Early Iron Age. The respective myths often relate pioneering activities. The early Greek heroes in the myths like Perseus, Heracles or Odysseus were revered by later generations because of the experiences they gained during their long distance travels. Strabo ('The Geography', I, 1; 16) concludes that *'Herakles was called "practiced in great deeds" because of his great experience and knowledge'*.

However, direct quotes of strategic or economic topics like metal procurement or trading processes are usually missing in the narrative element of the stories (cp. Helms 1988, 67f on motives for long distance travel in myth and ethnographic literature). It almost seems the Greek myths are told in an ancient 'tabloid style', *i.e.* focusing on people, their emotions and relationships, less on the abstract factual context. The question is: Why is this so?

The answer to this question remains to some extent speculative. One reason seems to lie in the value system of the targeted audience. The myths were conceptualized and sung for and about the martial elite of Greece. This elite had distinct values and a special 'code of conduct' amongst its members, such as the pursuit of martial fame (*'kleos'*) and virtue (*'arete'*), experience and learning about foreign countries (*'polytropos'*), a particular form of open hospitality (*'xenia'*) vs. visitors of the same class and a very direct and 'personal' relationship to the gods (cp. discussions in Mull 2017, 217ff and Kristiansen and Larsson 2005, 225 and 240ff).

The myths focus on contents, which 'paid into' this value system and interpreted the events of the time accordingly. Context, which did not fit into this code of conduct, seems to have been omitted. Purely mercantile contacts for this reason may not show up in the mythical record, which captures heroic explorations only. In this way some interpret a remark in the Odyssey (VIII, 162) as an indication that the Mycenaean nobility looked down on regular commercial activities, some of which may have been commissioned to and transacted by specialized merchants.[67]

The expeditions of the Bronze Age Greek explorers thus have to be interpreted in the a.m. context of the *'acquisition of rare and powerful wonders from legendary [...] distances'* (Helms 1988, 13). The 'ulterior motives' of long distance journeys, like access to mineral resources and the accumulation of wealth, were only much later rationalized by the geographers and mythographers. In the tale about the Argonauts the key motive to embark on a journey to Colchis on the Black Sea coast is a personal feud between Jason and Pelias about the succession to the throne of Iolkos. Strabo ('The Geography', I, 2; 39) on the other hand muses that *'the wealth of that land* [Colchis] *(from gold, silver and iron), for which Phrixos also went forth on his voyage at an earlier time, suggests a plausible reason for the expeditions'*.

---

[67] Manning and Hulin (2005, 11) remark that the status of merchants even in Classical Greece appears not to have been high.

8.5 The Historicity of Greek Travel Myths – Conclusions and Vantage Point

There is ample evidence for a considerable travel and trade during the LBA, probably exceeding the later commercial exchange in the Early Iron Age. The dimension of the extensive trade and commercial links during the LBA also relative to later periods would make us assume that this period would have left significant traces in the mythical records.

The ingoing assumption for this book is that Greek myths indeed contain bits and pieces of historical information, also when it comes to journeys to faraway places. The question is thus how to deal with the metaphorical framework and later distortions myths have been exposed to.

The structural analysis of Burkert has shown that myths use patterns and metaphors derived from ancient local and imported traditions. With regard to the question about an original historic nucleus of a myth, Burkert (1979, 75f) assumes that *'Historical reality, transmitted in the form of tales, is immediately shaped in accordance with these patterns.'* We are clearly not looking at strictly historical reports in a modern sense when we read the myths today.

Yet even 'Skepticists' would acknowledge that it should be possible to at least broadly locate various myths into the background of Bronze Age events or layers, which are historically or archaeologically attested. Maybe it is allowed to take the question regarding the historical roots of some myths even a bit further.

It seems conceivable that instead of being fictional 'topoi', the patterns and role models of Indo-European or Near Eastern provenience were applied to real and existing people in the Mycenaean Bronze Age, who stood out because of their achievements in battle or distant travels. The mythical character of Heracles, for instance, is often brought into connection with far older Levantine and Mesopotamian origins like the Levantine god Melkart, which even found entry into the Greek mythical nomenclature as Heracles Melikertes.[68] It would seem possible, however, that there existed a real king or local hero of Tiryns by the name of Heracles[69], who undertook journeys to distant places and to which these patterns of Levantine or Mesopotamian provenience have been applied.

If indeed this type of 'real' heroes were at the heart of some of the Greek travelling myths, this assumption then brings up the next question with which time span within the Bronze Age certain individual myths can be associated.

As mentioned above, the Greek mythical age spans about 14 to 15 generations from divine and cloudy origins to the aftermath of the Trojan War. With an average of 30 years for each generation this amounts to a time span of approx. 400 years. When we assume

---

[68] Also the Mesopotamian gods and heroes Ninurta and Gilgamesh seem to have influenced the Heracles figure (Burkert 1979, 80f; Lane Fox 2009, 204).

[69] Questioned by Burkert (1979, 83). However, with the decipherment of the Linear B Script of the Mycenaean Greeks on tablets found in places like Pylos and Knossos, next to administrative information also names of gods and heroes, which before were only known from the mythological canon, suddenly became tangible. Clearly for these names thus attested we can safely assume a Bronze Age origin. A closer look into the Greek myths as they are transmitted to us, reveals that the protagonists often carry not one but two names. Rohl relates a list, which contains the double names of Paris/Alexandros, Priam/Podarces, Pyrrhus/Neoptolemos, Heracles/Alceides, but these are just a few of the many examples. Whilst one name may be assumed to be the original, *i.e.* maybe 'historical' name, some of the additional 'given' names seem to be added later ascribing a certain quality or function within the myths. As many Greek heroes seem to have two names, of which one may be given to the mythical character, the other may be the 'historic' name (Rohl 2007, 333).

the Trojan War broadly contemporary to the archaeologically attested demise of the Mycenaean palace structures at around 1180 BCE, this would bring us back to about 1600 BCE as the beginning of the 'mythical age'. This coincides surprisingly well with the historically and archaeologically attested beginning of the LBA in Greece and provides a consistent frame for the analysis going forward.

The question dealt with in the following chapters therefore is, whether there are further specific hints in the various travelling myths, which would allow for a more detailed geographical and historical referencing and thus broad timing of the myths.

9

Mycenaean Contacts with the Civilizations in the Eastern Mediterranean

9.1 Mycenaean Contacts with Anatolia

9.1.1 Archaeological and Historical Evidence of Mycenaean Contacts with Anatolia

After a general discussion of myths and the cultures and traditions these myths have been embedded in, now let us turn to potential journeys of Mycenaean travellers to specific far away destinations and let us check the archaeological and historical background for these, but also the references within the transmitted mythological corpus for long distance travel. A special attention has to be given in this context to the question as to whether we have indications for *direct exchanges* between the Mycenaeans and people from far away countries or whether we have to assume *indirect exchange models* for Mycenaean goods having reached those distant places.

Due to its relative geographical proximity and the possibility of 'island hopping' across the Aegean, the Anatolian west coast was amongst the logical 'first targets' for a Mycenaean expansion to the west from about 1450 BCE (LH II B) onwards. Based on *archaeological findings*, contacts between Mycenaean Greece and western Anatolia were well established from the 15th to the 13th century BCE (Waal 2019, 24). Overall the material evidence for Mycenaean activity – trade and settlement – in western Anatolia is focused on the southwestern coast and may decrease somewhat to the north, an exception being the city of Troy (Mee 1998, 144f).

In terms of chronology, Mycenaean traces up to the period LH II A are still rare in western Anatolia overall except some ceramic shards and a few swords maybe indicating military ventures in this period (Mee 1998, 137). From the period LH II B onwards numerous traces of Mycenaean trade can be found on the Anatolian west coast and become more widespread in LH III, esp. in the cities of Milet and Troy, but also in Iasos, Ephesos, Clazomenai et al. (Niemeier 2000, 5f; Mee 1998, 138; McMillan 2016, 6f).

Before Mycenaean influences become visible in the material remains of *Milet*, the city was exposed to strong Minoan influence in the period LH II A, from architecture to ceramics and personal items. The finds indicate a Minoan settlement, probably as a base for metal trade. The excavations of Niemeier revealed a destruction level for this Minoan enclave dated around the middle of the 15th century BCE. A conquest by Mycenaean Greeks at this time cannot be excluded (Niemeier 2000, 6). From this time on, the material remains found in Milet strongly point towards a Mycenaean presence in the area and much more so than in any other western Anatolian settlement (Taracha 2018, 11).

The first significant evidence in this direction in Milet stems from the period LH II B, during which the expansion of Mycenaean influence in the eastern Mediterranean began. Mycenaean material remains become even more pervasive in the subsequent period LH III. Judging from the high percentage of Mycenaean ceramics, settlement level 'Milet V' from around 1450 to 1300 BCE had a decidedly Mycenaean character. This coincides with the period in which the Mycenaeans extended their influence in the eastern Mediterranean (McMillan 2016, 6f).

That Myceneans eventually settled also in other parts of western Anatolia is also supported by chamber tombs, *e.g.* in Mueskebi from LH III, but also on the eastern Aegean islands dating slightly earlier (LH II B). Regarding the sources of Mycenaean ceramics found in western Anatolia, there is a clear focus on Mycenae itself (including the Argolis) in LH III A, shifting to Thebes in LH III B (Troy, Ialysos), maybe indicating a power shift between the two palatial centres (Banyai 2019, 134ff; Mee 1998, 138).[70]

There are also *historical* sources for contacts between Mycenaean Greeks and Anatolians.[71] Diplomatic correspondence has been excavated in the form of clay tablets in the Hittite capital Hattusha between the Hittite ruler and a king of 'Ahhiyawa'. Most scholars today would equate Ahhiyawa with the Achaean kingdom or kingdoms in Greece (*e.g.* Mee 1998, 142). This correspondence seems to point at growing tensions between the two powers over time due to hegemony conflicts over the western Anatolian littoral and the neighboring islands.

Taracha (2018) puts the archaeological and historical information of a Mycenaean influence and presence in the cultural interface at western Asia Minor into context and paints an overall picture of the relationships to the Hittite kingdom:

The 'Indictment of Madduwatta' (a western Anatolian king) dating probably from the end of the 15th century BCE is an indication of early Mycenaean meddling in Anatolia and Cyprus at a time which in archaeological terms is classified as LH III A1 (Mantzourani et al. 2019, 108; Taracha 2018, 12). The text refers to an Myceanaen ruler or warlord named Attarissya based presumably in western Anatolia who gets into repeated conflicts with Hittite forces over a Hittite vassal named Madduwatta.

The Mycenaean colony at Milet was destroyed around 1315 BCE, probably in the context of conquests of parts of western Anatolia by generals of the Hittite king Mursilis II (Niemeier 2000, 6). A Hittite supremacy over Milet from this period on however is questioned by Taracha (2018, 13), who sees a continued Mycenaean character in the material remains until around the reign of Tudhaliya IV, *i.e.* ca. 1240 BCE. Mursilis II is the first Hittite king to refer to the king of Ahhiyawa as a kingdom (Taracha 2018, 13f).

In the 13th century BCE the conflict between the Mycenaeans and the Hittites continued over the Sporades. These islands formed an important steppingstone towards the Black Sea area, for which the diplomatic letters found provide some evidence. In the mid 1250s BCE the so-called 'Tawagalawa-letter' from the Hittite ruler (likely Hattusilis III)

---

70 Cp. also chapter 4 on the struggle for domination of the Mycenaean city states between Mycenae and Thebes.
71 Cp. chapter 7 ('textual and epigraphic evidence').

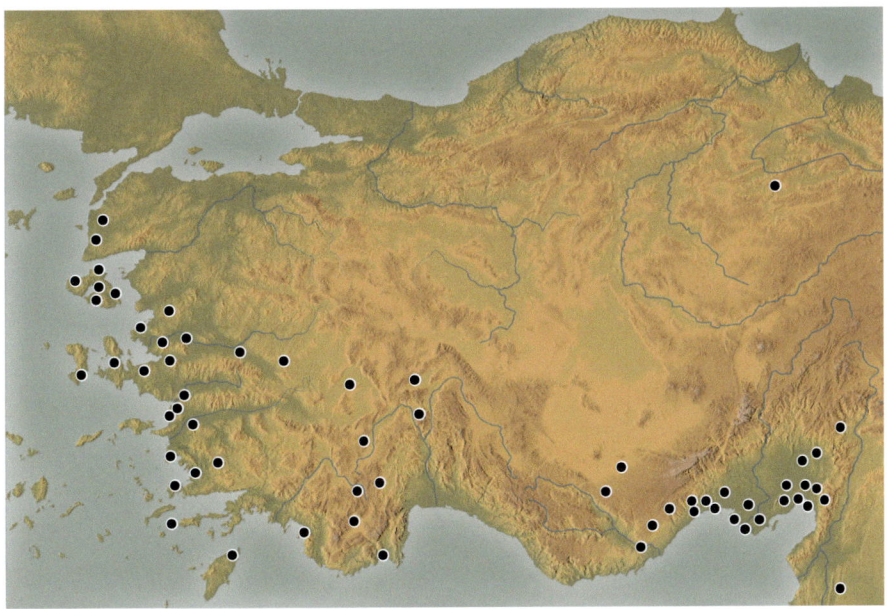

Fig. 9: Mycenaean finds in Anatolia (map: Olav Odé, after: van Wijngaarden in McMillan 2016, 54. Map of Cilicia: Olav Odé, after: 'Mykene – Die sagenhafte Welt des Agamemnon', Ausstellungskatalog, Badisches Landesmuseum, Schloss Karlsruhe, 2018/2019, Inside Cover).

to the king of Ahhiyawa Tawagalawas (maybe the mythical Theban king Eteocles, cp. Woudhuizen 2013, 8). In this letter the Hittite king complains about the protection granted by the Ahhiyawans for a rebel called Piyamaradu, who repeatedly ransacked Hittite controlled areas on the western Anatolian coastline and the islands.

The Tawagalawa-letter still indicates ongoing diplomatic relations on par between the rulers (Taracha 2018, 15). Only with the 'Sausgamuwa-letter' from the late 13th century BCE from the Hittite king to the ruler of Amurru about a trade embargo for Ahhiyawan ships the king of Ahhiyawa seems to have been no longer a player on the first level of power in the eastern Mediterranean (Taracha 2018, 17).

Overall, there are considerably less traces of Mycenaean material remains found in the inland areas of Anatolia (discussions in Waal 2019, 24f and Mcc 1998, 141). Exceptions are a Mycenaean sword and a ceramic shard showing a Mycenaean warrior excavated in the Hittite capital Hattusha. An interpretation for this remarkable paucity has been brought forward by Cline, who points at the potential consequences of a trade embargo imposed by the Assyrian king Tukulti Ninurta I on Mycenaean goods. The embargo is mentioned in a treaty between Hittite king Tudhaliya IV and Sausgamuwa of Amurru (first suggested by Cline 1991; discussed in McMillan 2016, 38ff, Schofield 2007, 114 and Waal 2019, 25).[72]

9.1.2 Reflections in Greek Myths

In the following paragraphs the attempt is made to give a tentative (genealogical) dating to the various myths based on cross-references between historical data and mythological time spans between different generations in the epics. The dates are speculative, because

---

[72] Cp. chapter 7; Waal (2019) offers alternative possible interpretations for this lacuna.

Fig. 10: Bellerophontes (Hans Weingartz).

we have neither archaeological nor historical proof that the mythological figures ever existed. Our information is based solely on the myths as they have been transmitted at first orally and then in written form, and finally quoted by later historians. The approach thus hinges on the reliability of genealogical dating approaches discussed above.

However, also the opposite applies: We have no proof either that the mythical figures and the genealogies they were embedded in did not reflect some historical elements as well. In fact, the myths often seem to contain a certain amount of historical information and it cannot be excluded that these nuclei contained the proper transmission of personal names as well. Some authors like David Rohl (2007) have tried to link some of the mythical names more or less plausibly to historically attested personalities. Also it needs to be reiterated that the overall timeframe of the mythical age fits quite well to the time we call the Late Bronze Age. So it may be worth at least a try to link some of the mythical information to historically attested data.

Bellerophontes

One of the initial advances of Mycenaeans towards western Anatolia may have been captured in the myth of Bellerophontes as it is related to us by Homer ('The Iliad', VI, 152) and Apollodorus ('The Library of Greek Mythology', 24). Bellerophontes, the son of Glaukos and grandson of Sisyphos, got caught up in disputes in the towns of Corinth and Argos and as a consequence was sent to Lykia on the south-western Anatolian coast. King Iobates of Lykia asked Bellerophon to destroy the Chimaira, a fire-spitting beast with a lion's head, the body of a goat and the tail of a snake (cp. also von Ranke-Graves 1986, 228ff).

With the help of the 'flying horse' Pegasus, Bellerophon manages to kill the Chimaira. He stays in Asia Minor and is subsequently sent to wage war against Anatolian tribes and pirates including the Amazons, who are further being referred to later in the chapter about the journeys to the Black Sea area (cp. chapter 11.2).

In terms of the metaphorical language used in this myth, the 'flying horse' Pegasus may actually stand for a swift Mycenaean galley, which may have been decorated with pictures of horses (cp. section 12.2.2 'Perseus'). The name 'Pegasus' may also have linguistic traces or origins in southern Cilicia, where a local Luwian-Hittite weather god called 'Pihassassi' is known, which was linked by the visiting Greeks with Zeus (Lane Fox 2009, 220).

Regarding the image of the Chimaira, similar pictographic motives with motives of a lion, snake and goat have been found in the Hittite city of Karkemish in northern Syria. The Chimaira depicted in a temple in this settlement was a symbol of the three-partite holy year of the Great Goddess (von Ranke-Graves 1986, 230).[73] The fire spitting image may go back to fires made by emissions of natural gas in the mountains behind Cape Gelidonya in proximity to Lykia, which were visible by night. The name 'Chimaira' may be connected to these fires and of Phoenician origin, where 'chmr' means 'fire' (Lane Fox 2009, 219f).

The theoretical dating of the myth based on mythological genealogies would take us to approximately three generations after the likewise mythical character Danaus (see section 9.4.2). If we can chronologically locate the Danaus myth in time roughly around 1550 to 1500 BCE[74], the expansion to Lykia in western Anatolia captured in the Bellerophontes myth would need to be placed around 1400 to 1450 BCE or slightly earlier. This timing coincides nicely with the initial expansion of Mycenaean activities in the Aegean and the western Mediterranean during the period of LH II B to LH III A.

Tantalos and Pelops

Further mythological links between Mycenaean Greece and Anatolia are to be found in the myths of Tantalos and his son Pelops. Tantalos, whose divine ancestry is contested since antiquity, was a mythical king of 'Lydia', from where he at some point of time set off to conquer Paphlagonia.[75]

---

73 Symbolized by a lion (for spring), a goat (for summer) and a snake (for winter).
74 Alternative datings are discussed below.
75 Strabo ('The Geography', XII, 8;21) sees Tantalos' origins in Phrygia. Both 'Phrygia' and 'Lydia' are toponyms describing parts of western Anatolia of late LBA and Early Iron Age origins and thus anachronisms. In Homer the country called Lydia is called 'Maionia'. Paphlagonia was located on the central Black Sea coast in northern Anatolia.

For crimes against his son Pelops, Tantalos was punished by the gods with the downfall of his kingdom. Later mythographers point to strong earthquakes in Lydia and Ionia during the reign of Tantalos, which 'destroyed Tantalis' (von Ranke-Graves 1986, 356). Pelops inherited the throne of Paphlagonia from the 'Lydians'. After ascending the throne, Pelops is harassed and defeated by 'barbarians', *i.e.* by king Ilus of Troy.[76]

As a consequence, Pelops is said to have migrated with his chariot and fabulous treasures to Elis in Greece. In Arcadia he took part in a chariot race to compete for the hand of the daughter of the Arcadian king Oinomaos, which he finished victoriously. He followed Oinomaos on the throne, married his daughter Hippodameia and went on to conquer the surrounding territories with the help of his charioteer Myrsilus. The latter word could be a Greek version of the royal Hittite name 'Mursilis' (Rohl 2007, 298). Pelops founded a dynasty in his new home and became the grandfather of Agamemnon.

The country subsequently changed its former names from 'Pelasgiotis' or 'Danaya' (after the mythical ancestor Danaus and his descendant Perseus, cp. section 9.4.2) to 'Peloponnes', or 'Isle of Pelops' (von Ranke-Graves 1986, 362). To the Hittites the country became known as 'Achaia' or 'Ahhiyawa'. Hyginus ('Fabulae', 124) lists Tantalos and Pelops in his list of the 'kings of the Achaeans'.

Behind the Pelops myth it is possible to see a migration and maybe minor conquest movement from Anatolia to Greece at around 1300 BCE (Rohl 2007, 298f). A genealogical date for the Tantalos myth would take us to a time broadly four generations before the Trojan War, or around 1310 BCE. Although linguistically problematic[77], it is tempting to see a connection to the Hittite client king Manapa Tarhunta (maybe in the contracted form Ta[rhu]nta + los), who became king of the Hittite province Seha River land (roughly identical to the later Lydia) around 1322 BCE and who wrote a letter to the Hittite king ca. 1295 BCE. This letter was discovered in the 1980s and contained references to conflicts in northwest Anatolia (cp. the a.m. mythical reference to the battles with king Ilos of Troy).[78]

Another interpretation of the Tantalos/Pelops myth is offered by Mosenkis (2016, 186), who sees in the two mythical figures the Hittite kings Tudhaliyas II and his son Suppiluliuma I (both 14th century BCE). Pelops' charioteer Myrtilos according to his theory would be Suppiluliuma's son and later Hittite king Mursilis II. In this interpretation the link to Mycenaean Greece is not entirely clear, though.

Overall the Tantalos and Pelops myths do not, however, belong to the Greek myths around exploration and long-distance travel, but rather to those about descent and origin of the Mycenaean dynasties ('Abstammungsmythen').

9.2 Mycenaean Contacts with the Levant

9.2.1 Archaeological Evidence of Mycenaean Contacts with the Levant

In the eastern Mediterranean, Mycenaean style pottery and other goods were in circulation for over two centuries and have been found at over one hundred sites in *the Levant* (Middleton 2015, 51). The Levantine coastline during the LBA was home to a number of different polities and smaller states stretching from the north down to the Carmel coast.

---

76   Ilus is the mythical character after which the citadel of Troy received its name 'Ilion'.
77   I am grateful for a warning in this respect from Ivo Hajnal.
78   The so-called 'Manapa-Tarhunta letter' also mentions an attack on Wilusa (Troy).

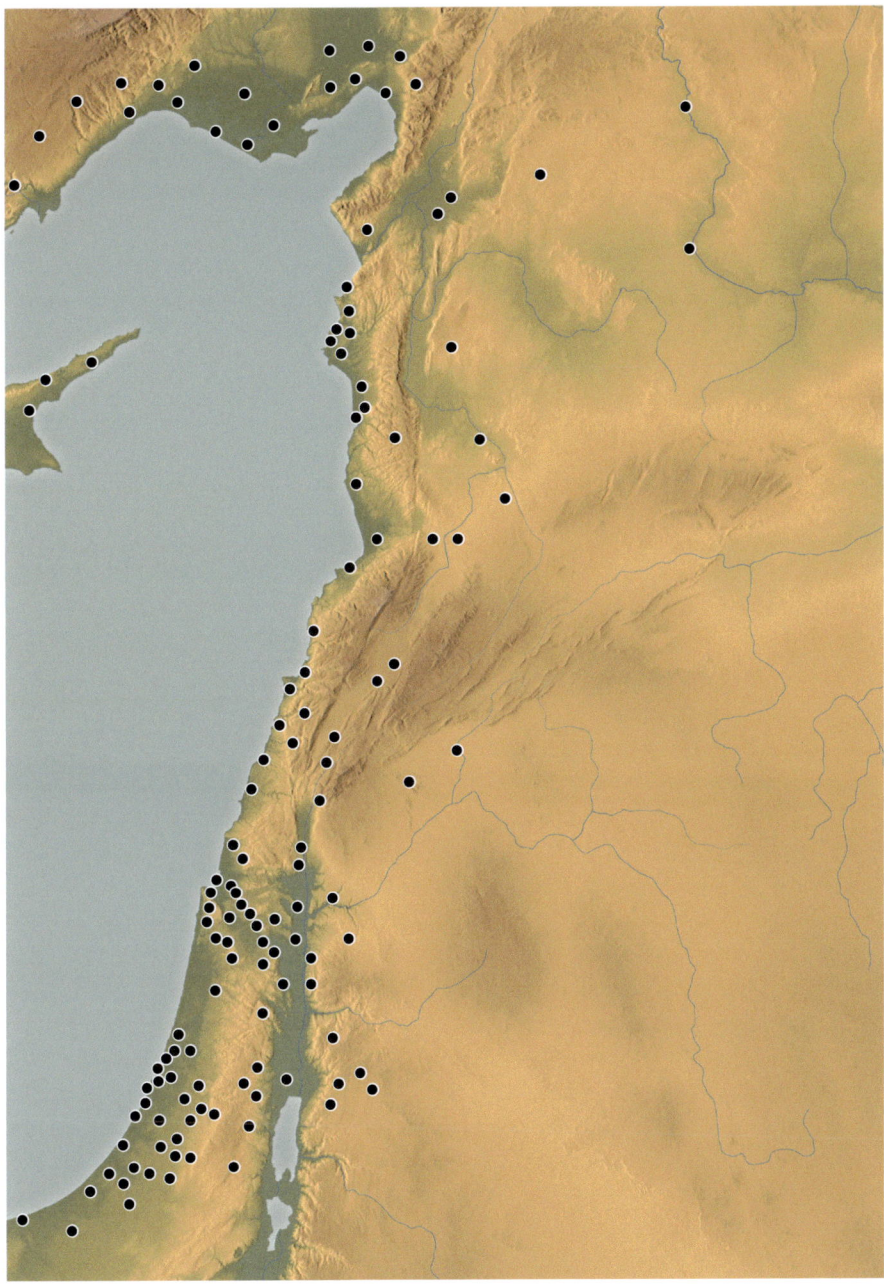

Fig. 11: Mycenaean material finds on the Levantine coast and Cilicia (map: Olav Odé, after: van Wijngaarden in McMillan 2016, 56).

Most of these independent city-states seem to have stood in contact with the Mycenaean Greeks (as demonstrated by McMillan 2016, 11f). In fact, overall the Levantine coastline provides archaeologically the highest number and density of Mycenaean artifacts in the Mediterranean starting from LH III A and found in all sorts of contexts. In Tell Abu Hawam a mix of Mycenaean pottery imports was found with origins in the Argolis (Tiryns, Midea) and Thebes (Mommsen and Maran 2000/1 in Banyai 2019, 137).

One of the most important sites in the Levant and international trading hub with links even to central Asia has been Ugarit. The city and its port have been a major gateway for tin from Asian sources into the Mediterranean world during the LBA. After the battle of Kadesh, the final stages of this route with the trading hub Ugarit were under control of the Hittite empire (Bell 2012, 181).

The question brought up before is, whether the contacts of Mycenaeans to the people from the Levant were of a direct or indirect nature. Mycenean ceramic finds from a number of settlements on the Syrian coastline (Tell Tweini, Tell Kazel (ancient Sumur), Tell Arqua and Tell Abu Hawam) point towards direct contacts by ship to the Aegean prior to the destruction of the settlements at the end of LBA II (Jung 2018, 293). Tartaron (2013, 29) and Bell (2012, 184) point out that only recently two letters have been found in Ugarit, which appear to render the Akkadian version of the Hittite name for the Mycenaeans. This new evidence could be another indication for a Mycenaean presence at Ugarit.

Next to the distribution of Mycenaean pottery in the Levant as shown in Figure 11, technological inventions seem to have had their origin on the Asian coastline and made their way from there to Mycenaean Greece (McMillan 2016, 11). In addition, 'cultural software' like Levantine gods, myths etc. may have 'travelled' from the Levantine coast to Bronze Age Greece (Lane Fox 2009, esp. chapters 14 to 16).

9.2.2 Reflections in Greek Myths

The Levant – 'Phoenicians' and 'Canaanites'

'Phoenicians' are frequently mentioned in the corpus of Greek myths. Io, for instance, had been abducted to Egypt on a Phoenician ship (Herodotus 'The Histories', I, 1). One origin of the ethnonym is related to the Greek word 'phoinix' meaning purple red and refers to the purple dye that the Levantine city-states were famous for (Lane Fox 2009, 21). In Greek mythology the name is connected to Phoinix, one of the sons of the Canaanite ancestor Agenor (see below).

Yet, the ethnonym 'Phoenicians' may not have been the name the people from the northern Levant used for themselves, at least not during the LBA. In fact, the Phoenicians under this ethnonym became tangible in the Mediterranean only from ca. 1000 BCE. In the older sources, they may have just been the 'people from Canaan', because Canaan is the other name that the northern Levantine coastline sometimes is referred to. In Mycenaean Linear B tablets the name may be rendered as 'ki-un-qa' with a reading of 'Kinahhi' or 'Kinahna' (*i.e.* Canaan; discussed in Woudhuizen 2010, 9).

In the near eastern mythological context the toponym 'Canaan' seems to be connected to 'Chnas', a Phoenician hero, who is sometimes equated with the a.m. Agenor from the Greek myths and is maybe the older denomination for the northern Levantine coast.

Sidon and Tyros have been some of the dominating municipalities in Phoenicia/Canaan in the LBA (Edwards 1979 in Woudhuizen 2013, 7). In the Odyssey, the Phoenicians seem to be referred to as 'Sidonians' at times, based on the city-state of Sidon, which for some time during the Early Iron Age dominated the sea trade off the Levantine coast.

Belos and Agenor

In Apollodorus' work 'The Library of Greek Mythology' (III, 1) we find the myth about the brothers Belos and Agenor. The name '*Belos*' seems to be a Greek rendering of the Phoenician title or deity 'Baal' (i.e. 'lord'). According to Apollodorus, Belos was a king of Egypt. The myth is thus very likely referencing to the 2nd Intermediate Period, where the northern parts of Egypt were under foreign (Hyksos) occupation, since at least a significant part of the Hyksos is likely to have had a Levantine origin.

Apollodorus reports about *Agenor*[79], the twin brother of Belos, that he left Egypt[80] to settle in Canaan/Phoenicia, where he became king of Tyre, married Telephassa (a seemingly Hittite name[81]) and fathered Europa, Cadmos, Phoinix and Cilix. The latter sons settled in different places after being unable to find their abducted sister Europa (see below). In the countries of destination according to Apollodorus they became name-givers to the countries Phoenicia and Cilicia (Apollodorus 'The Library', III, 1).

Genealogical analysis would make the brothers Belos and Agenor grandchildren of the Egyptian pharaoh Epaphos/Auserre Apophis (see below), which would lead to a dating of around 1525 BCE. This genealogically derived date is contemporary to – or slightly after – the Hyksos expulsion from Egypt and therefore fits well into the a.m. context.

Cadmos

Diodorus of Sicily in his Library of History (I, 23) mentions that Cadmus initially was an Egyptian citizen. If this was the case, he may have been part of the ruling stratum of foreign rulers in the northern Nile delta. If his leaving Egypt indeed was part of the Hyksos expulsion around 1550 to 1525 BCE, his name may be reminiscent of the last Hyksos pharaoh Khamudy (ca. 1550 BCE).

According to Apollodorus, Cadmos and Telephassa first followed their father Agenor to Tyre, but then left Phoenicia/Canaan, passed by Rhodes as well as Thera/Santorini and settled in Thrace, where Telephassa passed away. Still searching for his sister Europa, Cadmos asks the Delphian oracle for her whereabouts. The Pythia (priestess of the Delphian oracle) tells him to abandon his search and to found a city at a place where 'a cow takes a rest'. A cow he encounters and follows finally lies down in Boiotia, where Cadmos founds the city of Thebes, where the palatial complex and stronghold, the 'Cadmeia', are named after him.

Cadmos is also said to have brought the 'Pelasgian' alphabet back from Egypt to Greece.[82] If Cadmos is a son of Agenor, a genealogical chronological approach would lead to a date around 1500 BCE (Woudhuizen (2013, 7) argues for a date ca. 1600 BCE. The 'Parian Marble' puts the arrival of Cadmos in Thebes and the foundation of the Cadmeia into the year 1518/17 BCE (Rotstein 2016, 39).

---

79 Von Ranke-Graves (1986, 175) identifies Agenor with the phoinician hero Chnas, who is called 'Kanaan' in the Bible.
80 Rohl (2007, 495) equates the Egyptian Agenor with a 'well-attested, but unpositioned' Hyksos pharaoh named Akenenre Apophis.
81 In Greek mythology the name of Hittite kings 'Telepinu' seems to appear as 'Telephos'.
82 This cannot be the Phoenician alphabet yet, which reached Greece later in the Early Iron Age. Maybe this source is referring to a simplified rendering of Cretan hieroglyphs or the introduction of Linear B script (von Ranke-Graves 1986, 163).

Europa

Agenor's daughter Europa is abducted by Zeus himself, who takes on the shape of a bull, and brought to Crete. She there becomes the wife of the Cretan king Asterios and mother of his successor Minos together with his brothers Rhadamanthys and Sarpedon (Apollodorus 'The Library', III, 1).

With Minos being Europa's son, his reign would fall roughly into the period of 1480 to 1450 BCE or just before the Mycenaean occupation of Knossos.

As the record shows, the references to Phoenicians in the Greek myths are mostly *not* about Mycenaean exploration or pioneering adventures, but primarily about migration and descent ('Abstammungsmythen'). They put certain origins of the Mycenaeans into the broader context of eastern Mediterranean genealogies and migrations.

Menelaos

We find a reference to travel and trade of Mycenaeans to the Levant, albeit with a later date towards the end of the LBA, in the quotation by Menelaos referring to destinations he travelled to in the aftermath of the Trojan War:

> *'... for it took me seven years to amass this fortune and bring it home in my ships. My travels took me to Cyprus, to* **Phoenicia** *and to Egypt. Ethiopians,* **Sidonians***, Erembians, I visited them all; and I saw Libya, too.'* (Homer 'The Odyssey', IV, 80, my emphasis)

During these journeys he professes to have amassed an enormous fortune. One of his most treasured objects is later given to Telemachus, a mixing bowl made of silver that Menelaos according to his own accounts has received from *'Phaedimus, the heroic king of Sidon, when I stayed at his palace on my journey home'*. (Homer 'The Odyssey', IV, 610 and XV, 115; comments on Menelaos' stay in Sidon also in Strabo 'The Geography', I, 2; 33)

These later references belong to the time around 1180 BCE and are an indication for Mycenaean contacts with the Levantine coast either in the form of raid, trade or diplomatic exchange.

Mopsos

The myth of Mopsos' journeys in the eastern Mediterranean is transmitted to us by the Lydian Xanthos. Mopsos[83] had left the Trojan War already one year prior to its dramatic ending and had sailed down the Anatolian coastline to found new cities in Cilicia. After reaching Cilicia and subsequent to the foundation of some settlements in the vicinity of Adana, Mopsos continues his journey down the Levantine coast, reaches Canaan and participates in an attack on the city of Askalon (Rohl 2007, 393ff).

Inscriptions found in Cilicia and northern Syria support the assumption that Mopsos could have been a historical figure of Greek origin and stood in connection with Cilicia (Zangger 1994, 237; recently discussed in Kopanias 2018). The myth may fit into the context of Mycenaean migrations to Cilicia and even Canaan at the very end of the LBA.

---

83 The name 'Mopsos' is found in different languages of LBA origin: Mycenaean 'Moqoso', Luwian 'Muksa', Hittite 'Muksas'.

The Mopsos myth belongs into a similar timeframe as Menelaos' travels along the Phoenician coast. The attack on Askalon is often brought into connection with the Sea Peoples assaults on the Levantine coast. Rohl (2007, 399) and Kopanias (2018, 76) even assume that Mopsus was the leader of the contingent of 'Danana' warriors in the attacks on Levantine cities and Egypt.

Both myths – Menelaos's travels in the aftermath of the Trojan War and Mopsos' journeys – are thus not pioneering long distance travels to sources of metal supplies, but belong into the context of the convulsions at the end of the LBA. The absence of early pioneering journeys of Mycenaeans in the mythical record may have to do with the fact that from early times on the city states on the Levant were regular commercial partners for them.

9.3 Mycenaean Contacts with Cyprus

9.3.1 Archaeological Evidence of Mycenaean Contacts with Cyprus

Another key trading-partner of the Mycenaeans has been *Cyprus*, situated across the sea from the Levantine entrepot Ugarit and strategically positioned at the crossroads of three continents. The importance of Cyprus within the trading network of the Bronze Age lies in the abundance of copper sulphides mined since the EBA in the Troodos mountain range on the island. Based on textual evidence, Cypriot copper was traded to Egypt, Ugarit and via Levantine ports to cities in Mesopotamia already since ca. 1900 BCE. Archaeologically an upswing in the copper exploitation in Cyprus is noticeable only since the LBA (Kassianidou 2013; Mantzourani et al. 2019, 98ff; Pare 2000, 11).

The ramp up of copper production on Cyprus during the LBA may to some extent have been driven by demand from Mycenaean Greece. With over 4000 objects of Mycenaean origin found on the island, Cyprus has clearly been an important trading destination for the Mycenaeans (McMillan 2016, 28ff). Amongst these objects, a substantial amount of Mycenaean pottery has been excavated, both imported and – from the end of the 13th century BCE on – also produced locally (van Wijngaarden 2012, 67).

The Mycenaean contacts may have started in the LH III period and thus slightly later compared to the west coast of Anatolia, since the discovered pottery remains from the earlier periods LH I and LH II are rare. On the other hand, vast amounts of LH III pottery have been found on Cyprus. In the 13th and 12th centuries BCE, the Mycenaean pottery found on Cyprus can be interpreted as an indication for a transformation from exotic imports to objects, which were integrated into the everyday routines of the people on the island (see discussions in McMillan 2016, 24; Gillis 1993, 68 and Knapp 2012, 44).

Towards the end of the LBA, Cyprus due to its mineral wealth was fought over by the Hittites and maybe also by different elements of the Sea Peoples, who seem to have established strongholds on the island. In the aftermath of the conflicts at the end of the LBA, some Mycenaeans may have sought refuge on Cyprus in the context of the demise of the palace structures in Greece and have contributed cultural features to the Cypriot LBA and Early Iron Age culture (interpretation of Knapp 2012, 46). From this time on also an Arcadian dialect was spoken on Cyprus. Against this background it would probably be reasonable to assume that Cyprus was a familiar territory to the Mycenaeans.

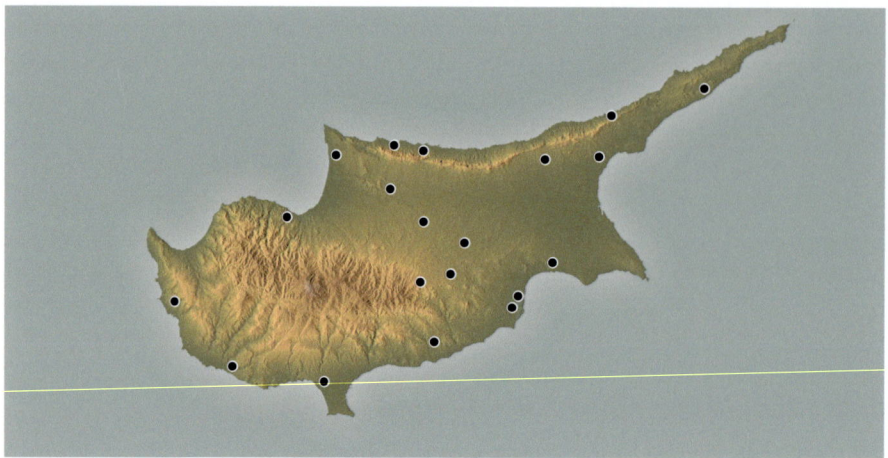

Fig. 12: Mycenaean material finds on Cyprus (map: Olav Odé, after: van Wijngaarden 2002 in: McMillan 2016, 55).

9.3.2 Reflections in Greek Myths

Regarding *Cyprus*, there is also a colourful and mixed reference in the catalogue of Greek mythology.

Aphrodite

According to Hesiod's 'Theogony' and to Apollodorus ('The Library', I, 1, 3), the goddess Aphrodite is said to be born in Cyprus. Like the story about Adonis (see below) this myth is based on an older tradition of Levantine origin (discussed in Lane Fox 2009, 362f).

Adonis

One of the Greek myths related to Cyprus is the story of Aphrodite's lover, the demigod *Adonis,* who was revered in Cyprus for a long period of time. The origins of the Adonis myth have to be sought in Mesopotamia and the Syro-Levantine coast and date back to times before 2000 BCE. It can be traced back to the Mesopotamian myth of Dumuzi the shepherd, who in Canaan was called 'Tammuz' and in his cult was referred to as 'Adonai' (*i.e.* 'Lord'), hence the rendering 'Adonis' in Greek language (cp. Lane Fox 2009, 240ff).

Teukros and Agapenor

Some myths with reference to Cyprus refer to the end of the LBA, when some Mycenaean veterans from the Trojan War resettle on the island. *Teukros* for instance is banished by his father from his home on the Greek island of Salamis due to the fact that he did not prevent the death of his brother Ajax. He travels via Egypt and Sidon to Cyprus and founds the city of Salamis on the island with the help of the Sidonian king (cp. Mull 2017, 252f).[84]

---

84 The 'Parian Marble' gives a date of 1202 BCE for Teukros' foundation of Salamis (Rotstein 2016, 41). This date would be about 20 years earlier than the chronology assumed here.

Agapenor, the leader of the Arcadian contingent in the Trojan War, gets blown off course during the return journey after the sack of Troy. Following some detours he ends up in Cyprus and founds the city of Paphos on the southwestern coast of the island. Should this myth have Bronze Age origins and an historical nucleus, it would help to explain why in the Classical Period of Greece an Arcadian dialect was spoken on Cyprus.

Overall, the Greek myths regarding Cyprus contain many elements that link these stories to Near Eastern origins. They need to be treated as 'cultural imports' and belong to the myths about descent and origins. Like in the case of the Levant, the lack of heroic early exploration myths around Cyprus may have to do with the fact that Cyprus was relatively well known and almost from the start belonged to the mercantile network of the Mycenaeans.

Other myths from the end of the LBA (Menelaos, Teukros, Agapenor) with reference to the Levant or Cyprus have a different background and have to be put into the context of the above-mentioned convulsions around the Sea Peoples, the migrations in the aftermath of the Trojan War and maybe the attack against Egypt under Ramses III.

9.4 Mycenaean Contacts with Egypt

9.4.1 Pictorial, Historical and Archaeological Evidence of Mycenaean Contacts with Egypt

Early Contacts (2nd Intermediate Period)
Some Egyptian goods have reached Crete as early as Early Dynastic times (*i.e.* ca. 2500 BCE) probably via *indirect* trade routes with Levantine cities as intermediaries. The first *direct* contacts between the Minoan Cretans and Egypt are assumed for the MBA. From the Middle Kingdom onwards (*i.e.* ca. 2050 BCE), Egypt seems to have become part of the Minoan trading network in the Mediterranean. This long-distance trading network connected the Aegean, the Levant, Cyprus, Anatolia, Egypt and part of the western Mediterranean and was also driven by the desire to obtain metals (early Minoan contacts with Egypt are discussed in Phillips 2010, 825; Duarte de Cunha 2013, 1; Kelder 2018, 10) .

There is evidence for ongoing contacts between the Minoans and Egypt during the 2nd Intermediate Period, esp. during the 'Hyksos period' of foreign domination of parts of northern Egypt from ca. 1640 to 1550 BCE, whilst Upper Egypt was in parallel ruled by local pharaohs of the 17th dynasty from Thebes. The Hyksos traded with the Levant, Cyprus and also with Minoan Crete. An alabaster lid with the inscription of the name of Hyksos pharaoh Khyan found in Knossos bears witness to these exchanges. In fact, Minoans in this period may have lived with and fought with the Hyksos at their capital Avaris in the Nile delta (Kelder 2018, 11; Rohl 2007, 8f).

There are also assumptions that during the 2nd Intermediate Period the first sporadic contacts between Egypt and the Mycenaeans occurred, which possibly have been employed as mercenaries by the Hyksos or the Egyptians, but these connections are not finally proven yet. Kelder (2016, 314) stresses that there are strong indications for silver objects from the El-Tod treasure found 20 km south of Luxor in Egypt dating to the final stages of the Middle Helladic period, *i.e.* to the 17th century BCE, being the produce of Mycenaean workshops. If proven right, this would point at trade connections between Mycenaean Greece and Egypt as early as the Mycenaean Shaft Grave era (the time of the first contacts of Mycenaeans to Egypt are discussed in McMillan 2016, 17; Kelder 2018, 13 and 2016, 314; Phillips 2010, 823).

Overall, for the 2nd Intermediate Period in Egyptian history under Hyksos domination new links to the international metal exchanges in the eastern Mediterranean and the Near East can be attested. Also during the 2nd Intermediate Period, tin bronzes become common in Egypt (Rahmstorf 2015, 194).

Contacts during the 18th Dynasty – From Diplomatic Visits to a More Diversified Exchange?

After the final expulsion of the Hyksos around 1550 to 1540 BCE[85] (or a bit later) and the establishment of the New Egyptian kingdom with the 18th dynasty, there used to be very little evidence in the subsequent years for direct Minoan, let alone Mycenaean contacts with Egypt, at least during the 16th century BCE under the pharaohs ascribed to the 18th dynasty 'A' (the dynastic 'split' follows Merrillees 1972, 283f, also Shaw 2000, 208), until recent excavations in Tell el-Daba (the location of the Hyksos capital Avaris) yielded new finds.

Lately substantial wall paintings in Minoan style were found in the remains of a palace built in Tell el-Daba by pharaoh Ahmose, the founder of the 18th dynasty (Shaw 2000, 204, 208), indicating a continuation or even increase of contacts between Egypt and Crete and maybe a Cretan presence in Egypt during this period. In spite of these new finds Dynasty 18 'B' begins with the female pharaoh Hatshepsut and the co-reign with her son Thutmosis III (1503 – 1482 BCE). During her reign, a maritime expedition to the land of 'Punt' was organized, a toponym which needs to be located most likely in northeastern Africa (Somalia), whilst some authors locate Punt in southern Arabia. The contacts with this southern region continue under her successors.

The picture regarding Mycenaean contacts with Egypt changes in the sole reign of Thutmosis III, *i.e.* from ca. 1482 BCE onwards. The combination of archaeological and pictorial evidence as well as written records points at an increase of Mycenaean contacts, whilst Minoan imports all but disappear. This is significant, because – as discussed earlier – it is assumed that around 1450 BCE the Minoan palaces on Crete have been destroyed by the Mycenaeans.

Various contacts with Mycenaeans as traders cum diplomats are attested during the time of Thutmosis III. The 'Tanaju' or 'Tanaja' are for the first time mentioned in the 'Annals of Thutmosis' visible as a monumental inscription on the walls of the Amun temple in Karnak (Panagiotopoulos 2006, 370ff and 394). These Tanaju are believed to be the Greek 'Danaans' of the Homeric myths (so Phillips 2010, 822 and Woudhuizen 2013, 7). The items sent by the 'prince of Tanaja' are interpreted as an act of diplomatic gift giving. The Minoans are absent in this inscription.

Contemporaneously, Mycenaean pottery begins to appear in Egypt, albeit in smaller volumes. It would fit to the a.m. interpretation to explain the arrival of this pottery in the wake of the *first diplomatic contacts*. Alternatively the appearance in this period due to the paucity of finds may as well still be the result of indirect and decentralized trade via Cyprus or the Levant (Kelder 2010, 130).

Additionally, wall paintings in the graves of various high ranking Theban officials from this period until the reign of Amenhotep II show contacts and different forms of exchange

---

85 Chronology after Kitchen (2006, 23).

with regions recently brought under Egyptian dominance (Nubia, southern Levant) and others from further away including the Aegean (Panagiotopoulos 2006, 377ff).

The paintings in the grave of Rekhmire, an Egyptian official and vizier and governor of Thebes under Thutmosis III and the first years of Amenhotep II display people of presumably Aegean origin bringing goods (commercial goods or offerings) to the pharaoh, some of them obviously Minoan Cretans.

Whilst the people from the Aegean are indiscriminately called 'from the isles in the midst of the Sea' by the Egyptians, the changing outfit from loincloths to kilts in an obvious over-painting of the pictorials in the grave of Rekhmire has been interpreted by some researchers as an indication of a Mycenaean takeover of trade routes to Egypt previously dominated by Minoans. The Mycenaean visitors seem to be bringing "greeting gifts" to the court including cups and jugs made from metal (interpretations by Merrillees 1972, 289ff; Panagiotopoulos 2006, 393ff and Kelder 2010, 125).

For the time of the subsequent pharaohs Amenhotep II and Thutmosis IV (18th dynasty 'C'), we have again less evidence for Aegean-Egyptian contacts (Merrillees 1972, 289). During the reign of Amenhotep III (1417 to 1379 BCE) a topographical list inscribed on the base of a statue at the funerary temple of the pharaoh at Kom El Hetan is interpreted as evidence for an Egyptian fleet, which at some point in time had sailed to various destinations in the Aegean in Crete and on mainland Greece (interpretations of the Kom El Hetan inscription in Matthaeus 2005, 336; Merrillees 1972, 290; Kelder 2018, 14 und 2010, 126).

This list of locations is taken as proof that the Aegean was to some extent familiar territory to the Egyptians at this time. A supporting fact for this assumption are the faience plaques found in the citadel of Mycenae with the royal cartouche of pharaoh Amenhotep III, which may have been sent as a foundation deposit for a shrine in Mycenae (Kelder 2009, 340 and 2010, 128f).

Kelder (2010) stresses that the Greek mainland – if this is behind the ethnonym or maybe toponym[86] 'Tanaju' – only is mentioned in written sources from the time of Thutmosis III and Amenhotep III onwards. As a consequence, he assumes that the contact between Egypt and the Mycenaean world during this time was of a direct and formal nature – i.e. between the royal courts – including the exchange of prestige goods (Kelder 2009, 340). Still, archaeological remains that indicate commercial or official direct contacts between Egypt and Greece from this period remain relatively rare (again Merrillees 1972, 291).

By contrast, the reign of Akhenaten, who started his reign under the name of Amenhotep IV (1379 to 1326 BCE), probably saw a *new intensity and quality of direct exchanges* between Mycenaeans and Egypt (so Kelder 2018, 14). The contacts are attested via considerable amounts of Mycenaean pottery found at Akhetaten, the newly founded capital under Akhenaten, where he moved in the 6th year of his reign.

These pottery remains are the first major Mycenaean ceramic finds in the Egyptian archaeological record and consist to some extent of containers for the transport of olive oils. This oil has been widely used in Egypt as a base for perfumes in ceremonies, but also non-perfumed for cooking, lamp fuel and to tend to horses and their equipment. The ceramics are all datable to the period LH III A2, a homogeneity that suggests one single

---

[86] Kelder (2010, 126) assumes the term 'Tanaju' to refer to a unified state headed by an over-ruler or king rather than a sub-group of Mycenaeans.

delivery. The style of the containers seems to point at the Argolid and potentially the area around Mycenae as the origin of the cargo. Olives at this time were not native to Egypt and had to be imported (discussions on olive oil as key export product from Mycenaean Greece to Egypt in McMillan 2016, 18 and Kelder 2009, 342 and 2010, 132ff).

Since some remains of Mycenaean pottery were found also in more humble dwellings outside the palatial area, Merrillees (1972, 291) assumes that the contacts were probably of a *commercial* nature and more diversified. Kelder (2010, 130f) on the other hand points to fact that the majority of pottery has been found in the central city around the palace. We thus have to assume some form of palatial control over the flow of important resources. He therefore interprets the advent of the olive oil containers as "greeting gifts" and as indication for (another) direct diplomatic mission between the palatial centres in Mycenaean Greece and Egypt during the Amarna period.

If Kelder is correct, this would overall potentially add up to at least three separately identifiable direct contacts from Mycenaean Greece to Egypt between the times of Thutmosis III and Akhetaten including the mission sent by Amenhotep III to the Aegean (cp. Kelder 2009, 347 and 2010, 133).

During the reign of Akhenaten, it furthermore seems that Mycenaean *soldiers* were employed in service of the Egyptian pharaoh. A papyrus fragment found in Amarna depicting what looks like Mycenaean mercenaries in the Egyptian army is interpreted in this direction. This interpretation is supported by the find of a boar tusk fragment in Qantir (the ancient Pi-Ramesse) of probable Mycenaean origin and by ceramic finds (Schofield 2007, 125; Kelder 2010, 126f and 2018, 17).

It is thus possible that Mycenaeans at this time *lived* in Amarna on a more permanent base, potentially employed as elite soldiers. There are also indications for another *Bronze Age Mycenaean settlement in Akhnim*, which the Greeks called 'Chemmis' (mentioned in Herodotus II, 91). One settlement with this name has been identified in upper Egypt, founded towards the end of the 2nd millennium BCE. This municipality existed as 'Khent-min' already under Thutmosis IV and Amenhotep II (von Ranke-Graves 1986, 221 and 475). Woudhuizen (2013, 7) refers to another location with the same name in the Nile delta, which due to its geographical accessibility is maybe a more likely base for Mycenaean settlers. These latter traces would also point to broader contacts between Egypt and Mycenaean Greece, which go beyond diplomatic niceties.

Contacts during the 19th and 20th Dynasty – Exchanges and Conflicts

The diverse contacts between Egypt and the Mycenaeans during the late 18th dynasty seem to have been maintained under the successors of Akhenaten until the long reign of Ramses II (1279 to 1213 BCE) and his successor Merneptah (1213 to 1203 BCE) of the 19th dynasty. This assumption is based on the earrings of queen Nefertari of presumable Aegean origin depicted on wall-paintings in her tomb. Also Mycenaean pottery is now found throughout Egypt though almost always as luxury goods. Overall around 1800 objects found in Egypt are of Minoan or Mycenaean origin, which makes Egypt the second largest trading partner for the Mycenaeans (contacts with Egypt in the late 18th dynasty are analyzed by McMillan 2016, 16 and Kelder 2009, 347, 2010, 136f and 2018, 17) .

Towards the end of the 13th century BCE, Achaeans under the ethnonym 'Ekwesh' seem to appear as opponents and prisoners of war during an attempted invasion from Libya into Egypt in the time of Merneptah in 1208 BCE. This ethnonym however does not seem to

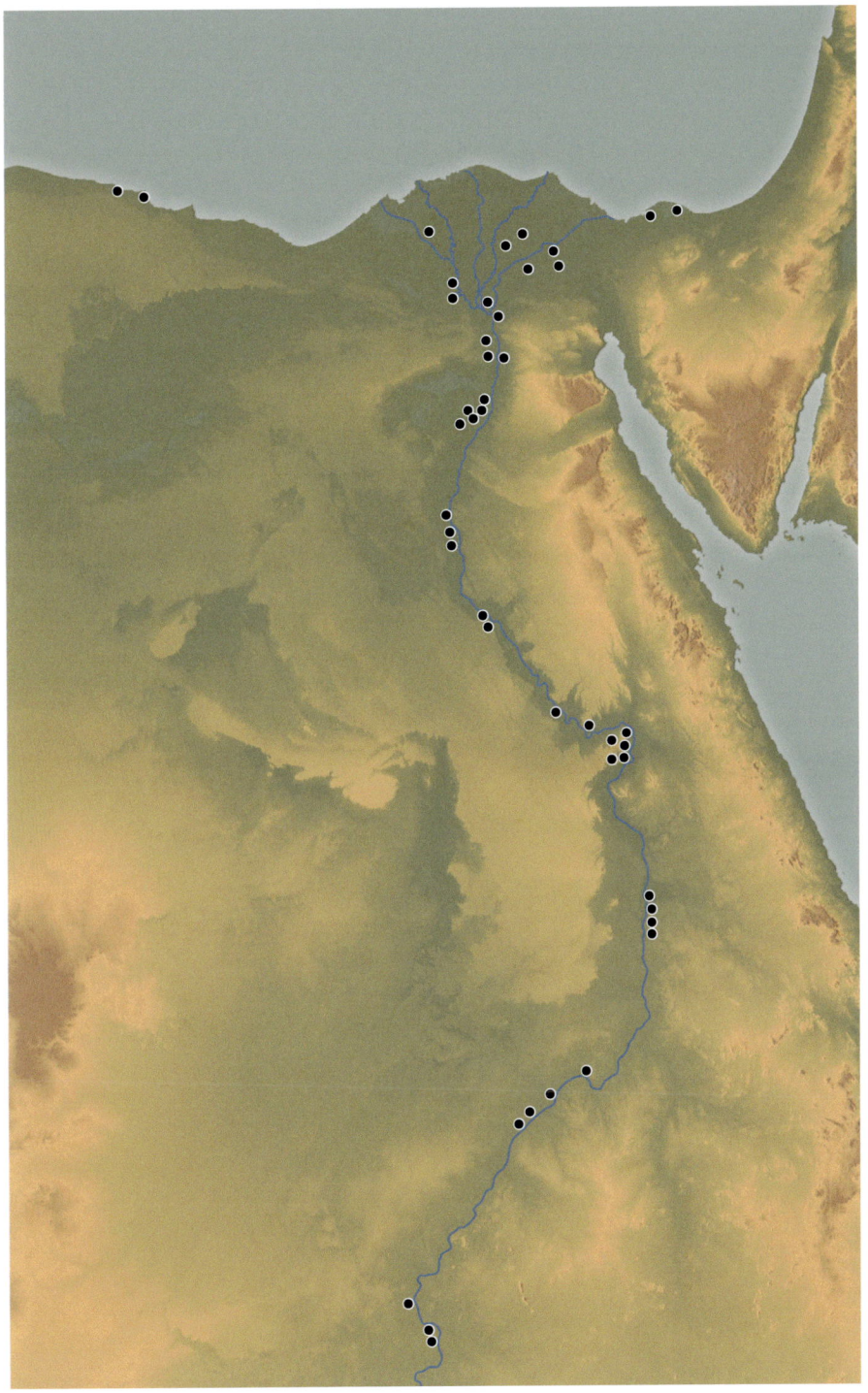

Fig. 13: Mycenaean pottery finds in Egypt (map: Olav Odé, after: van Wijngaarden 2002 in McMillan 2016, 57).

refer to a unified Mycenaean state, but rather denote a 'group of people', which may have its origin in Bronze Age Greece.

From these years onwards until the reign of Ramses III (1186 – 1155 BCE) of the 20th dynasty, Egypt and the other cultural centres in the eastern Mediterranean were threatened by the so called 'Sea Peoples', who disrupted the established trade routes, destroyed entrepots like Ugarit and contributed to the downfall of the Hittite empire. Since another group mentioned as part of the 'Sea Peoples' by Ramses III are the 'Denyen', who are often equated with the Danaans of the Homeric tradition, there are discussions as to whether the Mycenaeans were part of these raiders or whether their own palace structures fell victim to an attack by them.[87]

The last contacts between the Mycenaean Greeks and Egypt are attested for the time of Ramses III (Kelder 2018, 17). After a longer hiatus of several hundred years, contacts between Egypt and the Greeks only resumed on a more frequent level during the Iron Age under pharaoh Bocchoris of the 24th dynasty (725 to 720 BCE) residing in Sais in the Nile delta (Lane Fox 2009, 32).

Overall, as far as the existing material evidence goes, we thus have a varied picture of Aegean-Egyptian exchange over time with periods of high intensity and other times of a potentially lesser frequency. The range of contacts may have started with diplomatic missions and have become more diversified later on.

Gillis (1993, 68f) takes a 'minimalist' position and interprets the imbalance between Egyptian imports from Mycenaean Greece and the small amounts of potential exports from Egypt to Greece (mostly royal scarabs) as an indication against direct trade contacts between Egyptians and Aegeans.

On balance however, the huge amounts of Mycenaen pottery and even evidence for Mycenaean residents (as mercenaries?) in Egypt point to at least sporadic direct contacts between Egypt and the Mycenaean palatial centres perhaps since the 2nd Intermediate Period. The contacts may have been most intense during the reigns of Thutmosis III, Akhenaten and Ramses II. For the 18th, 19th and 20th dynasty, we have relatively clear indications for several direct missions of an official nature. Next to these maybe diplomatic connections, there is some evidence for Mycenaean soldiers in service of the Egyptian army from the 18th to the 20th dynasty in Egypt, and even of Mycenaean enclaves in Egypt (again Kelder 2009, 349 and 2010, 133).

The existing material record thus supports the assumption of relatively regular and direct contacts between the Mycenaean world and Egypt during the 18th and 19th dynasty up until the end of the palatial society in Mycenaean Greece around 1180 BCE maybe including conflicts towards the end of this period. A 'maximalist' position would assume many more and varied contacts of a commercial nature, for which the material or historical evidence is lost.

The question that now needs to be dealt with is, to which degree this varying level of contacts is reflected in and fits to the Greek myths.

---

87 A consistent sequence of events is suggested by Mull (2017) by including mythological sources; similar Getroux (2016).

9.4.2 Reflections in Greek Myths

Mythological references point to various contacts between Mycenaean Greece and Egypt during the LBA. These contacts seem to have started already during the Hyksos phase (2nd Intermediate Period) and in the early phase of the LBA.

Contacts during the Hyksos Period (2nd Intermediate Period) and the Early 18th Dynasty in Egypt

Dionysos

A very early reference to Egypt in the Greek myths is given in connection with the travels of the god Dionysos. It is said that Dionysos sailed with a shipload of wine to Egypt to the island of Pharos, where he was received by king Proteus, the grandfather of the a.m. Epaphos. During this time, 'Titans' were ruling in the Nile delta. Dionysos participates in a war 'to reinstate king Ammon' and achieves a military victory against the Titans in alliance with the Libyans of the Nile delta (Apollodorus 'The Library', III, 5; von Ranke-Graves 1986, 91).

A theoretical dating for this story takes us to the 2nd Intermediate Period of the Egyptian chronology and the Hyksos occupation of parts of the Nile delta, since Epaphos can probably be equated with the Hyksos pharaoh Ausserre Apophis (ca. 1585 – 1550 BCE[88]) and Proteus potentially with pharaoh Senakhtenre Tao (also called 'Ahmose the Elder', ca. 1600 – 1565 BCE) of the parallel 17th dynasty in Thebes. As Apophis is portrayed as a son of the Argive princess Io, one would arrive at roughly one generation before the Io tale and broadly in the first half of the 16th century BCE.

The ruling stratum of the Hyksos occupants would then probably need to be equated to the 'Titans' mentioned in the story of Dionysos' expedition to Egypt. Dionysos may have stayed or reiterated his travels until the expulsion of the Hyksos around 1550 BCE, if this is what is meant with the 'reinstatement of king Ammon' (since the Hyksos worshipped the god Baal, whilst the contemporary Egyptian pantheon had the Theban god Amun at its centre).

The shipload of wine may indicate an initial mercantile purpose for Dionysos' trip to Egypt and to Mycenaean export products other than olive oil. The apparent subsequent involvement in an armed conflict in Egypt may further point to Mycenaean mercenaries taking part in the power struggles towards the end of the 2nd Intermediate Period in Egypt.

Io

In the myth about Io, we have another immediate link to the a.m. Epaphos or Apophis. Io is said to be born in Argos being the daughter of the Pelasgian (*i.e.* pre-Mycenaean) king Inachus, who was a descendant of Iapetos (Rohl 2007, 151ff).[89] Herodotus ('The Histories', I, 1) relates two different versions of her later move to Egypt. In the Persian story of Io she arrived in Egypt as a captive of a (Bronze Age, *i.e.* Canaanite) Phoenician trading ship. In the Phoenician version ('The Histories', I, 5) she followed at her own will. Interestingly, in

---

[88] The chronology and precise dates for the reign of rulers during the time of the Hyksos occupation are not secured yet.

[89] Rohl (2007, 153) points to a common mythological heritage in the eastern Mediterranean and the possibility to identify Iapetos with the biblical Japheth.

the Greek myths professional merchants are often Phoenicians, whilst the Mycenaeans are portrayed as warrior heroes rather than traders (cp. Tartaron 2013, 134).

After her arrival in Egypt, Io gets married to an Egyptian king called Telegonos and gives birth to Epaphos, which we assume to be the later Hyksos pharaoh Apophis (von Ranke-Graves 1986, 169). Based on some form of linguistic analysis – with an element of conjecture -, Rohl (2007, 155ff) identifies Telegonos with pharaoh Seqenenre Taa (-ken) (Telegonos -> 'Tala ken'[90]) of the Theban 17th dynasty (around 1560 BCE), a brother of Kamose and father of pharaoh Ahmose, who finally liberated northern Egypt from the Hyksos rule. Sekenenre Taa (-ken) is likely to have lost his life in a conflict with the Hyksos. If one accepts the links stated above, a theoretical date for the Io tale would take us to the beginning to middle of the 16th century BCE.

Rohl (2007, 156ff) also equates Io with the Egyptian queen Ahotep (Yahhotep -> Yauna = Ionian), who seems to have played a decisive role in the war against the Hyksos.[91] Also Shaw (2000, 205) refers to Ahotep, the mother of pharaoh Ahmose, as the 'mistress of the Haunebut', an Egyptian toponym, which may refer to the Aegean isles. In queen Ahotep's grave, weapons were found with Aegean or east Mediterranean motifs on them (Shaw 2000, 208). Io in the Greek myths is connected to the moon cult and the pre-hellenic bull cult in Argos. In Egypt, she is often connected to the Egyptian goddesses Isis or Hathor, who also are often shown with cow horns.

Danaus

Herodotus[92], Apollodorus[93], Hyginus[94], Diodorus,[95] Manetho[96] and the Parian Marble[97] all relate a story about Danaos or Danaus, a descendant of Io/Yahhotep in the 4th generation, which is also directly linked to Egypt. According to Herodotus ('The Histories', II, 91), Danaus stemmed from Chemmis (Akhnim) in Egypt. His Egyptian name is rendered as 'Armais' by Manetho:

'Armais, also called Danaus, ruled five years. Then he was exiled from Egypt. Fleeing from his brother Aigyptos, he reached Greece, where he gained power in Argos and ruled over the Argives.' (Verbrugghe and Wickersham 2001, 142)[98]

According to Herodotus and Apollodorus, Armais/Danaus is said to have 50 daughters, which were to be married to the 50 sons of the Egyptian king Aigyptos. After a power-struggle with his brother Aigyptos, Danaus and his daughters decided to flee or were exiled from Egypt to Argos in Greece.[99] Upon arrival in Argos, Danaus claimed the kingdom there from the incumbent Pelasgian king Gelanor. Danaus won the contest and became the new king of Argos.

---

90 Von Pessl (1878, 23) renders the name as 'Tiaaken Raskenen'.
91 Kelder (2010, 127) notes that Ahotep possibly was of Cretan-Minoan birth.
92 Herodotus 'The Histories', II, 91.
93 Apollodorus 'The Library of Greek Mythology', II.
94 Hyginus 'Fabulae', 168.
95 Diodorus 'Library of History', I, 28
96 Verbrugghe and Wickersham 2001, 108, 142 and 159f.
97 Rotstein 2016, 39.
98 The names 'Aigyptos' and 'Danaos' may just indicate 'the Egyptian king' and/ or 'the Danaan noble'. Cp. Verbrugghe and Wickersham (2001, 108), where based on transmitted information by Manetho, different names for Danaos are given (Armesis, Armaios).
99 Herodotus speaks in this context of a Libyan migration or invasion of Argos (von Ranke-Graves 1986, 221).

Further according to Herodotus, his daughters brought a new cult of the godess Demeter to Pelasgian Argos. The 'sons of Aigyptos' eventually followed Danaus and his daughters to Argos. Then Danaus instructed them to get rid of all the husbands. After a feast, the daughters killed the grooms except one with the name of Lynkeus, who eventually became Danaus' successor as ruler of Argos.

Also remarkable in this context is the annotation that during his reign in Argos, '*Danaus [...] became so powerful a ruler that all the Pelasgians of Greece called themselves Danaans*'. (Rohl 2007, 291)[100] Interestingly, this quotation equates the 'pre-hellenic', *i.e.* autochtonous inhabitants of Greece, the Pelasgians, with the Danaans. The Homeric Danaans of the Trojan War would thus be descendants of those Pelasgian inhabitants of the Peloponnese.

Also the Danaus story – like the myths about Pelops and Cadmos – belongs to the traditions about migration (from Egypt) and descent (of the Argive kings) and is not primarily a myth about pioneering exploration.

There are several options for a genealogical dating of this myth. It is worth remembering that the Egyptians obviously called the Mycenaean Greeks 'Tanaju' since the time of pharaoh Thutmosis III (1504 – 1450 BCE) (again Phillips 2010, 822; Kelder 2018, 13). This approach would correspond well with a tentative dating based on genealogies, with Danaus living three generations after Epaphos (Apophis 1609 – 1569 BCE) and thus ca. 1500 to 1480 BCE, *i.e.* within the reign of Thutmosis III.

Genealogical chronology puts eight generations of Argive kings – or broadly 270 years – between Danaus and the destruction of Troy (von Pessl, 1878, 33). If the sack of Troy is an historical event and dated correctly at 1186 BCE[101], we arrive at roughly 1450 BCE for the Danaus myth, *i.e.* also towards the end of the reign of Thutmosis III, when Mycenaeans for the first time appeared in the historical records of Egypt. In a variation of this calculation, Woudhuizen (2013, 7) argues for an earlier timing of the Danaus myth 'around 1600 BCE' assuming the Trojan War as a reference point somewhere around 1280 BCE.

In a different approach, the myth about Danaus' emigration with his kin to Argos in Greece could also contain a memory of the final Hyksos expulsion from Egypt (based on Diodorus 'Library of History, I, 28, as suggested by Rohl 2007, 291; also Mosenkis 2016, 154ff), which happened probably ca. 1550 BCE under pharaohs Kahmose and Ahmose (ca. 1550 – 1525) or slightly later. This interpretation by Rohl would put Danaus into the ruling stratum of the Hyksos in the middle or second half of the 16th century BCE. In this case the a.m. three generations of distance to the reign of pharaoh Apophis need to be rather short ones. The 'Parian Marble' lists a date for the arrival of Danaus in Greece of 1510/09 BCE, which would broadly fit to this dating approach (Rotstein 2016, 39).

A third possibility to locate the myth considerably later in time would be to equate the Egyptian name of Danaus, Armais, with Horemheb or Haremhab (1348 – 1320 BCE), the last pharaoh of the 18th dynasty, and Aigyptos with Sethos I. This equation would be supported by Manetho as quoted by Flavius Josephus (Verbrugghe and Wickersham 2001, 159; also Dillery 1999, 95). However, in this case it would be difficult to correlate the chronology with the genealogies as given in the myths and would leave a difference of at least 120 to 150 years to be explained.

---

100 Cp. Apollodorus 'The Library of Greek Mythology', II, 1.4: "After he had taken control of the country, Danaos named its inhabitants the Danaans after himself"; also Strabo 'The Geography' V, 2.
101 As suggested by Mull (2017, 285).

Helios and Actis

Another early reference to Egypt in the Greek myths is connected with the isle of Rhodes. In this myth about the sun god Helios, the Bronze Age inhabitants of the isle of Rhodes were called 'Telchines'[102]. Some of them are told to have anticipated the 'Deucalian Flood'[103] and sailed away to Lykia (von Ranke-Graves 1986, 137). After the flood, the seven sons of Rhode and Helios governed the resurfaced island. One of them, Actis by name, got jealous of his brother Teneages and together with his brothers Triopas, Macar and Candalus murdered him. After the murder, according to the myth, Actis fled to Egypt and 'founded' the city of Heliopolis there (Diodorus Siculus 'Library of History', V, 57).

This myth seems to contain historical experiences of parts of the inhabitants of Rhodes in connection with the 'Deucalian Flood'. If we equate this flood with the inundations in the aftermath of the eruption of the Thera volcano, we can try to place the myth in a rough timing based on the relative and absolute attempts to date this epic eruption.

As discussed above, the timing of the Thera eruption that is potentially referenced to in this myth, is still disputed. Analyses based on C14 dating of an olive branch found in the ashes point at an early date around 1625 BCE. Recent publications have pointed at the margin of error in this dating method due to the growth patterns of olive trees (Roemer 2018, 2). The so-called 'Parian Chronicle'[104] dates the eruption at 1529 BCE, an archaeological chronology leads to a similar lower date around 1540 BCE (Schofield 2007, 69).

Manetho mentions that the Deucalian Flood according to his information occurred in the time of the 6th pharaoh of the 18th dynasty he calls 'Misphragmutosis', who reigned for 26 years (Rohl 2007, 193). This 6th king is likely to have been Menkheperre Thuthmosis III, whose sole rule indeed extended to 26 years after the co-reign with his mother Hatshepsut. Thus the name 'Misphragmutosis' seems to be a Greek contraction of Menkheperre Thutmosis.

If the Thera eruption falls into his sole reign, the Deucalian Flood would then need to be dated even lower between 1482 and 1450 BCE. As mentioned before, this reference may refer to the last and final eruption destroying the Minoan trading empire. It is possible that there were two earlier eruptions in years 11 to 22 of the reign of pharaoh Ahmose (ca. 1550 – 1525 BCE) based on an inscription found on a stelae[105] and another in the early years of Hatshepsut (ca. 1500 BCE). (Rohl 2007, 202f)[106] The Rhodian myth about Actis and his flight to Egypt after the Deucalian Flood would thus need to be placed towards the end of the first half of the 15th century BCE.

In total, the various mythical references regarding contacts between the Late Bronze Age Greeks and Egypt during the 2nd Intermediate Period seem to support

---

102 This name could be a variation of the word 'Tyrrhen' or 'Tyrsen' and would make the Telchines Tyrrhenians (von Ranke-Graves 1986, 168).
103 Named after a mythical son of the Cretan king Minos, Deucalion, who is told to have reigned on the island after the big flood. This flood is being connected with the eruption of Thera.
104 Also called the 'Parian Marble', a monumental marble list of chronological data originally placed on the island of Paros (Rotstein 2016).
105 The so-called 'Unwetter-Stelae' mentions various exceptional meteorological phenomena, which are brought into connection with an earlier eruption of the Thera volcano. The interpretation of the text on the stelae is disputed, though.
106 Rohl (2007) uses different dates based on his own 'new chronology', which is not generally accepted.

the assumption of Kelder (2018, 13) about first sporadic contacts already during the Hyksos era, even though there is no final archaeological confirmation in this regard as yet. As for the time of the subsequent 18th dynasty in Egypt, the existing historical and pictorial evidence pointing at contacts of 'Danaan' Mycenaeans with Egypt during the end or shortly after the reign of Thutmosis III, is broadly supported by the mythological transmissions.

Contacts with Egypt during the Later 18th Dynasty

Perseus

Sometime after Danaus, the Greek hero Perseus, the son of Danae and the king of Argos, is the next mythical figure with connections to Egypt, which he visited on one of his journeys. Perseus has been a descendant of Danaus and Lynkeus in the fifth generation (Herodotus 'The Histories', II, 91; Apollodorus 'The Library of Greek Mythology', II, 4).

Pausanias ('Description of Greece', II, 15; 4 and 16; 3) asserts that Perseus 'founded' Mycenae, whilst Apollodorus ('The Library of Greek Mythology', II, 4) writes that he rather 'fortified' the citadel as well as at Midea. It is also mentioned that Perseus finally took residence in Mycene. The later Greeks thus regarded Perseus as the founder of the 'Mycenean Age' and as an authentic and historical figure (von Ranke-Graves 1986, 218).

According to Apollodorus, Perseus had ancestral links to the a.m. city of Chemmis (presumably in the Nile delta) being a descendant from Danaus. On his travels to get the head of the Gorgo, Perseus thus stopped over in Chemmis to pay his respects (cp. also Herodotus 'The Histories', II, 91). If Apollodorus and Herodotus reflect LBA conditions in Egypt correctly in these quotes, we also have a mythological hint for a permanent Mycenaean presence in Egypt during this period.

Perseus then continued his journey to the Gorgo from Egypt via Libya, the Atlas Mountains and the 'Hesperides' all the way to the river Okeanos and then maybe north to the Hyperboreans (interpretation in Bridgman 2010 based on Pindaros 'Pythian Ode', X, 31 – 46). To the potential location of these places we will come back in chapters 10.3 and 12.2.

A genealogical dating of the Perseus myth with a distance in time of five generations to Danaus takes us broadly to the mid-14th century BCE, *i.e.* ca. 1350 to 1340 BCE. Rohl (2007, 298) reminds us that for this dating we have to consider another ancestor, Acrisius (Danae's father), having ruled in Argos over two generations. This genealogical date for the 'founder' of Mycenae interestingly coincides with the archaeological timing for the establishment of the first fortifications of Mycenae (Schofield 2007, 78).[107] The visit of Perseus to Egypt could thus have happened around the reign of the last pharaoh of the 18th dynasty, Haremhab (1348 – 1320 BCE) or slightly earlier.

Contacts with Egypt during the 19th and 20th Dynasty

Heracles (and Busiris)

For the Heracles cycle in general, Burkert (1979, 78ff) and Lane Fox (2009, 206f) pointed out the Hittite, Levantine and Mesopotamian parallels to the myths around the demigods Melkart, Ninurta and Gilgamesh, all of which are of a much older provenience. The

---

107 Schofield (2007,78) states that Mycenae was fortified in the mid-14th century BCE.

Heracles cycle of adventures also contains complex symbolisms around animal fights, cattle raids etc., which likewise have very ancient roots. Burkert (1979, 83) comes to the conclusion that *'there is not one myth of Heracles, there is not a character to start from, but a set of different stories involving the same name'*.

On the other hand, it also cannot be excluded that indeed a historical figure named Heracles existed, whose actual adventures and travels have been described and interpreted in light of these ancient role models.

If we assume that there was a historic figure in Greece around which the different stories have been shaped, it is the Heracles figure, who was the great-grandson of Perseus and who thus stands in the line of the rulers of Argos and Tiryns (contra Burkert 1979, 97). This Greek Heracles figure was also the protagonist in various travel myths.

For a time the great hero has been subject to king Eurystheus of Tiryns, who sent him to perform his famous labors. One of these epic labors brought Heracles to the 'Hesperides' to bring back the mythical 'Golden Apples', which were supposed to grant immortality.

On this journey according to myth Heracles stopped by in Egypt (Apollodorus 'The Library of Greek Mythology', II, 5.11) and was held up by king Busiris[108], one of the '50 sons of Aigyptos', who reportedly had the intent to sacrifice him to the gods. Heracles somehow managed to liberate himself and killed Busiris in battle.

With this episode we have an indication that not all contacts between the visiting Mycenaeans and the Egyptians were of a peaceful nature. Busiris is also known as an ancient city in Egypt, in local language 'Djedu', which held a necropolis of Osiris, the chief god of Busiris. A theoretical genealogical dating (3 generations after Perseus, one generation prior to the Trojan War) brings us to ca. 1220 BCE, *i.e.* towards the end of the reign of Ramses II. Another interpretation by Mosenkis (2016, 173) equals Busiris with Seti I (1290 – 1279 BCE), the father of Ramses II, who dedicated temples to Osiris and according to Mosenkis called himself 'Usiri'. This approach would require a slightly earlier dating of the Heracles cycle.

Orpheus

The mythic character Orpheus was a great singer or rhapsode in the Greek epics of probably Thracian origin, which later lived in Thessaly close to mount Olympus. The potentially Indo-European roots of the Orpheus myth have been pointed out by Nagy (1991, 207ff). Apollodorus ('The Library of Greek Mythology', I, 9.16; I, 3.1.) considers him to be the son of the Thracian king Oiagros.[109] Regarding his contacts with Egypt, nothing much more is reported by Diodorus Siculus ('Library of History', IV, 25 2-4) other than him having studied there. The remark, though, shows that there may have been more and diversified contacts also on the cultural level between Mycenaean Greece and Egypt.

Since Orpheus like Heracles according to myth was a participant in the expedition of the Argonauts to Colchis, a genealogical dating approach would need to place this character around the same time, *i.e.* around 1220 BCE. It needs to be stated though that in the chronographic tradition Orpheus is linked to the Argonauts only from the 6th century

---

108 Another reference to a 'king Busiris' is given by Hyginus ('Fabulae', 56), where a Greek augur named 'Thrasius' is summoned to the Egyptian court in order to stop a 9-year drought. Thrasius is reported to have suggested that a foreigner needs to be sacrificed and ends up being sacrificed himself.

109 Apollodorus is consistent with Pindaros in this respect.

Fig. 14: Menelaos and Helena (photo: Bibi Saint-Pol, Wikimedia Commons).

onwards (cp. Rotstein 2016, 106f). If we follow this late chronological positioning, Orpheus would have thus studied in Egypt in the later reign of Ramses II.

Different to this approach, the 'Parian Mable' lists a date for Orpheus of 1398/97 BCE and thus considerably earlier (the chronological conundrum is discussed in Rotstein 2016, 40, 107). This apparent inconsistency between the mythological and chronological record seems at present not to be reconcilable.

Menelaos

Several antique authors such as Homer, Herodotus and Strabo relate stories about Menelaos' journeys to Egypt. According to Homer ('The Odyssey', III, 270 – 310), Menelaos, the king of Sparta and brother of Agamemnon, in the aftermath of the Trojan war has been driven off course with his fleet and arrived in Egypt. He later tells Telemachos, the son of Odysseus, about his travels, which may include trade or raids:

> *'... for it took me seven years to amass this fortune and bring it home in my ships. My travels took me to Cyprus, to Phoenicia and to Egypt. Ethiopians, Sidonians, Erembians, I visited them all; and I saw Libya, too.'* (Homer 'The Odyssey', IV, 80)

Menelaos on his visit in Egypt tells about receiving a precious gift *'a gift from Alcandre, wife of Polybus, who lived in Egyptian Thebes, where the houses are furnished in a more sumptuous style than anywhere else in the world.'* (Homer, 'The Odyssey', IV, 120).

A theoretical dating of this episode can be tried with the help of Manetho in the epitome of Africanus, who remarks with reference to a pharaoh he calls 'Thouoris' that

'this is the king called Polybos, the husband of Alkandra, by Homer. Troy was captured in his reign' (Verbrugghe and Wickersham 2001, 108).

Behind the name 'Thouoris' we have to assume the female pharaoh Twosret (1187 – 1185 BCE), the last pharaoh of the 19th dynasty, during whose reign – according to Manetho – Troy fell. 'Alkandra' is the contemporary vocalization of her young son Akhenre Siptah, who is wrongly assumed to be female in Homer (Luban 2017, 80). Menelaos' visit to the Egyptian court would thus have to be placed ca. 1185 BCE.

Another story of Menelaos visiting Egypt is related by Herodotus ('The Histories', II, 118f). Herodotus relates stories told to him by Egyptian priests on the occasion of a visit to Egypt. According to this tradition, Helen was not brought back to Troy during the siege by the Greeks, but held up in Egypt and detained by a certain king Proteus. The story continues that Menelaos, after the sack of Troy and when Helen was not found in the city, went to Memphis in Egypt to recover his stolen goods and his wife and was received there by king Proteus.

This 'king Proteus' is called the 'man of Memphis' and presented as residing in Memphis being the successor to 'Pheron'. He is thus presented as having transferred the court and maybe as a founder of a new dynasty. He was succeeded by 'Rhampsinitus' (Herodotus 'The Histories', II, 112, 114 and 121).

Maybe it is possible to identify king 'Proteus' in this tradition with the pharaoh Setnakhte (Proteus = Userkhaure Setepenre, 1185 – 1182 BCE), the first pharaoh of the 20th dynasty, who succeeded Twosret, under whose reign Menelaos according to the a.m. story related by Manetho may have visited Egypt before. Setnakhte indeed moved his capital to Memphis after a coronation ceremony in Thebes. He was also the father of Ramses III, possibly the king 'Rhampsinitus' (in the regnal form 'Ra-mes-pa-sa-Neith') mentioned by Herodotus. Menelaos may thus have undertaken several journeys to Egypt during the transition from the 19th to the 20th dynasty (cp. Gertoux 2016, 4).

Strabo ('The Geography', I, 2; 23 and 32) further mentions that Menelaos *'is said to have come to Aithiopia, as far as the boundary with Egypt'*. This remark follows an earlier quote about Menelaos, who

'went up [the Nile] *as far as the Aithiopians and learned about the rising of the Nile and the soil that it puts on the land'.*

Maybe this information refers to a broader myth around the travels of Menelaos in the aftermath of the Trojan War which is now lost.

Interestingly also 'The Iliad' (IX, 383) contains a brief description of

'Egyptian Thebes, where the houses are stuffed with treasure, and through every one of a hundred gates two hundred warriors ride out with their chariots and horses.'

This quote in Homer, which is also familiar to Strabo ('The Geography', I, 1; 16), is another indication for a firsthand experience of Mycenaeans in Egypt.

Odysseus

Odysseus in 'The Odyssey' (XIV, 245-250) relates a fabricated story, which brings him into contact with Egypt, albeit this episode he needed to invent as an alibi ('the Cretan Lie'). In this story he tells about a trip to Egypt after having returned from Troy. Having re-equipped his ships, he reached Egypt in a 5-day journey. There his mariners plunder Egyptian farms, but are finally surrounded by Egyptian military. Many of his soldiers die in battle; Odysseus himself gets captured. He spends several years in Egypt, gains some riches and finally returns to Ithaca.

Whilst the story around Menelaos dates the end of the Trojan war to around 1186 BCE, the tale of Odysseus fits to the attack of the 'Sea Peoples' on Egypt in the years 1180 and 1177 BCE, which was beaten back by Ramses III.

Summary of Mythical Contacts with Egypt

In sum, the mythical 'records' show an astonishing number of direct contacts between the Late Bronze Age Mycenaeans and Egypt. Egypt obviously was a relatively familiar territory to the Bronze Age Greeks as far as the epic tradition goes. The assumption of Gillis (1993, 69) of only indirect trade contacts between Mycenaean Greece and Egypt is clearly not borne out by the mythological record.

Contrary to the archaeological, pictorial and historical evidence, where direct contacts between the Mycenaean palatial centres and Egypt seem to have started under Thutmosis III at around 1437 BCE, the mythological record seems to go a lot further back in time. The Greek myths know of various contacts between the Mycenaeans and Egypt already during the 2nd Intermediate Period and the time of Hyksos occupation, which ended around 1550 BCE. The Mycenaeans seem to have played a role – maybe as mercenaries – in the conflicts that ended the Hyksos rule (see the Dionysos myth discussed above).

There seem to be also references towards part of the foreign occupiers fleeing to Greece (Danaus). Especially the latter references in the Danaus myth belong into the broader context of myths about migration and descent for the Mycenaeans[110] and are not primarily stories of pioneering adventurers in the context of metal explorations.

During the later times from the 18th dynasty onwards, when pictorial evidence commences, we have both the archaeological and historical as well as the mythological evidence for direct (diplomatic or commercial) contacts. It is possible that there even were permanent Mycenaean presences in LBA Egypt, *e.g.* in Chemmis, which is mentioned at several instances in the mythological record.

For the late 19th (Merneptah) and the beginning of the 20th dynasty, we have mythological evidence also of contacts of a less peaceful nature (Heracles, Odysseus). This corresponds relatively well with the Egyptian records of conflict with the so-called 'Ekwesh', who are assumed to be the Achaeans.

Interestingly, the theoretical dating based on references to historical events and genealogical timespans would fit relatively consistently and plausibly into the historical context given above. Overall the picture emerging from the Greek myths regarding contacts with Egypt seems to broadly confirm the archaeological and historical record.

---

110   Cp. the comments on the myths of Agenor and Cadmos above.

10

Mycenaean Contacts with the Central and Western Mediterranean

10.1 Evidence of Mycenaean Journeys to Italy and Sicily

10.1.1 Archaeological Evidence

The central and western Mediterranean including Sicily, Sardinia (an important centre for copper) and the Italian coastline certainly have been familiar to the Bronze Age Greeks. This is confirmed by Lane Fox, who writes:

> 'Homer's epics show [...] that there was a long history of contact between the west and the Aegean before Greeks founded a clearly defined settlement in the western territory. (Lane Fox 2009, 124)

Overall, the western Mediterranean basin is more heavily mineralized than the eastern part (with the exception of the Balkans and northern Greece), especially around the 'south Iberian Pyrite Belt'. As a consequence of Mycenaean interest in those minerals, some authors assume direct contacts with the southern part of the Iberian Peninsula on behalf of the Mycenaeans, where in the Bronze Age important centres for metal production and trade existed. Mederos Martin (1999) even postulates that the primary direction of Mycenaean trade was directed towards the central and western Mediterranean area. Against this opinion, Blake (2008) cautioned that the Mycenaean contacts in this region, at least as far as Italy is concerned, were for the most time of a sporadic nature.

Judging from the archaeological record, the Mycenaeans entertained trade contacts and maybe temporarily settled in Italy including the island of Sicily. The varying intensity of exchange has to be interpreted in the context of the three phases of Mycenaean expansion in the Mediterranean as documented in the ceramic record of the phases LH I to LH III C1 (Blake 2008; cp. chapter 3).

Mycenaean contacts seem to have been established already in the early phases of the LBA (LH I) (discussed by Mee 2008 in Drews 2017, 215 and Blake 2008, 4f). Mycenaean pottery found in Italy including Sicily and the Aeolian islands and on the coast of the Thyrrenian Sea up to Massilia illustrates according to Maran (2004, 2007) some interest of the Mycenaeans in this area already in the first phase of Mycenaean power from 1600 to 1450 BCE, when the eastern Mediterranean was still predominantly Minoan trading territory.

One motivation to visit Italy may have been access to north Italian copper from ca. 1500 BCE onwards, which was traded also on transalpine routes towards the north (cp. Norgaard et al. 2021). The interest of the Mycenaeans may have additionally been triggered by the tin and amber trade down the rivers Rhine and Rhone into the western Mediterranean (Maran 2004). In similar terms Drews (2017, 215; cp. Blake 2008 and Mee 2008) stresses that

> 'already in LH I Mycenaean pottery appears in southern Italy, Sicily and the Aeolian islands. In these areas Minoan influence is minimal, and the Mycenaean presence may reflect a freedom to search for alternative sources of raw materials, probably metals'.

The fine pottery imported to Italy during LH I and LH II came mostly from the southern and southwestern Peloponnese as well as Kythera (Gillis 1993, 71). Increasing amounts of ceramics found not only in Sicily but also on the Italian coastline gave rise to expectations of very intense modes of exchange over time as expressed by Giardino (2000, 99):

> 'In the late Bronze Age the interactions between the Aegean peoples and the indigenous Italian communities (mainly in the islands and in southern Italy) are intensive, systematic and well documented by the archaeological evidence. These interactions are the results of a longer process which began during the Middle Bronze Age. [...] some centres [...] were involved in long-distance trade whereby the exchange seems to have been organized directly by the Mycenaeans...'.

This picture of growing and intense contacts seemed to have been even further supported, when it became evident that the archaeological record supported not only trade contacts, but over time also the establishment of local settlements of Mycenaeans in Italy since the 14th century BCE (Matthaeus 2005, 338). Kristiansen (2016, 160) interprets these finds as private traders and their families embedded within local chiefdoms.

In the recent years, a more diversified picture emerged, when it became evident that pottery in LH III A found in Italy to some extent consisted of local imitations, not imports. Vagnetti (2010, 894f) states that in the late Bronze Age

> 'the main new development of the period is the gradual change in nature of the interconnections [...] imported pottery is concentrated at specific spots [...], in other areas, imports become rarer and are gradually replaced by local production of Aegean-type wares. Trade is now integrated by a very impressive technology transfer that gives rise to several production centers [...].

Jung (2018, 279ff) confirms that the western (Thyrrenian) side of Italy sees a considerable decline of Mycenanean imports from the 14th to the 13th century BCE. This leaves southeastern Sicily as the only region of Italy to have received LH III A2 pottery in some quantity and even here imports from the 13th century are rare. On the other hand Jung sees the possibility that during LH III B some people of Italian origin spent time in Mycenaean Greece and later introduced Mycenaean style pottery in Italy (e.g. Termitito) after their return.

Judged by the LH I and LH II pottery finds, Mycenaens have probably sailed west to Italy and Sicily in this period and established an active commercial trade there (Gillis 1993, 73ff).

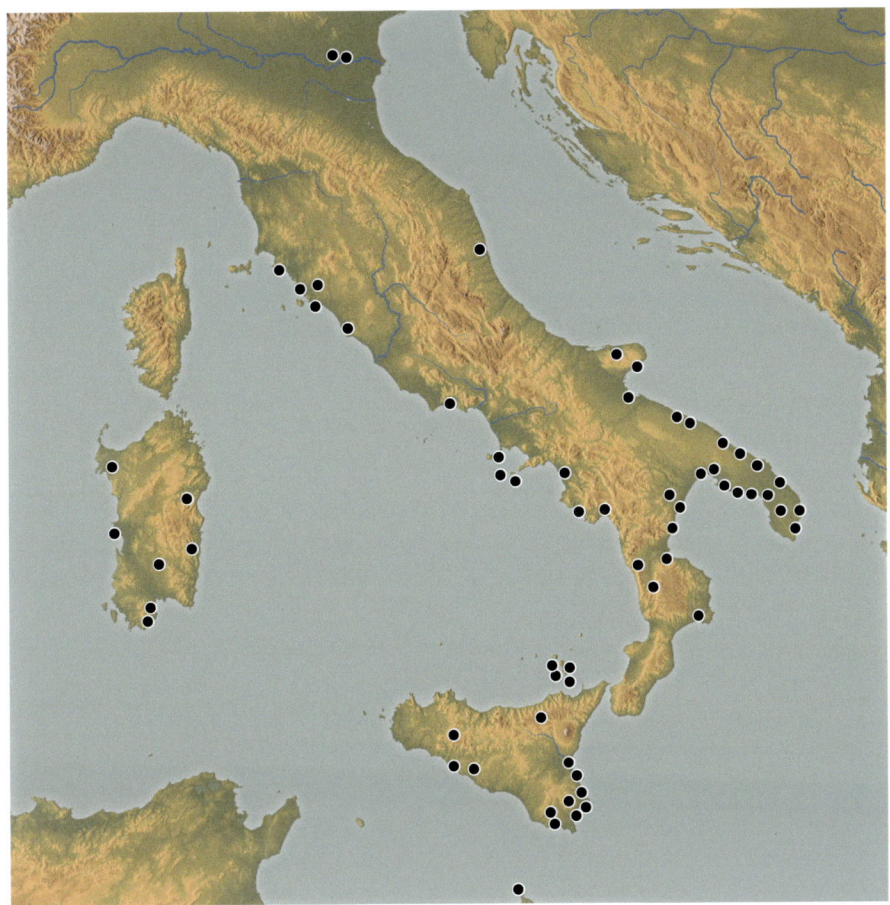

Fig. 15: Finds of Mycenaean pottery in Italy incl. Sicily and Sardinia (map: Olav Odé, after: 'Mykene – Die sagenhafte Welt des Agamemnon', Ausstellungskatalog, Badisches Landesmuseum, Schloss Karlsruhe, 2018/2019, Inside Cover).

However contrary to the picture of a continuous 'intense exchange' Blake (2008, 15, 23) classifies the contacts of Mycenaens to Italy and Sicily before the collapse of the palace structures in Greece (*i.e.* before LH III C1) as more of a sporadic nature and subject to seasonal changes.

As a consequence a two-fold picture regarding the Mycenaean contacts with Italy and Sicily emerges. On the one hand based on archaeological finds of pottery, the impression arises that *'As in the east there has been a lively history of contact between Greeks, part of Sicily and western Italy during the previous Bronze Age of the Mycenaeans.'* (Lane Fox 2009, 125; cp. again Kristiansen 2016, 160). On the other hand the nature and intensity of these contacts have been questioned lately. Jung (2018, 284) summarizes

> *'The Mycenaean palatial economy did not organise anything for the pre-state societies in the west that would have been even remotely similar to the bulk shipping of specially designed pottery towards eastern destinations.'*

More research seems to be necessary to substantiate either of the two assumptions.

10.1.2 Reflections in Myths

Diodorus Siculus ('Library of History', V, 1) explains that Sicily originally had been called 'Trinacria' (*i.e.* 'three capes'), then 'Sicania' after a tribe with this name that settled on the island and finally 'Sicily' after the tribe of the Siceli, who crossed over from Italy. Dionysius of Halicarnassus ('Roman Antiquities' 1, 22 in Moeller 2001, 246) relates that the Siceli left their previous homes in Italy three generations prior to the Trojan War, *i.e.* around 1275 BCE.

The Odyssey contains several references to Sicily, but also to 'Sicania', which according to the Iliad and to Herodotus may thus be just the older name for the island (Homer 'The Odyssey', XXIV, 308; Herodotus 'The Histories', VII, 170). The 'Siceli' furthermore are often equated to the 'Shekelesh' by contemporary scholars, who formed part of the Sea Peoples causing destructions at the end of the LBA.

Daidalos

Sicily in the Mycenaean mythical transmission is linked to the great craftsman Daidalos. The myth is transmitted at length by Diodorus Siculus ('Library of History', IV, 75 – 79) and again in passing by Apollodorus ('The Library of Greek Mythology', III, 6, 1) and by Herodotus ('The Histories, VII, 170).

Daidalos spent some time working under king Minos on Crete, from where he had to flee to Sicily. One version of the myth has him build wings from feathers and wax, which enabled the escape from the island together with his son Ikarus. The famous story with Ikarus flying too close to the sun, melting the wax and drowning in the sea is sometimes interpreted as a metaphor for an escape by boat with a recently innovated new type of sail (von Ranke-Graves 1986, 284).

Daidalos flees west to Sicily, where he is received and works for the local king Kokalos on the island's south coast, from where he moves on to Sardinia some time later. According to Herodotus, Minos went after Daidalos and followed him to Sicily, where the Cretan king found a violent death (Herodotus 'The Histories, VII, 170, also discussed in Lane Fox 2009, 197).

The Daidalos myth clearly has Bronze Age roots (analyzed by Lane Fox 2009, 199). Daidalos is also mentioned in passing already in Homer's 'The Iliad' (VIII, 590), where his story is assumed to be 'common knowledge' for the listeners.[111]

One genealogical date for the Daidalos myth puts it about three to four generations after the Deucalian Flood. If we could date this flood around 1540 to 1520 BCE (cp. section 9.3.2) we would arrive at a time around 1450 BCE for the Daidalos myth, or LH II B in archaeological terms. It is possible that the link to the Cretan king Minos points to a time before the destruction of Minoan palaces by the Mycenaeans, which is assumed to have happened sometime around 1450 BCE. Additionally, a reference to 'king Minos' in the Parian Marble would support a date around 1400 BCE or before (Rotstein 2016, 39f).

This early date for 'king Minos' clashes with a remark in the Iliad (XIII, 450) and in Herodotus ('The Histories', VII, 171) according to which Minos lived three generations before the Trojan War, or around 1275 BCE. Whilst there is thus another possibility to date the Daidalos myth, scholars have tried to reconcile this obvious inconsistency with the possibility that there may have been several Cretan kings with the name 'Minos'.

---

[111] Also in 'The Iliad', fine bronzework is sometimes called 'daidala'.

Heracles (in Italy)
Also the *Heracles* myth contains several links to Italy, in particular the return journey from his tenth labor, in which he captures the cattle of Geryon possibly in southern Spain. His journeys home take him through Liguria and Etruria (von Ranke-Graves 1986, 460f).

Also Heracles' friend Iolaus after having established a colony on Sardinia, spent some considerable time in Sicily as well, where he is received amicably (Diodorus Siculus 'Library of History', IV, 30).

Odysseus
As stated above, Sicily, the Sicels and also Sikania are mentioned occasionally in Homer's *'The Odyssey'* (*e.g.* XX, 383; XXIV, 307). In fact, most of the action of Odysseus' travels seems to take place around the island and southern Italy. Also one of the maidservants of Odysseus' father Laertes is of Sicilian origin (see XXIV, 211, 366, 389). It thus seems that Sicily in particular was a territory known to or familiar to Mycenaean Greeks, albeit on the boundary of their 'sphere of influence'.

Etrucscan Origins
Finally, the origins of the *Etruscans* in the mythical transmission are linked to western Anatolia, the founders being refugees from the Trojan War. Whilst many settlements around the Mediterranean have laid claim to be founded by heroes from the battle of Troy for reasons better or worse, in the case of the Etruscans, some linguistic research seems to support the mythical claim (cp. Mosenkis 2016, 64ff; discussion in Mull 2017, 96f).

The origin of the Etruscans according to this theory is to be found in the Tyrrhenians (or Tyrsenoi), who lived on the islands opposite the western Anatolian coast and were famous for their maritime skills. Herodotus relates a story how the Tyrrhenians split off the western Anatolian 'Maionians' in times of great hunger. Under the leadership of Tyrrhenus they sailed off to Italy, where they may have formed part of the later Etruscans (see Herodotus 'The Histories', I, 94). The Etruscan language indeed seems to have some roots in western Anatolia. There may also be a link to the 'Teres' from Egyptian sources, which formed part of the alliance of 'Sea Peoples'.

With the exception of the Daidalos myth, all of these mythical links need to be dated very late in the LBA, *i.e.* from about 1220 BCE onwards. Surprisingly there are few – if they exist at all – mentions of Italy in the earlier mythological transmissions, which would reflect the contacts archaeologically attested for in LH I. What is missing in particular is an exploration or pioneering myth along the lines of Bellerophontes, Perseus or the Argonauts. This lacuna in the mythological record still needs to be reconciled with the material finds.

10.2 Evidence of Mycenaean Contacts with Sardinia

10.2.1 Archaeological Evidence
Sardinia in the Bronze Age was home to the 'Nuraghen' culture, named after the monumental structures found on the island (nuraghi) and an important copper-producing centre in the Mediterranean. Copper was not only produced in, but also traded to Sardinia over some distance. Several ox-hide ingots – possibly of Cypriot origin – have been found in Sardinia, which point at trading connections of Late Bronze Age Sardinia to Cyprus. Lo

Schiavo (2005, 143f and 404ff) confirms contacts between Cyprus and Sardinia since the 13th century BCE. At the same time, ceramic finds on Sardinia also support contacts with the Mycenaean world (Blake 2008; Schofield 2007, 115). Blake (2008, 9) muses that

> 'the Mycenaeans may well have been involved to some extent in metals procurement on Sardinia, but if so, it must have been to a lesser extent than the Cypriot activity on the island'.

Furthermore, the finds of ox-hide ingots on Corsica and at the southern French coast between the Rhone estuary and Narbonne indicate a northern trading route including stations on Sardinia along the Garonne River to the bay of Biscaya and along the Atlantic coastline (or along the Rhone river). In addition, several Iberian weapons, ornaments and tools from Sardinia have been collected, amongst which a revolving 'obelos' (skewer) of an Atlantic type documents the far western link via Sardinia (Lo Schiavo 2005, 408).

Sardinia during the Early Iron Age, but certainly also during Bronze Age times, thus also acted as an intermediary for goods brought from the far west. It also served as a contact point for these western objects from Spain and maybe Britain (Lane Fox 2009, 127). Lo Schiavo (2005, 401 [translation by the author]) thus summarizes:

> *The nuraghic/sardic ceramics found in southern Crete and southeast Sicily confirm the existence of a western route [...]. Two ox-hide ingot fragments made of copper, which were found in Cannatello and Thapsos, bear witness of a mutual east-west trade and of different maritime routes during the time of the Uluburun ship.'*

These links to the Atlantic Ocean – next to the strait of Gibraltar there are also the Rhone river route and the Garonne route – have recently gained increasing attention and importance in the context of research on the Bronze Age trade routes in the western Mediterranean.

In terms of its population, the island of Sardinia in the context of the end of the Bronze Age is sometimes connected to the 'Sherden' mentioned in various Egyptian sources, who fought Ramses II, then became part of the Egyptian palace guard. They later formed part of the Sea peoples and were connected to destructions at the end of the LBA including the attempted invasions of Egypt.

During the Early Iron Age the westward trail of Greek and Phoenician colonists begins – or better resumes – ca. 800 BCE. Due to the earlier Bronze Age connections, Lane Fox muses about these Early Iron Age colonists in the sense that *'They did not enter a vacuum'.* (cp. Lane Fox 2009, 125 and 130)

10.2.2 Reflections in Myths

Daidalos

Already the early Greek historiographers speculated about the magnificent stone built Nuraghe structures in Sardinia and called them 'Daidaleia'. This name references back to the mythical Daidalos who is told to have fled from Crete to Sicily and Sardinia (cp. Lane Fox 2009, 197ff). There is, however, no further specific link to the Daidalos myth (except in the following story about Iolaus) and the tradition thus seems to build on the general reputation of Daidalos as a great craftsman rather than any specific mythical 'incident'.

Heracles and Iolaus
The Greek mythical transmission (esp. Diodorus Siculus 'Library of History', IV, 29ff) interestingly contains a reference to Mycenaeans trying to establish a colony on Sardinia. Heracles still being a young man sends 'fifty sons' (*i.e.* a penteconter) to Sardinia to found this colony under the general command of his trusted friend Iolaus. Iolaus then summons Daidalos from Sicily for support, who builds 'many great buildings' on the island, the so called 'Daidaleia'.

Iolaus had to overcome initial resistance of the natives in order to establish his colony. Diodorus Siculus reports that in later years the colony 'barbarized' (*i.e.* they converted from Greek to native languages), because the local inhabitants outnumbered the Mycenaean settlers. The members of the localized colony also later moved from the coast into the mountainous interior of the island.

If the Iolaus myth as quoted by Diodorus Siculus is of Bronze Age origin (and the Heracles cycle certainly is), it contains an interesting reference to the establishment of a Mycenaean trading colony on Sardinia around 1210 BCE or maybe earlier. We can assume that the main purpose of this colony was a regular access to Sardinian copper supplies and to the trade routes in the western Mediterranean. A (trading) colony also only makes sense in the context of subsequent visits of Mycenaeans to the island, however these follow-up journeys are not recorded in myths.

The a.m. reference to Daidalos in the context of the Iolaus myth feels a bit out of place and may be an anachronism if we follow the chronological dating given in section 10.1.2 regarding Daidalos with reference to Sicily. It may be a Mycenaean explanation for the existence of the '*nuraghe*' structures on the island of Sardinia, which were 'posthumously' ascribed to the mythical Daidalos.

Odysseus
About one generation later (*i.e.* relative to the Heracles/Iolaus myth), also Odysseus seems to have passed by Sardinia during his travails. The reception of the hero on the island however is a hostile one as the episode with the Laestrygonians shows, who attack Odysseus and his crew (Homer 'The Odyssey', X, 82 – 199).

A genealogical dating puts all of these contacts with Sardinia relatively late in the LBA, around 1220 BCE and later. Again, the incident shows that the islands of Sicily and Sardinia at this time were positioned at the outer fringes of what the Mycenaeans probably considered 'familiar territory'.

10.3 Mycenaean Contacts with the Iberian Peninsula

10.3.1 Archaeological Evidence
As discussed in Chapter 4, the southern Iberian Peninsula during the Early Bronze Age was home to the *Los Millares culture* (ca. 3200 – 2200 BCE) and during the Middle and Late Bronze Age to the *El Argar culture* (ca. 2200 – 1350 BCE). Further down the years, but latest since the Early Iron Age, southern Iberia also brought forward the '*Tartessian*' *culture* (from ca. 900 onwards; cp. Celestino Perez 2016). All of these population groups flourished on the basis of the rich minerals found *e.g.* in the Iberian Pyrite Belt – especially in the Rio Tinto area – and on metal trade. The Iberian Pyrite Belt is classified as

'one of the most heavily mineralized places on earth with and abundant supply of the prestige metals of gold, silver as well as copper and tin that is still being mined to this day.' (Sheppard Baird 2007, 15)

There is evidence that over time and already during the Bronze Age the people living in the southern part of today's Portugal and Spain came into contact with various other cultures. Koch (2013, 18) lists the influences from abroad in the sequence of appearance when he states that

'The Peninsula's Mediterranean coast came first into primary and strengthening contact from a succession of literate peoples from the east, including possibly the Minoans initially, then Mycenaeans, Cypriots and Phoenicians, the last eventually becoming full-blown colonists'.

Sheppard Baird (2007) mentions the possibility that the vast mines in the Rio Tinto area around Huelva have been exploited already since the 3rd millennium BCE, potentially by the 'Millarens', although there is no definite archaeological substantiation for this assumption yet (the assumption is based on a discussion by Nocete 2005 in Sheppard Baird 2007, 17). In spite of the absence of material proof he muses about some indirect evidence for early cross-incubations from the eastern Mediterranean to the southern Iberian cultures (on similar notes already Henning 1944 in Mosenkis 2016, 172). Sheppard Baird sees the 'tholoi' (funeral mounds) of the Los Millares as an indication of early maybe already Minoan cultural influence on the Los Millares culture. Also the near contemporary utilization of arsenic copper by the Minoans and the Los Millares culture is interpreted in this direction.

A cultural exchange at this early stage would potentially make the early Minoans the first commercial travellers from the eastern to the western Mediterranean, but this theory is not generally accepted yet. Betancourt (2008, 213) is more cautious, when he states that

'the western Mediterranean was not completely unknown to the people of the Aegean, but trade in this direction does not appear to have been a regular feature until later in the Bronze Age.'

Later Mycenaean contacts with the Iberian Peninsula during the LBA are slightly more plausible. From around 2200 BCE until about 1350 BCE the El Argar culture dominated in the region that is today southern Spain. There are some potential indirect clues for a cultural exchange with Mycenaeans from ca. 1500/1600 BCE onwards, however also for this period further archaeological proof is needed to ascertain the presumed contacts (again Sheppard Baird 2007, 19).

After the decline of the El Argar culture from around 1350 BCE, there are indications that the 'Atlantic route', which connected the copper-mines of southern Spain with Brittany and the British Isles became travelled more intensively (Ling et al. 2019, 32; Cp. section 12.2.1). This period falls into the time of Mycenaean expansion and presence in the eastern and western Mediterranean and needs to be looked at in more detail also in the context of the available archaeological evidence.

Fig. 16: Mycenaean finds in Iberia (map: Olav Odé, after: 'Mykene – Die sagenhafte Welt des Agamemnon', Ausstellungskatalog, Badisches Landesmuseum, Schloss Karlsruhe, 2018/2019, Inside Cover).

In the inland site of Llanete de los Moros close to the town of Montoro at the River Guadalquivir, Mycenaean pottery remains from the Bronze Age have been found (discussion in Mederos Martin 1999, esp. 248). These finds prove at least indirect contacts of Myceaeans with southern Spain during the LBA.

Access to the rich minerals in this broader area has been the often-quoted principal reason for these assumed exchanges. The trade route from the eastern Mediterranean to southern Spain according to Mederos Martin could have passed the strait of Messina in Sicily, touched the island of Lipari and the south of Sardinia before reaching Andalucia. The trade may have continued further – maybe via Atlantic traders – possibly to the Scilly Islands or Cornwall in Britain.

How Intense were the Mycenaean Contacts with the Iberian Peninsula?

Based on the archaeological findings by Ruiz-Galves and Mederos Martin, Koch (2013, 19) states that

> 'the archaeological record shows that the south-western [Iberian] Peninsula had been in contact with speakers of a variety of exotic languages from the eastern Mediterranean, including the Mycenaean Greeks from about 1500 BC followed by the Cypriots and Phoenicians'.

The intensity of these potential direct Mycenaean contacts with the western Mediterranean in general and the Iberian Peninsula in particular are still a matter of scientific debate. Mederos Martin (1999, 248 [translation by the author]) takes the first finds of Mycenaean pottery as an indication when he classifies these remains as

'simply the first examples which are securely documented in the western Mediterranean for commerce clearly directed at the Iberian peninsula from the Eastern Mediterranean.'

Cunliffe (2011, 200) to the contrary, is more cautiously stating

'The discovery of Mycenaean pottery and bronzework in Italy, Sicily, Malta and Sardinia shows that communications had been established between the east Mediterranean and the Tyrrhenian Sea after about 1600 BC, but to interpret this as evidence of Mycenaean exploration of the west is to force the material remains beyond their reasonable limits. All that can be safely said is that voyages took place between the two seas.'

Blazquez Martinez (2002, 18) equally professes that there is as of now no documented Greek pre-colonial presence in southern Iberia.

In sum, there may be archaeological indicators for Mycenaean contacts with the Iberian Peninsula. The intensity of those contacts is still debated and waits for further research.

Continuation of Contacts with the Iberian Peninsula in the Transition from Late Bronze Age to Early Iron Age – The Archaeological Evidence

In the subsequent Early Iron Age (10th to 6th century BCE) the so-called *'Tartessian Culture'*[112] became established in southern Iberia, esp. around the estuary of the Guadalquivir River. This Iron Age culture has been identified on the basis of artefacts, pictographical evidence, funerary customs and linguistic research (Celestino Perez 2016). Also a body of archaeological remains from the Late Bronze Age to Early Iron Age has been discovered. This includes the so-called 'Huelva hoard' of 400 items from the 10th century BCE (Koch 2013, 10).

Regarding the *origins* of this culture there are ongoing discussions around the so-called *'pre-colonization period'* – i.e. about the time during the Late Bronze Age and prior to a strong Phoenician influence in southern Spain. It is as of today uncertain, how far back in time we can date the autochtonous beginnings of the Tartessian culture and whether we can assume potential Mycenaean contacts at an early stage (see discussions in Celestino Perez 2016, 79ff and Blazquez Martinez 2002, 18).

A question to be asked in his context is, whether Bronze Age antecedents of the Tartessian culture – and a city of Tartessos – could have been the origin of the myth around the Hesperides in Greek mythology and what kind of archaeological evidence there is to support the mythical accounts.

---

[112] Koch (2013) assumes Celtic roots of the Tartessian culture based on linguistic evidence. Celestino Perez (2016, 11, 78ff) muses about even earlier roots and beginnings of the Tartessian culture, which seems to have started to flourish under Phoenician influence.

This assumed Bronze Age city of Tartessos, which is mentioned in various mythical and later historical sources (*e.g.* Celestino Perez 2016, 21ff), has not yet been found. Some authors assume it is covered by the modern city of Huelva[113], others assume it was located around Jerez de Frontera, around the estuary of the Guadalquivir river, or close to Gibraltar.

Whilst there are thus still uncertainties regarding the Bronze Age roots of the Tartessian culture and its reflection in the Greek myths, we have a slightly clearer picture of the long-distance connections between Greece and southern Iberia during the subsequent Early Iron Age. The contacts from Greece to southern Spain continued – or were resumed – in this period.

'We know that by the later 9th century BC Greek pottery had been carried, some of it surely by Greeks, to Huelva.' (Lane Fox 2009, 124)

Huelva is situated near the mouth of the river Guadalquivir, known as the river Baetis[114] in antiquity. It was thus located in a region known for its metal production already since the 2nd millennium BCE. Pottery finds from about 625 BCE onwards point towards a Greek presence around Huelva during the late 7th century BCE. The Ionian city of Phocaea in particular stood in contact with the 'King of Tartessus' (Nesselrath 2005, 158). From the historian Avienus we hear about a 'Periplous' dating back to the 6th century BCE, which bears witness to Greek maritime exploration *beyond* the Straits of Gibraltar (Dihle 1994, 26f).

This period was followed by a near monopolization of the trade routes in the western Mediterranean by the Phoenicians/Carthaginians after the Phocaeans lost many of their ships in a battle against a joined Carthaginian and Etruscan fleet between 540 and 535 BCE (Nesselrath 2005, 159; Dihle 1994, 27). The subsequent monopoly served the Carthaginians to procure tin from the Britain from the 6th century onwards. Remains of Phoenician trading posts on the Portuguese Atlantic coast dating back to 600 BCE have recently been discovered (Wachsmann et al. 2009 in Moerner and Lind 2015, 136). So latest in this period regular maritime journeys via the Straits of Gibraltar and through the Atlantic Ocean are attested. The question remains, when these journeys started and who the first travellers were.

In the subsequent years, *i.e.* from the 6th century BCE onwards, the Carthaginians monopolized the trade routes in the western Mediterranean and the tin trade with Britain on the Atlantic route. From this time on and with few exceptions, the Greeks of the Classical Period were unable to leave the Mediterranean at its western exit.[115] As a consequence, the Greek knowledge of the western Mediterranean went into decline (again Dihle 1994, 27; Nesselrath 2005, 159).

---

113 This identification goes back to the German archaeologist Adolf Schulten (1922) and is taken up by Wouidhuizen (2010, 7).
114 Antique Graecolatin sources also call the Baetis the 'Tartessos river' (*e.g.* Strabo 'Geographica', III, 2; 11).
115 A notable exception is the journey of Pytheas from Massilia to Britain, who probably travelled into the Atlantic Ocean via the riverine routes (Nesselrath 2005, 159, 162f).

Fig. 17: Vix Crater with Head of the Gorgo Medusa (photo: Karsten Wentink).

10.3.2 Reflections in Greek Myths

Of the Mycenaean travelling heroes, two are particularly connected with journeys in the far west, Perseus and Heracles.

Perseus (and the Hesperides)

As discussed earlier, Polydectes demanded from Perseus to obtain the head of the Gorgo Medusa. Athena instructed the hero to find the 'Hesperides' in the far west. The Hesperides as the probably most western point known to the Mycenaean Greeks were told to have a garden in which the 'Golden Apples, which grant immortality', can be found.

According to Apollodorus ('The Library of Greek Mythology', II, 4,2), Perseus first travelled from Egypt via Libya to the Atlas Mountains and on to the 'Hesperides', where he obtained the weapons to overcome the Gorgo: a sword, a helmet and a knapsack as well as a shield and 'winged sandals'. Hesiod ('Theogony', 274f), further specifies, the Gorgons dwelled 'beyond the famous Okeanos on the fringes of the night' and in the vicinity of the Hesperides. Hesiod thus indicates that Perseus potentially could have ventured even further, *i.e.* all the way to the 'river Okeanos' (*i.e.* into the Atlantic Ocean; von Ranke-Graves 1986, 216).

With a genealogical dating of the Perseus stories to around 1350 BCE (see section 9.3.2), his trip to the southern Iberian Peninsula would have taken him there just around the demise of the El Argar culture and towards the beginning of the more intense utilization of the 'Atlantic route' between the Iberian Peninsula and Britain for metal trade (discussed above with Ling et al. 2019, 32). Maybe the power shift in the context of the demise of this cultural centre triggered the interest of the Mycenaeans at that time. Did Perseus at this most western point known maybe turn north towards the 'Hyperboreans'? To this potential – and admittedly for the most part hypothetical – second part of his journey we will revert later.

Heracles (and Geryones)

The adventure of Heracles (being the great-grandson of Perseus) and the giant Geryones at the western end of the ancient world has been put in the context of very old Indo-European cattle raid myths (Burkert 1979, 83ff). Yet the setting of the myth may also reveal traces of another Mycenaean journey to southern Spain.

Various classical Greek historians, mythographers and geographers report the journeys of Heracles to southern Iberia.[116] As his tenth labor, Heracles was asked to steal the cattle of Geryones of Erytheia or Erythrea, an island *'now called Gadeira'* in or near the Okeanos (Apollodorus 'The Library of Greek Mythology', II, 106). According to the myth, Geryon was called the 'king of Tartessos'.[117] As stated above, the existence of a city or kingdom of Tartessos which stood in contacts with the Mycenaeans already during the Bronze Age is assumed by some researchers, but still needs to be proven (again Celestino Perez 2016, 78ff).

For this job, his tenth labor, Heracles travelled into the far west and built the eponymous two pillars at the strait of Gibraltar. He even had to go beyond the strait into the 'Outer Sea' to the island of Erytheia (discussion in Nesselrath 2005, 156).[118] Erytheia and Tartessos seem to have been in some proximity to each other and accessible with a short sailing trip. Strabo ('The Geography', I, 1; 4) is outspoken about the true motivation for Heracles' trip being 'Iberian wealth'.

Erytheia may have been the island on which the city of Gades (Phoenician Gadir/Gadeiros) was situated, whilst the 'Pillars of Heracles' could be either symbolically the mountains visible on both sides of the Gibraltar strait or later Early Iron Age reflections of the columns of a Phoenician temple in the city of Gadeiros (discussion about the possible origins of the 'Pillars of Heracles' in Dihle 1994, 10 and Lane Fox 2009, 209).

Overall the travels ascribed to Perseus and Heracles may thus have taken them to the far western Mediterranean and possibly beyond. The question of 'how far beyond?' will be discussed in a later chapter. At this point just the additional remark of Diodorus Siculus ('Library of History', V, 24) will be quoted *'Now in the course of his campaign against Geryones, Heracles visited Celtica and founded there the city of Alesia.'* Even though the southern Iberian Peninsula was potentially populated also by Celtic people from the 8th century onwards (Koch 2013), this may be another hint that Heracles went even further than Spain on his journey.

Heracles (and the 'Golden Apples' of the Hesperides)

As his eleventh labor, Heracles was asked to get the 'Golden Apples' of the Hesperides, which grant immortality. The garden of the Hesperides[119] is described to be situated in the far western corner of the known world near the Atlas mountains in North Africa and bordering the encircling ocean (Okeanos). Apollodorus ('The Library of Greek

---

116 Hesiod 'Theogony', 287 – 290; Apollodorus 'The Library of Greek Mythology', II 5, 10; Herodotus 'The Histories', IV, 8; Diodorus Siculus 'Library of History', II, 17,1-2; 18, 2-3; Strabo 'The Geography', I, 1; 4 and III, 2; 13.
117 As discussed above, 'Tartessos' is an Iron Age culture in southern Iberia (and maybe a city yet to be discovered), whose roots may go back to the Bronze Age (Celestino Perez 2016, 78ff).
118 Erytheia has been identified already in antiquity with Gadeiros/Cadiz.
119 'Hesperides' (cp. lat. 'vesperum') as an expression for the extreme west, the 'land of the sinking sun'.

Mythology', II, 5) additionally mentions *'These apples were not in Libya, as some have said, but on Mount Atlas in the land of the Hyperboreans'*.

If we position the mythos around the Hesperides to the southern Iberian Peninsula, the '*Golden Apples*' of the Hesperides could be identified possibly as either yellowish apples or some other kind of other fruit, which at that time was still unknown to the Bronze Age Mycenaeans. The stories about reaching a state of 'immortality' when eating these 'Golden Apples' maybe due to the related vitamin C intake after a long journey by ship (prevention or cure of scurvy).

In the time of the Renaissance the 'Golden Apples' were believed to be oranges.[120] Citrus fruits however were first described a long time after the end of the Bronze Age by Theophrastus[121] in his work 'Historia Plantarum' around 310 BCE and later by Roman authors (*e.g.* Pliny). The origin and earliest cultivation of citrus fruits is thought to lie in southeast Asia around 500 BCE and they are first mentioned in Chinese literature in the 4th century BCE. From east Asia the knowledge about citrus fruit cultivation travelled westward and reached the Levantine coast and the Roman Empire via India and Persia in the first century BCE. Lemons were introduced to Italy after the Arab conquest of Sicily in the 10th century AD. Sweet oranges were cultivated around 1200 CE in Asia and reached Europe via the Portuguese explorers following Vasco da Gama.

In the context of this book, Apollodorus' a.m. geographical reference is very interesting also from a different angle. At first glance, it does not seem to fit the geographical directions, since the Atlas Mountains and Spain lie in the west, but the Hyperboreans were believed to have lived in the far north (cp. section 12.3.2). In order to make sense of this quote, one could assume that the journey first to the west and then to the north, *i.e.* to the Hyperboreans, referred to in this quotation were part of the same trip and followed the Atlantic route. It is thus possible that Heracles has gone further than southern Spain on this journey. This topic will be taken up later again.

As mentioned above, Strabo ('The Geography', III, 2; 11) has identified the Hesperides with the later Tartessos in southern Spain. Since a LBA settlement which could be identified with Tartessos has archaeologically not been found yet, what more can be said about this location from ancient sources?

Early Greek sources starting from the 1st millennium BCE refer to Tartessos also as a river. Strabo mentions the river Baetis (ancient name for the Guadalquivir) in connection with Tartessos (cp. again Strabo 'The Geography', III, 2; 11). These quotes form the basis of the a.m. assumption that Tartessos could have been situated around modern day Huelva at the estuary of the river Guadalquivir. Deviating from this hypothesis, Strabo ('The Geography', III, 2; 14) quotes also a different contemporary belief, which links Tartessos with the city of Carteia near modern Gibraltar.

Herodotus ('The Histories', I, 163 and IV, 152) mentions that Tartessos was situated 'beyond the Pillars of Heracles'. It was also believed to be rich in metals[122] and the earliest European civilization. Especially tin[123], but also gold and copper 'from the Celtic lands' were brought in connection with Tartessos.

---

120 Thus *e.g.* Giovanni Pontano around 1500 CE.
121 Successor of Aristoteles as the head of the Peripatetic School.
122 The Rio Tinto lies in relatively close proximity.
123 Ephorus 'Historiai', cp. section 8.2.5 'Historiographers during the Classical Period'.

Fig. 18: Heracles in the Hesperides (The Minnich Collection).

In the Greek mythical transmission, Tartessos was assumed to be not far away from Gadeiros (Cadiz), which was situated on an island. If we position Tartessos in proximity of modern day Huelva, the two localities are broadly separated by a ca. 150 km distance. In the Bronze Age this would have made a 2-day journey by boat. Gadeiros – as mentioned above – was the Greek version of the Phoenician name for the modern city of

Cadiz (-> Gadir). Both destinations are already past the Strait of Gibraltar, so technically already on the Atlantic coastline of Europe.

One later source, Rufus Festus Avienus, in the 4th century CE actually equates both locations in his geographic poem 'Ora Maritima', when he writes *'hic Gadir urbs est dicta Tartessus prius' (here is Cadiz, formerly called Tartessus).* (in Koch 2013, 9) He is assumed to have described a status in this poem from the LBA-Iron Age transition maybe even before the Phoenician city of Gadir was 'founded'. Velleius Paterculus (19 BCE – 30 AD) is even more precise when he writes *'Tyre's colony at Cadiz north west of the straits, was founded 80 years after the fall of Troy.'* (in Koch 2013, 10)

Now if we continue to refer to two separate locations – Tartessos/Huelva/ Carteia /the Hesperides and Cadiz/Gadeiros – there are currently no material Bronze Age remains that have been found. Gadeiros/Cadiz definitely is a very old settlement, but is archaeologically assumed to be a Phoenician foundation, its origins probably dating back to around 1050 BCE, which had extensive trading relation to the – presumably Celtic – Tartessian culture from around the 8th century BCE (Koch 2013). It was home to a temple of the Phoenician god Melkart, who is often identified with Heracles by Greek authors.[124] Two large pillars at the entrance of the temple could have been the origin of the myth regarding the 'Pillars of Heracles' (Lane Fox 2009, 209). As we stand, an Early Iron Age origin – or re-interpretation – of the myths of Heracles and the Hesperides cannot be excluded.

If there were Bronze Age journeys from Mycenaeans to southern Iberia, these contacts continued into the Early Iron Age. Latest by the 8th century BCE, Greek pottery has been carried to Huelva (here assumed to be the ancient Tartessos). From the 6th century on, Phoenician trading posts were established on the Atlantic coast of modern Portugal (Wachsmann et al. 2009 in Moerner and Lind 2015, 136).

From these locations in Spain and Portugal, regular trade contacts have existed to Britain and Ireland, which is stated in the poem 'Ora Maritima' of Avienus (in Koch 2013, 9):

'Tartessiisque in terminus Oestrumnidum negotiandi mos erat' (the Tartessians did business as far as the Oestrumnides).

These islands called 'Oestrumnides' were rich in tin and lead mines and were to be found two days of sailing from Ireland and the Irish (*'gens Hiernorum')*, which were close to the *'insula Albinorum'*, i.e. Britain.[125] In his poem Avienus thus confirms trading contacts of early Tartessians to Britain and Ireland.

Avienus may refer to trading contacts in the Early Iron Age. As outlined in the previous chapter, we also know that southern Spain during the preceding Bronze Age was home to significant cultures based on metal exploration and trade. The question remains, how far back those commercial contacts went and whether or how frequently already the Bronze Age Greeks reached southern Spain. If we assume a Bronze Age origin of the myths around Perseus and Heracles these myths would support this kind of early contacts.

---

124 *I.e.* 'Heracles Melikertes' (Lane Fox 2009, 206ff; von Ranke-Graves 1986, 427). Melkart was a Tyrian god and the protector of the city (Phoenician melq = king; quart = city).
125 Avienus relates knowledge of trade routes to the Britain and Ireland covered by the Carthaginian Himilco already around 500 BCE (Nesselrath 2005, 160).

Fig. 19: Rio Tinto, the 'Pyriphlegeton'? (photo: Luis, stock.adobe.com).

Odysseus

Strabo ('The Geography', III, 2; 13) muses that 'the expedition of Odysseus' may also have reached southern Iberia. Whilst most of the locations mentioned in the Odyssey probably need to be placed around Sicily and Sardinia, there may be indeed one instance that potentially connects also Odysseus with southern Spain. After his pleas with Circe to leave her island have been granted, she informs him that he first has to visit the underworld. After he asks for the way there, she tells him:

> *'The North Wind (Boreas) will blow her on her way; and when she has brought you across the River of Ocean, you will come to a wild coast and Persephone's Grove, where the tall poplars grow.'* (Homer 'The Odyssey', X, 513). Odysseus sets sail and finally gets to the place described: *'So she reached the furthest parts of the deep-flowing River of Ocean where the Cimmerians live, wrapped in mist and fog...'* (Homer 'The Odyssey', XI, 14).

Odysseus approaches the underworld at the confluence of two rivers meeting a rock. One of the rivers is called 'Pyriphlegeton', which translates into 'flaming with fire' and stands for a red-watered river according to Lane Fox (Homer 'The Odyssey', X, 513, discussed in Lane Fox 2009, 124).

There is an interesting theory by the historian Adolf Schulten that this Homerian river named 'Pyriphlegeton' actually reflects the Rio Tinto in southern Spain, whose waters even today are reddish. The confluence is still visible where Rio Tinto meets the Rio de Huelva near present day Huelva (Lane Fox 2009, 124). For this location a potential identification has already been given as Tartessos in the context of the Heraclean myths. It may thus be that also Odysseus reached the area of the later Tartessos during his journeys.

So if the Pyriphlegeton is the Rio Tinto, the journeys to the Iberian Peninsula have been connected with going to the Atlantic Ocean and potentially further north to countries of 'mist and fog'. This topic will be taken up later on again.

Nostoi

After the Trojan War several Mycenaean veterans encountered problems and upheavals upon their return home and were forced to emigrate into other areas in the Mediterranean Basin. The stories of their homecoming and ongoing travels are transmitted as the 'nostoi'.[126]

According to these myths, some of the heroes migrated westward (Idomeneus, Menestheus, Ocelas, Diomedes, Teukros) to various places in Italy and also the Iberian Peninsula. Whilst these migration myths clearly have to be interpreted also in connection with later Early Iron Age colonization of Greek settlers in the western Mediterranean, who sought to legitimize their new territories with reputable ancestry, there are also historical analyses and interpretations of Mycenaean contacts with Spain for this period at the very end of the Late Bronze Age (the mythical 'transmission' process in the Early Iron Age period of colonization is discussed in Lane Fox 2009; Celestino Perez 2016, 22 does not exclude some LBA migration background in some cases).

Summary of Mythical Contacts with the Central and Western Mediterranean

The myths referring to the central and western Mediterranean contain some strong elements of pioneering explorations. In the Iolaus myth we may have a specific reference to the establishment of the Bronze Age colony on Sardinia.

The mythological record also contains two journeys to the Hesperides, which lie in the southern Iberian Peninsula. There the mythological record points to various contacts of Mycenaean travellers to southern Iberia already between 1350 (Perseus) to ca. 1250 to 1180 BCE (Heracles, Odysseus). The Mycenaean explorations to Iberia may have started broadly contemporaneously to the increase in importance of the 'Atlantic route' for metal trade between the Iberian Peninsula and Britain (Ling et al. 2019, 32).

These contacts must have occurred at a time when the El Argar culture had already disappeared and the Early Iron Age Tartessian culture had not flourished yet. The mythical record would suggest that these contacts remained rare and had the nature of heroic adventures. Further analysis on the so-called 'pre-colonization' period of the Tartessian culture seems necessary to fill the void.

---

126 Amongst other authors related by Hagias of Troezen and Strabo 'Geographica', III, 2; 13 and III, 4; 3f.

11

Mycenaean Journeys to the Black Sea Area

11.1 The Historical, Archaeological and Epigraphic Evidence of Mycenaean Contacts with the Black Sea Area

When analyzing the archaeological evidence of Mycenaean contacts with or presence in the Black Sea area, it needs to be noted upfront that overall the material traces of Mycenaean activity in the Black Sea area are still scarce (Romey 2003, 28; de Boer 2007). Compared to other regions around the Mediterranean, the Black Sea coast in general, but especially bordering the southern Caucasus mountain range (Colchis in antiquity) has been subject to limited archaeological research over the last 70 years and some areas were closed to western archaeologists for a long time (cp. Drews 2017, 220). Hiller (1991) has summarized the material finds of Mycenaean origin (or likely Mycenaean origin) around the Black Sea in 1991 and the archaeological status quo has not changed significantly since.

Existing archaeological finds of items with Mycenaean origin in the Black Sea region may point to some form of trade contacts into this region from the Aegean during the Late Bronze Age. Mycenaean pottery found in Anatolia (the Hittite settlement of Masat Hoeyuek, northeast of Hattusha) may have gotten there via the Black Sea route. There are also ox-hide ingots found in Bulgaria (*e.g.* Sozopol on the Bulgarian coast) and maybe some swords and double axes found around the Sea of Marmara, which could be of Mycenaean origin. Additionally stone anchors found on the Bulgarian coastline may be Mycenaean, though the exact identification and dating of the finds is difficult (on possible Mycenaean finds in the Black Sea area cp. Mee 1998, 144; Hiller 1991, 208ff; Dimitrov 1979 in Romey 2003, esp. 28f; Andreadou 2015; McMillan 2016).

These material finds may indicate potential trade links or maybe even a limited Mycenaean presence in the southern and western Pontic zone (Andreadou 2015, 3; contra: de Boer 2007). However, uncertainties regarding the origin of Mycenaean goods found in the Black Sea area vs. the possibility of local copies and the routes how these goods have reached the Pontic zone still prevail.[127]

The paucity (bordering on an absence) of Mycenaean ceramic finds in the Black Sea area has been also pointed out by Blazquez Martinez (2002, 17) as a notable difference

---

[127] It is often unclear whether Mycenaean goods arrived via a sea route or whether they have been traded down land routes through Anatolia (Andreadou 2015, 18f).

Fig. 20: Mycenaean material finds in the Pontic region (map: Olav Odé, after: Hiller 1991, LVIII).

to the situation in Italy and even southern Iberia. Additionally the notable scarcity of Mycenaean pottery finds makes even the relative dating of material remains difficult. The unclear archaeological situation does thus not unequivocally support a Mycenaean presence in the Pontic area and leaves the possibility that the few finds reached the region via indirect trade, maybe via intermediaries from Troy.

In spite of this scarcity of Mycenaean material remains found so far, some authors consider the possibility that contacts of Mycenaean Greeks with the Black Sea region are historical. One reason for this is the epigraphic evidence of Mycenaean Linear B tablets, which contain toponyms from the Propontis and the Black Sea area up to Colchis at the Caucasus range (Woudhuizen 2010, 6).

Another reason for the assumption of Mycenaean contacts with the Pontic zone are recent archaeological discoveries on the Thessalian coast in Greece, which allude to contacts with parts of the Black Sea coast during the Late Bronze Age. Archaeological finds in Dimini point to trade links during this time between Thessaly and the Colchis area. Dimini is identified with ancient Iolkos, the take off port for the mythical Argonauts (Andreadou 2015, 10ff and 50).

Andreadou assumes that the interest of the Mycenaeans in the Pontic area may have been triggered by the metal ores found in the southeastern Black Sea region and the areas bordering the Caucasus mountain range (Colchis), but also by tin traded down the Danube into the Pontic and Aegean basins.

Colchis and its river Phasis in the Classical Greek period marked the northeastern boundary of the world known and familiar to the Greeks during the Classical Period (cp. Dihle 1994, 19). The region has been known probably since Bronze Age days to be rich in minerals, including gold. Additionally, the Chalybes on the southeastern shore of the Black Sea were mentioned already by Homer (Alybe) as being experts in mining and metal processing (Homer 'The Iliad', II, 850; discussions in Manoledakis 2013, 20 and 25f; Mull 2017, 89f).

Another indication for Mycenaean contacts with the Black Sea area are names found on Linear B tablets in Pylos, which can be read in a way to render the names of mythical personalities with links to the Black Sea area (Hiller 1991, 214).

If these assumptions regarding a Mycenaean presence in the Pontic region prove to be right, the paucity of archaeological finds would indicate that this presence cannot have been very significant during the LBA and not have been maintained over a long period of time. The access to the Black Sea via the Dardanelles and the Bosporus may have been difficult for the Mycenaeans and may have been obtained only late in the LBA due to three different reasons.

For one, the passage through the Dardanelles, the Marmara Sea and the Bosporus has always been a difficult navigational challenge due to the prevailing winds and currents. The winds allowed a passage only in the summer months. A discussion has evolved, actually when the Bronze Age Mycenaeans had ships capable of mastering this difficult task (*e.g.* Andreadou 2015, 24). The Mycenaean galley may have played a decisive role as a technological precondition for this nautical endeavour (Emanuel 2013, 3). Only when it was nautically as well as politically possible and the Mycenaeans finally were able to enter the Black Sea, its denomination changed from *'axeinos pontos' (hostile sea)* to *'euxeinos pontos' (welcoming sea)* (Wood 2011, 4).

Secondly, based on the archaeological finds, Hiller (1991, 207f) and Andreadou (2015, 23) discuss the critical role of Troy as a gatekeeper to the Dardanelles and for the access to the Black Sea routes. The question is whether Troy marked a terminal or an intermediary port for further travels into the Black Sea for the Mycenaeans. Troy seems to have made good use of the fact that ships had to wait often for days and weeks for favorable winds in its harbor. The Trojans may have been eager to retain their trading monopoly with Black Sea partners and may have tried to keep the Mycenaeans out.

Thirdly, control of the Hittite kingdom not only over Troy as a vassal state, but also over the southern coastline of the Black Sea and its mineral riches seems to have been an impediment to Mycenaean endeavors in the Pontic area for a long time. A plausible assumption is that the Hittites were eager to monopolize the access to these areas. Only when Hittite control began to loosen in the final years of the Hittite empire (*i.e.* from probably 1230 BCE onwards) and the Mycenaeans had gained control over the Sporades, Mycenaean expeditions into the Black Sea became feasible. The dispute between the Mycenaeans and the Hittites about the Sporades is documented in historic documents and dates to the years around 1250 BCE.[128]

Later on in the Iron Age and the period of Greek colonial expansion, the colonization of the Black Sea coast was undertaken primarily by the cities of Megara and some Ionian cities like Milet. In the subsequent chapter we will take a look whether the rather late access of the Mycenaeans to the Black Sea during the LBA is borne out by the mythological record.

---

128 The conflict around the Sporades is likely to be the background for the correspondence between the Hittite king Hattusilis II and a Mycenaean king named Tawagalawas (assumed to be Eteocles of Thebes).

11.2 Reflections of Mycenaean Journeys to the Black Sea Area in Greek Myths

Strabo ('The Geography', I, 2; 10) reports that in very ancient times the Black Sea – the 'Pontos Euxeinos' – was believed to be an 'outer Ocean' and that *'those sailing there went beyond the limits of the world, just like those who went beyond the Pillars'* [of Heracles]. We find mythical evidence for Mycenaean travels to the Black Sea area in the tale about Phrixos, the epic labors of Heracles and the tale of the Argonauts.

Phrixos and Helle

The myth about Phrixos and Helle is transmitted as part of the 'Athamas' myth by Apollodorus ('The Library of Greek Mythology', I, 80) and Hyginus (III).

The story about the siblings escape to the Black Sea area is some sort of a precursor to the later journey of the Argonauts (see below). The twins were children of the Boiotian king Athamas. Their step mother Ino conspired to have the kids sacrificed. They were saved from a sacrificial death by their real mother, who sent a golden ram to take them away on his back.

With the help of the 'golden ram' the children fly towards the Black Sea area. On the way, Helle falls into the sea and drowns. The 'Hellespont' being the entry point to the Black Sea for the Mycenaean Greeks is named after her.

Phrixos manages to escape to Colchis, a country bordering the Caucasus mountains called Aiaia or Aia in the myths. He is accepted there by the local king Aeetes and marries his daughter Chalciope. The golden ram is sacrificed to Zeus and his fleece given to king Aeetes.

With the 'golden ram' we may have – similar to the 'flying horse' Pegasus – possibly another metaphor for a fast sailing ship with a different décor at the bow. The destination of Colchis as a renowned mineral producing area points at metal exploration as a hidden motive in the story. A further significance regarding the image of a golden ram in particular connection with Colchis lies in the technology to wash metals out of mountain streams with the help of sheep fleeces, which took on a metallic glimmer in the process. The area of Colchis bordered the Caucasus Mountains and was reportedly rich in gold. Finally a ram's fleece hung on a pole used to be a Hittite regnal symbol.

The story around Phrixos and Helle based on genealogical chronology needs to be positioned around 1250 BCE, *i.e.* a generation before the Argonauts and two generations before the Trojan War. The 'baptism' of the Hellespont may indicate a first contact with this area for the Mycenaean Greeks.

Heracles (and the Amazons)

The very ancient Near Eastern or Mesopotamian parallels to – and maybe origins of – the Heracles myth have already been discussed. This analysis focuses on a potential Mycenaean travelling hero with the name of Heracles to whom these foreign attributes seem to have been later ascribed.

Heracles may have been one of the first explorers on the newly discovered or now accessible route (for the Mycenaeans) to the Black Sea areas. His ninth labour is reported to have ventured to the land of the Amazons at the Thermodon river. The Thermodon is today's Terme river between the cities Ordu and Samsun at the southern coast of the Black Sea (the myth is related by Herodotus 'The Histories', IV; Strabo 'Geographica' III, 2; Diodorus Siculus 'Library of History', IV, 16).

Heracles travelled with up to nine ships in the company of Telamon and Peleus, both fathers of Mycenaean heroes at Troy, and passed the island of Paros and Mysia. Upon reaching the estuary of the Thermodon he anchored the ships at the harbour of Themiskyra.

He obtained the desired belt from the Amazon's leader Hippolyte after some violent clashes. The return journey of Heracles and his crew included raids on several other southern Pontic settlements and also an attack on Troy and its then king Laomedon, to ensure future access to the Black Sea (the 'first Trojan War').

The Amazons are described by Greek historians as a warlike steppe tribe dressed in furs, which has migrated to the southern Black Sea coast from the northern Pontic area around the river Tanais (Don). They may have been related to the later Scythians and Sarmatians, both of which are Iranian peoples, even though Herodotus ('The Histories', IV, 111ff; 114) reports that they initially spoke a different language.

Archaeological discoveries of burial sites with female warriors in the Pontic steppe may be indications to support this theory (Anthony 2007, 329). From their new settlements at the Black Sea they seem to have conducted several raids on different areas in Asia Minor.

As in the Egyptian adventures of Heracles, also for this myth a theoretical timing of approx. 1220 BCE is suggested, which puts the 'historical' Heracles figure in the final stages of the Late Bronze Age.

The Argonauts

The myth about the Argonauts is already mentioned in Homer (*e.g.* 'The Odyssey', XII, 69) and much later by Apollodorus ('The Library of Greek Mythology', I, 9; 3). Its best known version however was compiled in Hellenistic times by Apollonius of Rhodes, a librarian at Alexandria (Romm 1992, 31).

The mythical background of the story about the Argonauts is the claim of Jason to the throne of Iolkos in northern Greece (today's Dimini near to present day Volos). His incumbent uncle Pelias makes the handover of the throne conditional on returning the 'fleece of the golden ram' to him, which Phrixos brought to Colchis. Jason takes on the task, assembles an illustrious crew of 50 mariners – amongst them some of the greatest heroes of the time – and has a ship build for him, the 'Argo'.

In the myth, the Argo is introduced as a ship with 50 rowers. We are most likely looking at a Mycenaean galley, and clearly a pentaconter judging from the number of the crew. As stated above, the introduction of fast pentaconters like the Argo could have been an important precondition and an enabler for the Mycenaeans to venture past the Dardanelles and the Bosporus due to the difficult conditions regarding winds and currents.

In order to return the 'Golden Fleece' from Colchis to king Pelias, the Argonauts managed to enter the Black Sea with this ship. The destination of the Argonauts was the country of 'Aia' or 'Aiaia' in the far east of the known world, a toponym, which is archaeologically not finally attested yet (Wood 2011,4).[129] They stopped en route at major metal producing areas (*e.g.* the 'Chalybes') on the southern Black Sea shoreline. The tale of the Argonauts later developed into the founding myth for many towns along this coast.

---

129 An ancient gold treasure has been found in the region at an ancient site near the town of Vani, and it has been suggested that this site may be the location of Bronze Age Aia, even though no Bronze Age settlements have been found there yet.

Fig. 21: Map 'Argonautica' by Ortelius, 16th century, rendering various mythical locations (Inritter).

MYCENAEAN JOURNEYS TO THE BLACK SEA AREA

After many adventures the 'Golden Fleece' is finally obtained. It is unclear whether the Golden Fleece was an original part of the myth. However, in the Hittite Empire a fleece hung upon a pole represented royal power as well as prosperity and the labours of Jason resemble Hittite initiation rites (Mosenkis 2016, 176). Furthermore, as stated above fleeces were a method to filter metals (also gold) out of mountain streams. The fleece over time took on a metallic glitter.

The Argonauts are reported to have travelled back on the northern shore of the Black Sea, probably passing the estuary of the Danube. Strabo quotes sources, which say that Jason and his crew went up the Istrus (Danube) for quite some distance, maybe to scout out tin deliveries from the north via this route (Strabo 'The Geography', I, 2; 39).

The historicity and origin of the Argonautica are disputed. The first definite connection of the Argonautica with the Colchis goes back to Hesiod (quoted in Apollonius of Rhodes), who mentioned that the travellers sailed along the river Phasis. Nesselrath (2005, 158) ascribes the first connection being made to Colchis as the destination of the Argonauts to Eumelus (Corinthiaca) during the mid-sixth century BCE.

Von Ranke-Graves (1986, 456) on the other hand considers the mythical record essentially to reflect a historical process of LBA Mycenaean travel and contacts with the Black Sea region. There are also indications that the myth of the Argonauts may indeed go back to Bronze Age roots (discussed in Wood 2011, 2: Parke in Bridgman 2010, 141). Karl Meuli has shown that the Odyssey presupposes an earlier epic of the Argonauts (Dihle 1994, 12; cp. also Bridgman 2010, 142). If these assumptions are correct, we may indeed be dealing with a metal exploration to Colchis at the Caucasus at the background of the Argonautica.

The myth about the journey of the Argonauts underwent significant changes during the transmission in the Classical and Hellenistic Periods of Greece. The number and composition of the crew, initially 50 mariners, as well as the list of places visited changed in this time. There are variants of the Argonauts further destinations with different authors.

It is possible that there were two different travel myths later combined in the Argonautica. The first one describes a trip to the Black Sea and Colchis at the Caucasus mountain range with a crew consisting mostly of Thessalian people from Iolkos. The second journey would take a different crew of Minyans up the Adria in the east and into the Po River (discussed in von Ranke-Graves 1986, 543f, 552; Bridgman 2010, 141; Nesselrath 2005, 157). This latter journey would thus have to be dealt with in the context of western explorations.

Overall the exploration of the Black Sea by the Bronze Age Mycenaeans seems to have started relatively late, much later than journeys undertaken to Egypt or Anatolia. The myths of Heracles and the Argonauts with reference to the Black Sea coast point to the very end of the Bronze Age. A theoretical timing of the Argonaut myth needs to be seen as contemporary to Heracles and about a generation before the Trojan War, thus also around 1220 BCE. This timing coincides well with the a.m. gradual loss of control of the Hittite empire over the vassal states in northwestern Anatolia incl. the city of Troy from approx. 1230 BCE onwards.

12

The Mysterious Countries 'Beyond'

In ancient Greece, geography in general, but especially within it the records of countries and peoples far away 'at the edges of the earth' often was more about adventure and the supernatural than about science (Helms 1988; cp. Romm 1992, 3, 47). Reports and speculations about the edges of the known world followed certain patterns, which themselves were subject to changes over time, and created a literary genre on its own.

Exotic people like the Ethiopians, Hyperboreans, Arimaspians and Scythians belonged to those far away populations of which not much was known and that yet fascinated the Greeks. Herodotus ('The Histories', IV, 16 and 32) for instance relates stories about 'Indians' in the far south-east, about 'Hyperboreans' in the far north and about the 'springs of the Nile' in the far south. The traditions regarding these remote places and peoples in Herodotus are also not told as a result of travels and direct experiences by the author, but rather as indirectly related by third parties. Herodotus uses these stories to define the limits of possible knowledge in his space and time (Luraghi 2001, 145).

Some authors point to the fact that descriptions of the remote territories in ancient times encompassed connotations of 'mythical paradises' and stereotypical elements mirroring or contrasting Greek self-perception and thus a form of 'created reality' (Rausch 2013, 50f). To relate these stories on the other hand to the potential knowledge and concrete experiences of much earlier Bronze Age travellers naturally includes an element of speculation, because there are very few archaeological or historical cornerstones to build on.

Yet, like in the traditions related by Herodotus, not all knowledge needed to be acquired first hand by the Mycenaeans. When they travelled to the edges of their known world they would have encountered different people and 'middlemen', who told them stories about what lies 'beyond'. Due to the lack of firsthand experience, these stories will have been even more prone to include an element of the fantastic, but maybe sometimes also experiences of other mariners on the 'borders of the Bronze Age'.

12.1 The Far South and East – The Ethiopians, the Red Sea and the Indian Ocean

If Egypt has been relatively familiar to the Mycenaean Greeks in the Late Bronze Age, one is tempted to ask, whether their geographical knowledge extended even further to the south and east. Did the Mycenaeans hear about or have conceptual knowledge of Africa south of Egypt, the Red Sea or even the Indian Ocean and the people living there?

The word 'Ethiopian' is already attested in Mycenaean Greek from the 2nd millennium BCE. Since the literal translation means 'people with burned faces', the word seems to have denoted darker skinned people from the south, about which the Mycenaeans probably had some knowledge via their trade with Egypt, where Nubians were present as mercenaries and traders (Dihle 1994, 7ff; Romm 1992, 50).

The Ethiopians also feature in the Homeric epics, living 'on the edge of the world' ('eschatoi andron') and being particularly just and 'loved by the gods' (Homer 'The Iliad', I, 421 – 423; XXIII, 206 – 208; Homer 'The Odyssey', I 21 – 23; IV, 81 – 84; V, 282- 287; XXIII, 205). Regarding their location, they were associated as well with the far west as with the far southeast. This concept may reflect Homeric knowledge of dark skinned people living on *'opposite coasts of a dimly perceived African continent'* (Romm 1992, 49f; already Strabo ('The Geography', I, 2; 26) discusses the Homeric remarks in this way).

So if the Mycenaeans had a word for African people with dark skin, what did they actually know about the geography south and east of Egypt, *i.e.* about Africa, the Red Sea and the Indian Ocean?

In Roman times, *i.e.* a good thousand years after the end of the Bronze Age, detailed knowledge about the Indian Ocean existed and a regular direct travel to India was conducted (McLaughlin 2010). The Romans got access to the Red Sea ports after the conquest of Egypt in 30 BCE and sent regular fleets of large transporters to India until about the middle of the second century CE. The knowledge of trade routes and direct contacts between the Romans and India are summarized in a so-called 'Periplous', a detailed description of the maritime way from the Red Sea to India dating from ca. 54 CE, a period of extensive contacts between Rome and the Far East during imperial Roman times.

How far back in time does this familiarity with India, the Red Sea and the Indian Ocean reach? The Malabar Coast of India was discovered for trade by crossing the Indian Ocean in the year 117 BCE by the Greek captain Eudoxos. During these days, the term 'Erythraean Sea' (*i.e.* the Red Sea) and 'Erythraean Ocean' (*i.e.* the Indian Ocean) were differentiated (Dihle 1994, 78, 86).

Further back in the Classical Greek Period (480 – 323 BCE) probably due to a lack of knowledge in detail about the maritime expanses, the Red Sea and the Indian Ocean were both still indiscriminately called the 'Erythraean Sea', *e.g.* by Herodotus (484 – 425 BCE).[130] Herodotus describes ('The Histories', II, 11, translation by Rohl 2007, 152):

> *'There is in Arabia, not far from Egypt, a gulf of the sea entering in from the sea called Red; its length and narrowness are as I shall show. For length, if one begins a voyage from its inner end, to sail right through into the broad sea is a matter of forty days for a boat that is rowed.'*

According to Herodotus, this knowledge about the Red Sea and the Indian Ocean was based on another Periplous reflecting a voyage, which took place between 520 and 510 BCE and which was undertaken by a certain Scylax (Herodotus 'The Histories', IV, 44; discussed in Romm 1992, 35 and 84). Scylax was an Ionian mariner from Karyanda in Karia, who was forced into service by the Persian king Darius I (550 – 486 BCE). India – the toponym then

---

130 The name 'Erythraean Sea' denoting the Red Sea only came into use from Agatharchides of Knidos on, *i.e.* from the 2nd century BCE onwards (Dihle 1994, 86).

denoted roughly today's Pakistan – at this period of time belonged to the Persian Empire. The voyage started on the river Indus, went downstream to the Indus estuary, along the coastline of the Indian Ocean, around the Arab peninsula and up the Red Sea (Dihle 1994, 24f). The Periplous contained detailed descriptions of the coastlines thus visited.

So by ca. 450 BCE the Greeks had positive and specific knowledge about the Red Sea, Africa and India. The question is, did this knowledge already exist during Bronze Age times? Do the Homeric myths mention the Erythraean Sea?

As it stands and as shown above, the African Ethiopians feature in the Homeric myths. In the Odyssey, Menelaos also mentions the 'Erembians', which may be people from Arabia, he encountered on a tour through the eastern Mediterranean.[131] Finally, in mythical traditions outside the Homeric epics, Dionysos is told to have travelled to India (Diodorus Siculus 'Library of History', II, 38). So we do find some faint references in the mythical tradition with maybe Bronze Age roots to Africa, Arabia and India.

Homer does however not explicitly mention the Erythraean Sea, nor India. Also no Mycenaean remains have been found on the Red Sea coast. Overall, as of yet there is thus no record or material hint of Mycenaeans having possessed a direct knowledge of this part of the world.

On the other hand, as shown above, the Mycenaeans probably were relative regular travellers to Egypt. The contact with the Red Sea and from there with the Indian Ocean obviously went via Egypt. During the late Bronze Age, the pharaohs of the 18th, 19th and 20th dynasties continued expeditions to the land of 'Punt', which probably needs to be located in northeastern Africa. The first contacts between Egypt and Punt already date back to the Old Kingdom and are attested for the 6th dynasty. Also during the Middle Kingdom Punt has been contacted during the 11th and 12th dynasties (under Pharaoh Senusret). Only after the time of Ramses III the contacts with Punt seem to have ceased.

If in the days of Hatshepsut, Thutmosis III and their successors of the 18th and 19th up to the 20th dynasty Mycenaean Greeks visited Egypt, they may have heard about the stories around the Egyptian naval expeditions to northeastern Africa. In fact, they could have seen the colorful representation of it in the mortuary temple of Queen Hatshepsut. It is highly plausible that Egyptian travellers could have told the Mycenaean visitors about the Red Sea region. All in all the Mycenaean Greeks based on their contacts with Egypt could have formed a picture of the world to the southeast of Egypt.

12.2 The Far West – 'The Isles of the Blessed'

To reiterate upfront, in archaeological terms Mycenaean finds currently go no further west than southern Iberia (Montoro, Llanete de los Moros). The Mycenaean pottery found there may serve as a general indication about the reach of Mycenaean goods, but they are neither a proof that Mycenaeans themselves regularly went to the Iberian Peninsula, nor a proof to the contrary that they did not venture even further in incidental journeys without traces being visible today[132].

---

131 'My travels took me to Cyprus, to Phoenicia, and to Egypt. Ethiopians, Sidonians, Erembians, I visited them all; and I saw Libya, too.' Homer 'The Odyssey', IV, 80; Strabo ('The Geography', I, 1; 3) already identifies the 'Erembians' as Arabs.
132 For a regular exchange one would expect to find archaeological traces though.

As far as mythological records go, at least the Perseus myth and the adventures of Heracles indicate direct contacts of Mycenaeans beyond the Pillars of 'Heracles'. In later Archaic, Classical and Roman times, several authors write about territories or isles even further west, the *'makaron nesoi'*, the 'Fortunate Isles' or the 'Isles of the Blessed'.

The Isles of the Blessed are mentioned already by Hesiod (Works and Days 167ff, discussed in Rausch 2013, 48). In geographical terms, this toponym seems to have been a moving target over time. After Hesiod one of the first to mention these remote islands has been Pindaros ('Olympian Ode', II, 57ff) in the years around 476 BCE. There the islands are mentioned as the abode for the afterlife of mythical heroes like Peleus, Cadmos and Achilles, albeit without being specific about their location. It seems, the concept of their whereabouts moved from initially the western Mediterranean towards somewhere in the Atlantic Ocean. During later Roman times Plutarch was specific that there are two of them and located them 1250 miles from Africa with a seemingly subtropical or tropical climate (Plutarch 'Life of Sertorius', VIII). Also Strabo ('The Geography', I, 1; 5) mentions that the *'Blessed Islands are to the west of the farthest part of Maurousia [Morocco; Mauretania], the portion that comes close to the limit of Iberia'*.

These remarks by later authors have been brought into connection with Homer's *'Elysian Fields at the world's end [...] where no snow falls'* and to which heroes like Menelaos or mythical figures like the Cretan Rhadamantys go after death (Homer 'The Odyssey', IV, 562). So maybe already Homer had a vague concept of tropical territories or islands in the far west.

There has been some speculation as to whether the Cape Verdes, the Canary Islands, the Azores or even the Lesser Antilles could be a fit for the description (cp. Mosenkis 2016, 171). Of these locations, only the Canary Islands are proven to be occupied in pre-historic times. The question to be dealt with here is, how far back in time we can assume some knowledge about islands beyond the 'Pillars'.

In terms of substantiated knowledge in antiquity about locations west of the Pillars of Heracles, we know from Herodotus' accounts ('The Histories', IV, 42-44) of a circumnavigation of Africa by Phoenicians under Pharaoh Necho II (610 – 595 BCE). Interestingly Herodotus describes Necho's orders ('to come round by the Pillars of Heracles') in a way that may infer that his was not the first expedition around Africa. Also Euthymenes of Massilia travelled down the African coastline up to the mouth of the Senegal River by the mid-6th century BCE (Dihle 1994, 27).

Additionally, the Phoenicians have sailed beyond modern Gibraltar regularly from about 1000 to 900 BCE. They have established settlements on the Moroccan Atlantic coast and up the shoreline of modern Portugal.[133] Even much earlier, members of the Atlantic Bell Beaker culture have travelled up and down the Atlantic coastline.

Whether any of those travellers encountered islands in the Atlantic Ocean is unclear. If they did and if ever Mycenean mariners should have ventured beyond the straits of Gibraltar – two big ifs -, at least a passive knowledge in Mycenaean times about islands in the Atlantic Ocean can probably not be excluded and may have formed the base of the myth about the 'Isles of the Blessed', the origin of which is still cloudy.

---

133 The name of the modern city of Agadir in Marocco is of the same Phoenician origin as Gadeiros/Gadir (Cadiz) in Spain.

12.3 'Hyperborea' – The Mysterious 'Far North'

12.3.1 The Archaeological Evidence of Contacts from Mycenaean Greece with Northern Europe

The question being dealt with in the following chapter is whether Mycenaean Greeks during the LBA had positive knowledge of and possibly contacts with people in the north of Europe. Schofield (2007, 115) calls the extent of Mycenaean trading links to the countries of northern Europe 'obscure'. We therefore need to investigate whether whatever indications we can arrive at from the archaeological remains is being backed up by the mythological record.

While Rahmstorf (2010, 685) points out that Aegean – north European contacts prior to Mycenaean times (*i.e.* before ca. 1700 BCE) are likely to have been negligible, Kristiansen and Larsson (2005, 210) have stated that cultural transmissions from the Aegean to northern Europe are assumed for as early as the 18th century BCE:

> 'We have demonstrated that there existed well-organized trading networks that connected southern Scandinavia with the Carpathian tell cultures during the eighteenth to sixteenth centuries BC, and from here there were similar networks to the Circum-Pontic Zone, Anatolia and the Aegean.'

For these early connections via the Carpathian basin the Danube must have played an important role as a transmission route (discussions in Earle et al. 2015, 641; Cunliffe 2011, 169f).

Already during the first stages of the Mycenaean Late Bronze Age amber and tin seems to have been traded from Britain (Cornwall), France (Brittany) the Baltic Sea coast and Bohemia via the European riverine systems to the western and eastern Mediterranean.[134] Maran (2004) illustrated the close connection between Mycenae and the southern British Wessex culture based on an analysis of the amber necklaces found in the Mycenaean shaft graves of the 16th century BCE and their close counterparts in southern England.[135] He stressed the importance of the 'western route' down the Rhone and along the Italian coastline during the early stages for the Mycenaeans when trade in the eastern Mediterranean was dominated by the Minoans.

Maran's assumption regarding the transmission routes for amber and tin from northern Europe to the Mediterranean is backed up by a remark in Diodorus Siculus, which may be based on the much later journey of Pytheas to Britain in the 4th century BCE. Diodorus ('The Library of History', V, 22) mentions the connection for the trade of tin from northern Europe via land routes through Gallia to the estuary of the river Rhone (Maran 2004, 55).[136] From there the transport according to Maran was continued via

---

[134] Muhly (1973 in Maran 2004, 58) was the first to classify the amber found in Mycenaean graves as a 'by-product' of the tin trade from northern Europe. Cp. also Rahmstorf 2010, 685.
[135] The parallels range from specific boring holes in the amber over the context of the necklaces only found in burials (Maran 2004).
[136] Diodorus Siculus ('The Library of History', V, 22) states 'The inhabitants of Britain [...]. They it is who work the tin, [...]. On the island of Ictis the merchants purchase the tin of the natives and carry it from there across the strait of Galatia or Gaul; and finally make their way on foot through Gaul for some thirty days, they bring their wares on horseback to the mouth of the River Rhone.' Cp. also Cunliffe 2011, 45.

ship along the Italian coastline into the eastern Mediterranean. This central European connection to the north via the Rhine/Rhone systems may also go back to Bronze Age networks and trading routes.[137]

Furthermore, Herodotus ('The Histories', IV, 32) – quoting Homer and Hesiod – mentions an amber route to the north up to the Baltic Sea. It needs to be asked whether Homer and Hesiod transmitted knowledge here that dates back to Bronze Age origins.

Next to the amber that found its way from northern Europe to the Mediterranean during the LBA, there are recent finds of Egyptian glass beads in Denmark from the time of pharaoh Tutankhamun (mid 14th century BCE) indicating a maybe reciprocal exchange of goods from southern Europe to the north (Varberg et al. 2014).[138]

Overall it is assumed that amongst the rivers frequented during LBA times for trade with northern Europe were the Vistula/Danube system as well as the Rhine/Rhone and the Seine/Rhone routes (Bridgman 2010, 107ff). Maybe also the ocean route from Britain down the Atlantic and via Gibraltar into the Mediterranean was in use already in the Late Bronze Age. It was certainly known to the Phoenicians just a few hundred years later (Cunliffe 2011, 299; cp. section 10.3.2). For the Bronze Age, some authors hypothesize over the knowledge available about this Atlantic route and the travellers on it. We will come back to this question a bit later on.

For the next phase of the Late Bronze Age (15th – 14th century BCE), increasing contacts and transmissions can be demonstrated as well towards northern Europe. Mycenaean ceramics like kylixes have been found not only around the Mediterranean basin, but also in northern Europe as far as northern Germany (Kleinhubbert 2018, 123).

Compared to a 'first stage' of exchange in the LBA, which was dominated by Minoans and Hittites in the eastern Mediterranean, whilst Mycenaeans traded on the western routes,

> *'the second stage marks a heavier transmission of the social and ritual institutions of warrior aristocracies. It reflects increasing interaction between Mycenaean culture and central and northern Europe characterized by increased borrowing on both sides, e.g. flange-hilted swords. What is now transmitted is the whole set-up of ruling elites.'*
> (Kristiansen and Larsson 2005, 212)

Again, the question needs to be raised regarding the form of contact between these far away regions. Are we looking at *indirect* trade networks or do we need to assume *direct* contacts via long distance shipping?

Maran (2004, 57f) ponders both forms of exchange, but considers the *indirect* exchange for the most likely transmission mechanism via overlapping networks of trade in which specialized traders organize a regular transfer of goods. Interestingly he dismisses the alternative theory of Harding (in Maran 2004, 57), who considers a *direct* transmission over large distances the most probable form of exchange.[139] This theory would be supported by the lack of finds of the particular amber necklaces or parts of them anywhere on the trade route in between Britain and Mycenae. Also Andreadou (2015, 16) stresses the existence

---

137 As discussed in earlier chapters, he trading routes via central European riverine systems may even be much older and go back to Neolithic origins, if we follow Cunliffe (2011, 123f).
138 The glass beads were found in a woman's grave south of Copenhagen.
139 Cp. the comments in chapter 5 on the transactional costs and risks of an indirect trade over several intermediaries.

Fig. 22: Ships carved into the rocks of Tanum, Sweden (Designium) (photo: Mattis Kaminer, stock.adobe.com).

of an 'amber route' from the Baltic to Mycenae, but she finds it *'difficult to argue that the Mycenaeans during their travels reached the Baltic area'*.

On the other hand, Kristiansen and Larsson (2005) have illustrated the breadth of cultural influences between Britain, Scandinavia and the cultural centres in the eastern Mediterranean during the entire Late Bronze Age. Pictographic evidence of ships in rock carvings in Sweden may – some authors claim – point to a maritime extension of trade routes from those centres around the Mediterranean Basin all the way to Britain and possibly Scandinavia. Also the remains of Bronze Age weapons, tools and luxury items as part of a maritime cargo claimed to be of Minoan origin found in the shallow waters of the North Sea belong in this context (Berger, 2013, see below).

A controversial theory of Moerner and Lind (2002) already touched upon earlier regarding *direct* trade contacts between the eastern Mediterranean and Scandinavia possibly also via the Atlantic route is based on pictorial representation of what they consider to be Aegean ships on rock-paintings in southern Sweden and Norway. Interestingly these pictorial representations of ships seem to appear just at the same time as amber (and tin?) from southern Britain appears in Mycenaean shaft graves and the beginning of the Bronze Age in Scandinavia based on imported Bronzes, *i.e.* around 1750 to 1600 BCE.

Moerner and Lind (2002, 5) believe that both occurrences at broadly the same time in history are an evidence for long distance migration and trading. Further, seemingly Mediterranean signs, symbols and ornaments found in Scandinavia are taken as an indication of cultic parallels and ultimately of direct exchanges across the continent. This exchange is believed to have happened also via the Atlantic route rather than only the riverine systems due to the size of the ships shown on the pictorial representations.

Olsson (1999 in Kristiansen and Larsson 2005, 71), Moerner and Lind (2002) as well as Sheppard Baird (2007) interpret the carvings of ship images as essentially *foreign*, i.e. Mediterranean, and as evidence for cultural exchange via a direct trade connection between Scandinavia and the eastern Mediterranean via the Atlantic route since ca. 1500 BCE. Also various other authors (*e.g.* Drews 2017, 159) assume the ships to be an externally stimulated innovation, since they appear so suddenly and are very much advanced vs. their local Neolithic predecessors, which were dugouts or made of skin. The ships represented on the Swedish and Norwegian rocks according to these assumptions would essentially go back to some form of external influence and need to be seen as an indication of a direct trade between the Baltic and the eastern Mediterranean possibly via an Atlantic route.

Drews (2017, 159) muses about a direct connection between Scandinavia and the eastern Mediterranean stating

> *'The maritime tradition of the Nordic Bronze Age was apparently initiated by contact with the eastern Mediterranean cultures, and it is very likely that the amber trade lay behind the extension of the Mediterranean maritime tradition to Scandinavia. Before amber was carried over a land route through central Europe, that is, it seems to have been brought to Greece by ships: from the North Sea through the English Channel, around Gibraltar, and then through the Mediterranean.'*

However, not all scholars follow this line of thinking. Cunliffe (2011, 217ff) identified the *Atlantic Bell Beaker culture* as the initial agent to organize the maritime transport along the entire european Atlantic coastline. After the end of the Bell Beaker phenomenon around 1800 BCE the people living subsequently on the Atlantic fringe may have maintained the know-how about routes and boat building including British and Scandinavian mariners.

The carvings in Sweden from the beginning of the LBA according to his view may thus represent Scandinavian, not Mediterranean, ships. Similarly Kristiansen (2016, 161ff) classifies the carvings as part of a shared Nordic culture. Earle et al. (2015, 644) reckon some scholars would agree that rather than foreign visitors, *Scandinavians* participated in long distance trade in the Bronze Age and the boat finds and depictions as rock art in Scandinavia represent a long *local* boat-building tradition. Ling and Uhner (2014, 36) confirm that the local sewn-plank boats were capable of long-distance sea journeys already around 1800 to 1600 BCE and could transport a cargo of 700 kg.

The 'Atlantic Route'

Irrespective of the speculations whether the travellers on the Atlantic route were of eastern Mediterranean – possibly Mycenaean – origin or of maybe Iberian or local Scandinavian provenance, it is fairly certain that the route was already in use throughout the Bronze Age. It is thus worth some words on where this route may have led.

Mariners in the Late Bronze Age coming from the Mediterranean probably had the option to cut across southern France on the Aude-Garonne connection and by this way circumvent the Iberian Peninsula (Cunliffe 2011, 43). Since this route had the disadvantage of a portage of some kilometers, it was probably not suitable for bigger ships and larger cargoes.

Fig. 23: The 'Atlantic Route' (conjecture) (map: Olav Odé).

The other route would have led around the southern tip of the Iberian Peninsula, crossing the 'Pillars of Heracles' with possibly a stop in the Bronze Age precursors of Cadiz and/or the location later called 'Tartessos'. From these vantage points further advance could be made up today's Portuguese coastline. As mentioned above, considerable Bronze Age settlement remains have been uncovered along the estuary of the river Tagus, some 350 km from Cadiz and 160 km from Huelva (Cardoso 2015). Further Phoenician remains from the later Iron Age have been found up along the estuaries on the Portuguese coastline. It remains speculative whether the Phoenicians followed outposts already established during the Bronze Age.

Another likely stopover would have been the Garonne estuary on the Atlantic coastline, where the riverine passage across southern France would be met. From here access to the minerals of Brittany was only about 400 km away. One conceivable final target of the journey could have been the 'tin islands' off the southwestern coast of Britain.

The Scilly Islands may be a possible candidate for the 'Cassiterides' (*i.e.* the 'tin islands'), of which Diodorus Siculus ('The Library of History', V, 22) says that they are located between Europe and Britain. Next to Diodorus these tin islands are also mentioned by Herodotus and Strabo ('The Geography', II, 5; 15; cp. Woudhuizen 2010, 7). On the Scilly

Islands, Bronze Age graves from 2500 to 800 BCE are still visible today. The tin supply for the Cassiterides would have come from Cornwall and Devon. A shipload of tin ingots found on the Salcombe boat bear witness to this trade (Wang et al. 2016).

The overall journey would have covered around 2.400 km from Cadiz. Including the return trip a Late Bronze Age galley may have been able to cover this distance in around 80 to 100 days.

Did the Mycenaeans Travel the Atlantic Route?

If one is allowed to assume some form of direct contacts of the Mycenaean world to southern Iberia during the LBA – and considering that the Phoenicians already ventured into the Atlantic Ocean possibly as early as around 1000 BCE (again Cunliffe 2011, 56) -, the largely hypothetical question arises whether the Mycenaeans travelled even further than the Straits of Gibraltar.

Against a lack of archaeological evidence that could prove this point, there is the a.m. vast amount of speculation regarding the commencement of western and northern trade journeys by Aegean peoples. It is intriguing indeed that the ship renderings found in Scandinavia date to a period, when amber made its first appearance in the Mycenaean shaft graves and when new types of weapons, which go back to Carpathian origins, start a breakthrough in the Nordic Bronze Age (Maran 2004; Drews 2017, 156).

On the other hand Cunliffe (quoting Pindaros) points to the fact that the Straits of Gibraltar may have posed a psychological barrier for the Mycenaeans that may have prevented journeys beyond. This more limiting approach for Mycenaean Atlantic journeys is supported by Romm (1992, 17f), who states that the 'Pillars of Heracles' were being looked upon by mythographers and historiographers alike as a forbidding 'non plus ultra' and a warning not to proceed any further. To pass them was a prerogative of the gods or demigods like Heracles, who actually did venture beyond the pillars.

So are there any archaeological clues that would support the hypothesis of Mycenaeans in the Atlantic region?

Matthaeus (2005, 338) points to the fact that according to the archaeological record as it stands today the most western point of the earlier Mycenaean far distance travel in the Mediterranean was Andalucia, where the a.m. Mycenaean ceramics have been found in the LBA settlement of Llanete de los Moros.

Recent archaeological research in the Tagus estuary on the Atlantic coast of Portugal reveals that this region formed an important link between the Atlantic trading zones and various Mediterranean influences (Cardoso 2015). The cultural exchange is most pronounced in the time between 1000 to 800 BCE and thus later than the LBA investigated here. By this time we are facing an established commercial axis up to Sardinia and can assume Phoenician settlers in the area.

The region around the mouth of the Tagus however has been settled already by the Atlantic Bell Beaker people from 2800 BCE. The sites analyzed by Cardoso reveal settlement traces from after the Bell Beaker period around 1500 BCE and we have evidence of foreign presence in the area from the central and maybe eastern Mediterranean from broadly 1400 BCE onwards.

Also further north, some recent isolated finds point towards the possibility of an exchange of people from the eastern Mediterranean with northern Europeans during the Bronze Age. Skeleton finds on the island of Thanet in the Thames estuary indicate that Scandinavians interacted with groups from the Mediterranean during the LBA (McKinley

2013 in Ling and Uhner 2014, 35; cp. Earle et al. 2015, 643). In trading places like these there may have been direct exchanges between people from northern Europe with people from the western and eastern Mediterranean.

Further singular material traces in northern Europe could indicate that the theory of direct contacts with people from the eastern Mediterranean may receive further substantiation in the future: Mosenkis (2016, 19) mentions a Minoan inscription found engraved on a rock face of a Bronze Age cult site in Norway. Additionally a German periodical in 2013 reported about seemingly Minoan finds of the ethnologist Hans Peter Duerr in the shallow North Sea waters (Berger in 'Focus', 2013). The items recovered from the ocean floor consisted of Crete-manufactured cups and plates, a Minoan seal turned into an amulet with Linear A inscriptions, a lance tip and a few luxury items. The pieces were reportedly found under a layer of peat that started to form only after 1300 BCE. Neutron-analyses indicate that the ceramics have been shaped around 1300 BCE in central Crete and resemble similar vessels found in Kommos at the south coast of the island.

The fact that the items recovered were mostly household goods favours their arrival in a direct exchange pattern rather than as a result of indirect trade, which is assumed to have been in place mostly for luxury goods. Some researchers quoted in the article like Burkert consider it in principle possible that Minoans found their way to the North Sea cost. Matthaeus suspects Cornwall as the likely destination of the trip, where tin could be obtained, with a subsequent detour to the German coastline maybe to trade amber.

It needs to be reiterated that even if there may be faint traces of 'eastern Mediterraneans' on the Atlantic route, there is as yet no definite archaeological proof to back up an Atlantic travel of Mycenaeans during the late Bronze Age. If these journeys happened, they were likely to be exceptional trips in very individual cases and the source of fame and fortune. Further finds will hopefully contribute to a clearer picture about the nature of the commercial exchanges between the western Mediterranean and the regions on the European Atlantic border as well as their protagonists.

12.3.2 The Mythical Record of Mycenaean Contacts with Northern Europe

If we assume that indirect – and in some instances maybe also direct – trade contacts existed between the eastern Mediterranean and northern Europe during the Late Bronze Age, possibly via the riverine system but maybe even on the Atlantic route, the question comes up, whether there are reflections of these contacts as well in the mythical record.

The name for the 'far north' in the Archaic and Classical Greek records is 'Hyperborea'. Various classical sources contain information about 'Hyperborea' and its inhabitants, the 'Hyperboreans', a region that has been located 'beyond the Northwind' (Boreas) and was often connected with extreme cold and snow.[140] We find references to 'Boreas' already in Homer[141] and Hesiod, however, the myth around the Hyberboreans may be considerably older and may also have Bronze Age origins (Rausch 2013, 12; discussed also in Bridgman 2010, 145f).

---

140 The ancient Greeks actually had two possibilities to express their idea of the 'far north'. Next to the 'northwind' Boreas also the constellation 'Arktos' served as a pointer to the north, but in case of the latter one only since the end of the 5th century BCE, whereas we find references to Boreas already in Homer and Hesiod (Rausch 2013, 9f).
141 The Hyperboreans, however, are not mentioned in the Homeric epics.

Strabo ('The Geography', I, 1; 6) assumes that already Homer knew the principle of the Arctic Circle. The star constellation used to identify the extreme north is described in the Iliad and the Odyssey as *'the Great Bear [Greek: Arktos], sometimes called the Wain, [...] which never sinks below the horizon to bathe in the Ocean's Stream'.*(Homer 'The Odyssey', V, 275. Similar Homer 'The Iliad', XVIII, 480). If Strabo is right, we have to assume at least some passive knowledge about the northern territories around 700 BCE. In the same passage he points out that Homer knew of some potentially nomadic people living in the north he calls the Hippemolgi ('mares-milk drinkers') and the Abii (Homer 'The Iliad', XIII, 5; Strabo 'The Geography', I, 1; 6).

In comparison to the Ethiopians in the extreme south, who did not interfere with the people living in the 'oikoumene', the Hyperboreans at various times seem to have come in contact with the Mycenaean Greeks (Romm 1992, 61). In fact, according to Pausanias and Herodotus, the Hyperboreans are reported to have founded the Delphic oracle with two maidens (Arge and Opis) under the leadership of a prophet named Olen, who may have been Lycian (Herodotus 'The Histories', IV, 35; discussed in Romm 1992, 61 and Bridgman 2010, 49).

In similar manner, Herodotus links the ancestry of some shrines on Delos to Hyperborean visitors. The Artemis temple on Delos has been identified to be the oldest on the island and dates back to Mycenaean times. The Hyperborean myths thus were closely related to the goddess Leto and her divine twins Apollo and Artemis, to all of whom a direct contact and visits to the northern regions were ascribed, and centered in Delos and Delphi. Even the delivery routes of offerings brought to these sanctuaries from the north was discussed amongst the ancient historians (*e.g.* Pausanias and Herodotus, discussed in Bridgman 2010, 87ff). Apollon is sometimes linked in this context to the Celtic god Belenus (Mosenkis 2016, 171).

Another Hyperborean who according to Herodotus and Hecataeus came into direct contact with the Greeks was a traveller from northern countries called Abaris, who renewed the goodwill and kinship of the Hyperboreans to the Delians (Herodotus 'The Histories', IV, 36; Hecataeus in Bridgman 2010, 135; discussed in Romm 1992, 63ff). Also Pindaros ('Olympian Ode' III, dated around 468 BCE, cp. Rausch 2013, 51) mentions Abaris and positions his visit into the time of the reign of Lydian king Kroisos, *i.e.* around 550 BCE. On the other hand, the god Apollo and some heroes like Heracles have reportedly ventured north and visited Hyperborea.

At some point in time, Hyperborean visits to Greece seem to have ceased, maybe because the emissaries did not return to their northern homes. Overall the contacts must have been of a very sporadic nature, because contrary to normal cultic patterns, according to which local heroes were regularly claimed as ancestors by the local population, the Hyperboreans were not perceived as ancestors of later-day Greeks.

So where exactly was the location of Hyperborea? Hyperborea according to Pindaros marked the northern limits of the world known to the ancient Greeks and was contrasted with the Pillars of Heracles as the western, and the rivers Phasis (today's Rioni river flowing from the Caucasus mountains into the Black Sea at ancient Colchis) and the Nile as the eastern and southern limits. Whilst various Greek authors placed the location of Hyperborea in the far north beyond a mountain range called the 'Rhipean Mountains'[142],

---

142 Cp. the comments on Anaximenes in section 8.2.5, who was one of the first ancient geographers to place the Rhipean mountains on his world map.

its exact location is undetermined or varied between different authors and different historical periods (cp. Rausch 2013, 22ff).

The early historians and historiographers (*e.g.* Aristeas of Proconnessus, Dionysius of Miletus) located Hyperborea in the steppe north of Thrace. Dionysius in particular wrote that the Rhipean mountain range ran in east-west direction far to the north above the Tanais river (the river Don) and the Black Sea areas. Above these mountains, so Dionysius, lived the Hyperboreans, whose lands stretched to the 'other sea' (Bridgman 2010, 28ff, 45ff).[143]

With later historians the assumed location of Hyperborea obviously was transposed from east to west together with the shifting geographical focus of the ancient Greek colonization efforts. Various of these later authors then identified Hyperborea with the Celtic territories north of the Alps (so Stephanus of Byzantium, Antimachus etc.) and in particular with Britain (Hecataeus of Abdera) (Bridgman 2010, 63ff on Stephanus and Antimachus, 66f and 137 on Hecataeus).[144] The mountain chain of the Alps in this process became the 'Rhipean Mountains'.

Hecataeus mentions an island called Elixoea in the context of the Hyperborean myth, in which a significant temple of Apollo is to be found. This temple has been identified by several authors with Stonehenge and Boreas with the Celtic sun god Borvo (discussion in Bridgman 2010, 135ff).

Regarding these potential links to Britain, Diodorus Siculus ('Library of History', II, 47) quotes Hecataeus at some length, when he professes to

'discuss the legendary accounts of the Hyperboreans. Of those [...] Hecataeus and certain others say that in the regions beyond the land of the Celts there lies in the ocean an island no smaller than Sicily. This island, the account continues, is situated in the north and is inhabited by the Hyperboreans, [...]. And there is also on the island both a magnificent sacred precinct of Apollo and a notable temple [...]. The myth also relates that certain Greeks visited the Hyperboreans [...].

Also von Ranke-Graves points out that Britain was a centre of the cult around Boreas (von Ranke-Graves 1986, 475).

Apart from these later Archaic and Classical links of Hyperborea to Britain or the Celtic lands, do we have myths rooted in Bronze Age lore, which would support contacts or travel of Mycenaean Greeks to the far north?

Perseus (in Hyperborea?)

We have already learned that in the story of Perseus, Polydectes demands from the hero to bring back the head of the Gorgo Medusa. Athena instructs him to find the Hesperides, where he obtained the weapons to overcome the Gorgo, a sword, a helmet and a knapsack as well as a shield and 'winged sandals'.

Regarding the metaphors used in this story, the 'winged sandals', with which Perseus went to the land of the Hyperboreans, are already mentioned in the 'Pythian Ode' of

---

143 Theories as to whether this 'other sea' refers to the Caspian Sea, the Baltic Sea or the North Sea remain speculative to date.
144 The Celts until the late 5th century were not recognized as a 'nothern' people, but rater located in the far west, a bit north of the Iberians (Rausch 2013, 32f).

Pindaros ('Pythian Ode', X 30-49). Maybe these winged sandals and the additional image of Pegasus as a 'flying horse' helping Perseus to speed up his journey are both metaphors for fast sailing ships. Phoenician and Greeks ships were often decorated with pictures of galloping horses on the prow. Lane Fox (2009, 125) points at *'Phoenicians, whose boats had prows shaped like horses galloping through the water.'* Equally, Strabo ('The Geography', II, 3;,4) mentions ships from Gadeiros in southern Iberia when he writes *'it was Gadeiran, for although their merchants sent out large ships, poor men would have small ones that they call "horses" from the devices on their prows..'.*

With respect to the potential final destination of Perseus' journey, three quotes from our ancient mythographers are interesting:

As one of the oldest sources, Hesiod ('Theogony', 270ff) writes about the Gorgons

'who dwell beyond glorious Ocean at the edge toward the night, where the clear-voiced Hesperides are,..'.

So in the first instance the trip must have carried Perseus west into the Atlantic Ocean beyond the 'Pillars of Heracles'.

Apollodorus ('The Library of Greek Mythology', II, 5) further writes – albeit in the context of one of Heracles' journeys (see below) – about the Hesperides and the 'Golden Apples' found there that

'These apples were to be found not in Libya as some have claimed, but on mount Atlas in the land of the Hyperboreans'.

This quote links the Hesperides in the far west with Hyperborea, which was located not west but north of the Mycenaean world.

Pindaros ('Pythian Ode', X, 31) finally mentions the

'rain-washed inhabitants of Hyberborea and the petrified sculptures of men and beasts',

which were found by Perseus upon arrival in the north. The latter are assumed to represent the menhirs found in western France, esp. Brittany, and Britain. Perseus according to this ode participated in a feast at the Hyperboreans after slaying the Gorgo and had the chance of observing their customs. Pindaros also states that Perseus escaped to the safety of the south after cutting the Gorgo's head off, which implies that he had travelled north to get there in the first place (interpretation of von Ranke-Graves 1986, 216). He returns passing the Atlas Mountains on the north African coastline and finally arrives in the Aegean Sea.

Bridgman (2010, 16) thus considers that

'it is probable the two episodes [i.e. the killing of the Medusa and the visit to the Hyperboreans] took place on the same trip and that the Gorgons and the Hyperboreans were neighbors.'

It has been mentioned above that some scholars interpret the mythical record of Perseus' trip to the Gorgons as the description of a journey beyond the Hesperides in the far west (*i.e.* southern Spain) into the Okeanos (*i.e.* Atlantic Ocean) and then potentially north to

Fig. 24: Perseus with the head of the Gorgo Medusa (photo: Flutreiz, stock.adobe.com).

the Hyperboreans. Is it therefore possible to interpret the three mythographical fragments taken together as a potential reflection of a metal exploration via the Atlantic route to the tin mines in Cornwall or to the Scilly Islands off Britain?

As a tentative timing for the Perseus myth based on genealogical dating, we had earlier established the period around 1350 to 1340 BCE. The amber in the Mycenaean shaft graves as an indicator for indirect or potentially even direct links between northern and southern Europe goes back to a much earlier date (1600 to 1500 BCE). Perseus may thus have travelled on some paths already known. It is also intriguing that the genealogical date for the Perseus adventure of ca. 1350 BCE coincides with the period, when the 'Atlantic route' of metal exchange along the Atlantic seaboard from the Iberian Peninsula up to Britain gained in importance.

Heracles (in Hyperborea?)

Next to Perseus, the incredible feat of 'crossing the Ocean', *i.e.* venturing into the Atlantic Ocean, in antiquity was only ascribed to Heracles (Romm 1992, 138). Apollodorus ('The Library of Greek Mythology', II, 119f) mentions that Heracles found his way to the Hyperboreans in the connection of a trip to Atlas and the Hesperides.[145] This journey seems to have led the hero along the coast of northern Africa (Libya) '*to the outer sea*' (*i.e.* the Atlantic Ocean), from where he crossed over to the '*continent on the other side*', which may be a reference to Europe's Atlantic coast or maybe even Britain. It is thus possible that this journey was a continuation of the trip to the Hesperides.

---

145 This myth seems to mix up two different trips, since it also refers to Prometheus, whose myth is usually connected with the Caucasus mountains.

There is also another mythical transmission, which links Heracles to Hyperborea, albeit in the context of a journey east maybe in the context of one of his ventures into the Black Sea. In Heracles' third labor, the 'Cerynitian Hind', Pindaros ('Olympian Ode', III, 24 – 34) mentions the hero and his pursuit of 'the doe (female deer) with the golden antlers' up to 'Istria' and the Hyperborean lands before finally catching the animal in Arcadia after one year. According to Pindaros, Heracles followed the doe to the 'sources of the Istros' (in this case probably the river Don), which in Pindaros' time were assumed to lie somewhere in the north[146], and brings back olive trees from this region. Branches of these olive trees were later awarded to winners at the Olympic games.

Whilst this story seems to be full of symbolisms and metaphors (discussion in Bridgman 2010, 37), it is interesting to note that the only subspecies of deer where the females wear antlers are reindeer in the far north of Europe. Indirect transmission of information about distant countries may be at work here. The 'doe with golden antlers' is also linked to the goddess Artemis, who has close connections to the north and Hyperborea as well. It is overall striking that Heracles is not only brought into connection with a visit to the remote west but in different sources also to territories in the northeast.[147]

Further Mythical and Historical References to Hyperborea

Later Greek historiographers offer further identifications of Hyperborea, other than Britain. As discussed above Pindar located Hyperborea near the sources of the Don (Istrus) and thus in the far northeast. In modern times, Moerner and Lind (2002, 130) in a recent interpretation identify Hyperborea with southern Scandinavia based on the amber found in Mycenaean graves, which may originate in southern Sweden.

This last interpretation of the origin of the Hyperborean myth seems to be supported by some apparently firsthand information of conditions in or around the Arctic Circle, such as

- an unbearably cold climate (Herodotus 'The Histories', IV, 28-31)
- creatures, who sleep for six months of the year (= hibernation) (Herodotus)
- 6 months of continuous daylight (Pliny)
- 24 hours of sunlight (Pomponius Mela)

A frequently asked question in the context of the tales around Hyperborea is: How old are the roots of this myth? Like the myth about the explorations to the east by the Argonauts, the Hyperborean myth dates back at least to the 8th century BCE, but likely to earlier Mycenaean times (Bridgman 2010, 58, 97, 107 and 145f). The myth may thus indeed well contain a reflection of early trading contacts of the Mycenaean Greeks with northern peoples to obtain tin and amber and then later during the 'dark ages' to the Celtic Hallstatt culture and/or Britain (discussed also in Rausch 2013, 49).

---

146 Rausch (2013, 51) points out that in old mythical traditions the Istros as a toponym was not only given to the Danube, but also to the river Don, on which travellers from its estuary in the Sea of Azov towards its sources indeed had to journey north.

147 It needs to be reiterated that the geographical identification of far away destinations was often not as clear cut in antiquity as it is today. The phenomenon of geographical transposition has been mentioned already in connection with the shifting focus of early Greek colonization efforts. Additionally different distant regions may have been identified by different people with the same name. Cp. also Helms 1988.

13

Summary and Conclusions

The archaeological record delivers some indications that extensive trade networks may have existed in the entire Mediterranean region and possibly beyond in the Late Bronze Age (ca. 1600 to 1180 BCE) often driven by the need to get access to metals, esp. to copper and tin, the components of Bronze. The frequency and volume in this multilateral exchange of goods is disputed between researches, some of which assume only sporadic and directed exchange between the royal houses vs. others who postulate an intense, diversified and largely commercial trade (*e.g.* discussed in Tartaron 2013, 24).

Regarding the extent to which Mycenaean travellers participated directly in these various forms of exchange is likewise disputed. One position interprets Mycenaean trade as transacted via intermediaries, such as Cypriot or Canaanite merchants vs. others, who assume that the Mycenaeans were active participants in the exchange and finally some, who are of the opinion that both was the case.

The LBA broadly coincides with the so-called 'mythical age' of Mycenaean heroes. In the transmitted stories, these heroes often undertook long distance journeys to exotic destinations. In spite of a long and complex transmission process through the subsequent centuries, we can assume some considerable Bronze Age nuclei were contained in these myths. The stories told contain metaphors in various forms. The heroes often 'fly' to their destinations (Bellerophontes on the 'winged horse' Pegasus, Perseus as well, but additionally on 'winged sandals', Daidalos on self-made wings, Phrixos on a 'golden ram'). Maybe we have to imagine a narrative element here, by which the bridging of incredibly long distances via new and fast sailing ships was communicated to a more rural and sedentary audience at home.

Via the archaeological record and including the mythical references it is possible to form a rough picture of the geographical knowledge of Mycenaean Greeks, although it is difficult and near impossible within the individual myths to discern between Bronze Age experiences and later additions and interpretations. Even if it is therefore incorrect to take myths literally and assume they reflect history directly, the synopsis of all Mycenaean journeys in the mythical record paints a broad picture that is surprisingly consistent with the most recent status of archaeological discoveries around the Mediterranean regarding Mycenaean long distance contacts – albeit with some notable exceptions.

The picture that emerges is one of a relatively detailed and specific knowledge of Mycenaeans regarding the *eastern Mediterranean*, the people living there as well as their customs. With few exceptions (Bellerophontes), the early myths regarding contacts within the easten Mediterranean are primarily about origins, migrations and descent (Danaus, Cadmos) and they show the degree to which Mycenaean history was embedded in the broader Mediterranean context. The later myths datable towards the end of the LBA with references to Egypt, the Levantine coast, Cyprus and western Anatolia could be interpreted as a mix of commercial, cultural, diplomatic and also hostile contacts reflecting a certain familiarity with the region.

In terms of the regional focus, *Anatolia* has been one of the 'natural' early targets for Mycenaean expansion to the east. The beginning of this expansion around LH II B coincides comfortably with the mythical record, where Bellerophontes seems to have been one of the early travellers to the Anatolian coast broadly around 1450 BCE.

Regarding *Cyprus and the Levant*, the locations with the most intense archaeological remains from the Mycenaean palatial centres, we also have various older myths of migration and descent, partially of Near Eastern provenience. References in various myths indicate a familiarity of Mycenaean travellers with these destinations. The stories point to commercial contacts and to Cyprus as a refuge after the convulsions and disruptions in connection with the Sea Peoples at the end of the Bronze Age.

The mythical record would also suggest that some of the earliest contacts have been established with *Egypt* already around 1550 BCE during the Second Intermediate period and the Hyksos occupation. These early contacts suggested by the mythical record are not yet borne out by archaeological finds. In later times, relatively frequent and diverse contacts and even Mycenaean settlements in Egypt could be extracted from the mythological transmission.

The travel myths that lead beyond this familiar environment *e.g.* into the *central and western Mediterranean* or the *Black Sea* area are of a somewhat different nature. The Greek travel myths regarding those more remote areas are often the stories of heroic explorers and 'first movers' regularly including conflict and warlike activities. The motivation for these long distance trips seems to lie primarily in the access to metal supplies. This objective shines through in various myths (Argonautica, Perseus, Heracles, Iolaus) *e.g.* via the selection of travel destinations and stopovers, but is not made explicit in the myths due to their distinct narrative style. In view of the remoteness of the destinations and reflecting a lesser degree of knowledge and familiarity about the areas and the customs of the people, these myths often contain elements of the supernatural (a common phenomenon in ethnographic literature as shown by Helms 1988).

With regards to the *central and western Mediterranean*, we have various mythical references about contacts with *Sicily* in the Greek myths albeit probably more of a sporadic nature. With reference to *Sardinia*, a tradition about the foundation of a (trading?) colony on the island has been transmitted via an account in Diodorus Siculus' work. Both islands seem to have been located on the outer rim of what the Mycenaeans perceived to be 'familiar territory'.

Concerning *Italy*, where Mycenaean contacts may go back as far as LH I, mythological references only exist with a focus on LH III B. This absence of a pioneering myth for Italy dating back to LH I is one of the most interesting lacunae in the mythological transmission.

In the far western Mediterranean, whilst the archaeological record would indicate contacts with the *Iberian Peninsula* already from 1500 BCE, the mythical record would suggest these journeys to have commenced around 1350 BCE, significantly at just the point in time when the Atlantic metal trading route to Britain began to open up. The archaeological finds of Mycenaean origin on the Iberian Peninsula are at this point in time still very limited and maybe inconclusive. Jung (2018, 284) postulates overall much more intense trade relations of Mycenaeans in the eastern compared to the western Mediterranean.

A notable absence in the epigraphic evidence of toponyms from the western Mediterranean overall may also indicate a lesser familiarity or lower commercial intensity of this region to the Mycenaeans (Woudhuizen 2010, 6).

Finally, the *Black Sea area*, for which appropriate ships were required and the passage via the Dardanelles needed to be secured, would have been travelled by the Mycenaeans probably only from about 1230 BCE as far as the myths are an indicator. Control of the Hittites over northwestern Anatolia and the political obstruction of a prior access to the Black Sea may have played a critical role in preventing earlier journeys of the Mycenaeans into this area.

The heroes in the Greek myths are portrayed primarily as explorers and warriors and only to a minor extent as traders.[148] Also the ships they used – the Mycenaean galley – would support exploration as a target, but not bulk trade. Yet, Tartaron (2013, 134) asserts that there is *'no reason to believe [...] that elites of Homer's time did not participate in trade voyages.'* In view of the fact that trade, piracy and raids did not have clear-cut borders in the LBA, the mythological record would still suggest that there were direct contacts of Mycenaeans to key destination for the metal supply and that Mycenaeans at least to some extent were also active participants in the Mediterranean trade networks.

The intensity of direct and distant metal trade conducted by the Mycenaeans themselves is not easy to assess via the mythical record. The pioneering journeys transmitted as myths are few, but maybe only some pioneers received mythical status and were followed by regular traders, for which the records of the respective journeys are lost. The various specific pieces of information in the myths regarding Mycenaean long-distance travel and trade are not easy to reconcile with the minimalist position that Mycenaean trade was sporadic and primarily transacted by intermediaries and support the theory of a more active role on behalf of the Mycenaean mariners.

Information about more distant destinations like the Atlantic Ocean, the Red Sea or the territories north beyond the Alps is likely to have existed as well already in the LBA and was in some instances possibly based on indirect transmissions via travel and trade, but hypothetically on rare occasions also via first hand experiences. It is interesting that many travelling myths connected to the Iberian Peninsula actually also seem to contain conjectures to the misty countries up north and further west.

However – and maybe due to less frequent contacts – the picture about these more remote locations is partially blurred, includes conjectures and guesswork and is particularly subject to later geographical transpositions, interpretations and relocations during the later Iron Age colonization period.

Especially intriguing in this context is the question whether already the Bronze Age Mycenaeans could have travelled the Atlantic route as far as Britain. As far as the mythical record and the notes of ancient historians go, this cannot be ruled out, even though we do not have sufficient archaeological proof as of yet to back it up.

---

148 A few journeys are mentioned in the myths that imply some form of commercial purpose: Dionysos brings a shipload of wine to Egypt, Menealos 'amasses a fortune abroad'.

Most researchers would probably concede that the knowledge obtained by the Mycenaean Greeks about the far northern countries as well as distant areas like the Red Sea could have reached them indirectly via extensive trade networks. The general possibility of long distance journeys as far as Britain on the Atlantic route can on the other hand not be completely excluded, even if conclusive archaeological evidence is still missing.

In sum, a comprehensive reflection of the Greek travel myths allows us to decode some of the underlying concrete experiences already during the Late Bronze Age, even taking later transpositions and re-interpretations into account. Economic exchange and trade emerges as a key background to early travel and exploration.

14

References

ANDREADOU, Maria: 'The Mycenaean Presence in the Black Sea Region', Masterthesis, International Hellenic University, Thessaloniki, 2015

ANTHONY, David W.: "The Horse, The Wheel and Language: How Bronze-Age Riders from the Eurasian Steppes Shaped the Modern World', Princeton, 2007

APOLLODORUS 'Library' and HYGINUS 'Fabulae' – Two Handbooks of Greek Mythology (translated by Smith, R. Scott; Trzaskoma, Stephen M.), Indianapolis, 2007

APOLLODORUS 'The Library of Greek Mythology', (translated by Hard, Robin), New York, 2nd ed., 2008

BAIKOUZIS, Constantino and MAGNASCO, Marcelo O.: 'Is an Eclipse described in the Odyssey?', in: Proceedings of the National Academy of Sciences of the United States of America, 24.06.2008, Online Publication

BANYAI, Michael: 'Die Mykenische Staatenwelt: Zwischen Mykene und Theben', in: Kelder, Jorrit M. and Waal, Willemijn J.I. (eds.) 'From "Lugal.Gal" to "Wanax" – Kingship and Political Organization in the Late Bronze Age Aegean', Leiden, 2019, pp. 131 – 147

BELL, Carol: 'Merchants of Ugarit: oligarchs of the Late Bronze Age trade in metals?', in: Kassianidou, Vasiliki and Papasavvas, George (eds.) 'Eastern Mediterranean Metallurgy and Metalwork in the Second Millennium BC', Oxford, 2012, pp. 180 – 187

BERGER, Olaf: 'Kretas Hochkultur im Watt', Focus Online, 25.11.2013

BETANCOURT, Philip P.: 'Minoan Trade', in: Shelmerdine, Cynthia W. (ed.) 'The Cambridge Companion to the Aegean Bronze Age', Cambridge, 2008

BIETAK, Manfred and HOEFLMAYER, Felix: 'Introduction: High and Low Chronology', in: 'The Synchronisation of Civilisations in the Eastern Mediterranean in the Second Millennium B.C. III', Bietak, M. and Czerny E. (eds.), Proceedings of the SCIEM 2000 – 2nd EuroConference, Vienna, 2007, pp. 13 -23

BLAKE, Emma: 'The Mycenaeans in Italy: A Minimalist Position', in: Papers of the British School at Rome, Vol. 76, 2008, pp. 1 – 34

BLASQUEZ MARTINEZ, Jose Maria: 'The Greek colonization in the Black Sea and Iberia: similarities and differences', in: Pont Euxin et commerce: la genese de la "route de la soie". Actes du IXe Symposium de Vani (Colchide, 1999) Besancon: Institut des Sciences de'l Antiquite, 2002, pp. 15 – 21

BRIDGMAN, Timothy P.: 'Hyperboreans: Myth and History in Celtic-Hellenic Contacts', digital reprint (from original 2005), 2010

BRILLANTE, Carlo: 'Myth and History – History and the Historical Interpretation of Myth', in: 'Approaches to Greek Myth', Edmunds, Lowell (ed.), 2nd ed., Baltimore, 1991, pp. 91 – 138

BURKERT, Walter: 'Structure and History in Greek Mythology and Ritual', Berkeley, 1979

CARDOSO, Joao Luis: 'Between the Atlantic and the Mediterranean: the Late Bronze Age around the Tagus estuary (Portugal). Economic, social and cultural aspects', in: Rivista di Scienze Preistoriche LXV, Firenze, 2015, pp. 149 – 170

CELESTINO PEREZ, Sebastian: 'Tarteso – Territorio y Cultura', Barcelona, 2016

CLINE, Eric H.: '1177 B.C. – The Year Civilization Collapsed', Princeton, 2014

CONSTANTINOU, George: 'Late Bronze Age copper production in Cyprus from a mining geologist's perspective', in: Kassianidou, Vasiliki and Papasavas, George (eds.) 'Eastern Mediterranean Metallurgy and Metalwork in the Second Millennium BC', Oxford, 2012, pp. 4 – 14

CUNLIFFE, Barry: 'Europe between the Oceans 9000 BC – AD 1000', London, New Haven, 2011

DE BOER, Jan: 'Phantom-Mycenaeans in the Black Sea', in: Talanta (Proceedings of the Dutch Archaeological and Historical Society) XXXVIII – XXXIX, Stronk, J. P. and de Weerd, M. D. (eds.), 2006 – 2007, pp. 277 – 302

DICKINSON, Oliver: 'What conclusions might be drawn from the archaeology of Mycenaean civilization about political structure in the Aegean?', in: Kelder, Jorrit M. and Waal, Willemijn J.I. (eds.) 'From "Lugal.Gal" to "Wanax" – Kingship and Political Organization in the Late Bronze Age Aegean', Leiden, 2019, pp. 31 – 48

DIHLE, Albrecht: 'Die Griechen und die Fremden', Muenchen, 1994

DILLERY, John: 'The First Egyptian Narrative History: Manetho and Greek Historiography', in: Zeitschrift fuer Papyrologie und Epigraphik 127, 1999, pp. 93 – 116

DIODORUS SICULUS: 'Library of History', Volumes I – IV, Loeb Classical Library 279, 303, 340, 375, (translated by Oldfather C. H.), 1950

DREWS, Robert: 'Militarism and the Indo-Europeanizing of Europe', Abingdon, New York, 2017

DUARTE DA CUNHA, Marcos Davi: 'The maritime contacts of Minoan Crete with Egypt', in: Revista Mundo Antigo – Ano II, V. 02, No. 01, 06/2013

EARLE, Timothy, LING, Johan, UHNER, Claes, STOS-GALE, Zofia and MELHEIM, Lene: 'The Political Economy and Metal Trade in Bronze Age Europe: Understanding Variability in Terms of Comparative Advantage and Articulations', in: European Journal of Archaeology 18 (4), 2015, pp. 633 – 657

EDMUNDS, Lowell: 'Introduction: The Practice of Greek Mythology', in: Approaches to Greek Myth', Edmunds, Lowell (ed.), 2nd ed. Baltimore, 1991, pp. 1 – 20

EMANUEL, Jeffrey P.: 'Odysseus' Boat? New Mycenaean Evidence from the Egyptian New Kingdom", part of the lecture series 'Discovery of the Classical World, Harvard University, 2013/14

EMANUEL, Jeffrey P.: 'The Late Bronze – Early Iron Age Transition: Changes in Warriors and Warfare and the Earliest Recorded Naval Battles', in: 'Ancient Warfare: Introducing Current Research, Volume I', Lee, Geoff, Whittaker; Helene and Wrightson, Graham (eds.), Newcastle upon Tyne, 2015, pp. 191 – 209

FINLEY, Moses I.: 'Myth, Memory and History', in: 'The Use and Abuse of History', London, 1975, pp. 11 – 33

GERTOUX, Gerard: 'The Trojan War – Chronological, Historical and Archaeological Evidence', Lulu, 2016

GEUS, Klaus: 'Greek and Greco-Roman Geography', in: The Cambridge History of Science, Vol. I 'Ancient Science', Jones, Alexander and Taub, Liba (eds.), Cambridge, 2018, pp. 402 – 412

GIARDINO, Claudio: 'Sicilian hoards and protohistoric metal trade in the Central West Mediterranean', in: 'Metals Make The World Go Round – The Supply and Circulation of Metals in Bronze Age Europe', Pare, C.F.E. (ed.), Oxford, 2000, pp. 99 – 107

GILLIS, Carole: 'Trade in the Late Bronze Age', in: Gillis, Carole, Risberg, Christina and Sjoeberg, Birgitta (eds.) 'Trade and Production in Premonetary Greece: Aspects of Trade', Proceedings of the Third International Workshop, Athens, 1993, pp. 61 – 86

GRAFTON, Anthony: 'Tradition and Technique in Historical Chronology', in: 'Ancient History and the Antiquarian: Essays in Memory of Arnaldo Momigliano', Crawford, M.H. and Ligota, C.R. (eds.), London, 1995, pp. 15 – 31

GRAZIOSI, Barbara: 'Inventing Homer – The Early Reception of Epic', Cambridge 2002

GUTTANDIN, Thomas, PANAGIOTOPOULOS, Diamantis, PFLUG, Hermann and PLATH, Gerhard: 'Inseln der Winde – Die maritime Kultur der bronzezeitlichen Aegaeis', Heidelberg, 2nd ed., 2014

HAJNAL, Ivo: 'Troia aus sprachwissenschaftlicher Sicht – Die Struktur einer Argumentation', in: Innsburger Beitraege zur Sprachwissenschaft, Band 109, Meid, Wolfgang (ed.), Innsbruck, 2003

HAARMANN, Harald: 'Wer zivilisierte die alten Griechen? Das Erbe der alteuropaeischen Hochkultur', Wiesbaden, 2017

HARDING, Anthony: 'Horse-Harness and the Origins of the Mycenaean Civilization', in: Autochton: Papers Presented to O.T.P.K. Dickinson on the Occasion of his Retirement, Oxford, 2005, pp. 296 – 300

HELMS, Mary W.: 'Ulysses' Sail – An Ethnographic Odyssey of Power, Knowledge and Geographic Distance', Princeton, 1988

HERODOTUS: 'The Histories', New York, 11th ed., 1997

HESIOD: 'Theogony, Works and Days, Testimonia', Most, Glenn W. (ed. and translation), Loeb Classical Library 57, Harvard, 2018

HILLER, Stefan: 'The Mycenaeans and the Black Sea', in: Thalassa. L' Egee prehistorique et la mer [Aegaeum 7], Laffineur, R. and Basch, L. (eds.), Liege, 1991, pp. 207 – 216

HOMER 'The Iliad', Translation by E.V. Rieu, London, 2003

HOMER 'The Odyssey', Translation by E.V. Rieu, 4th ed., London, 2009

HORNBLOWER, Simon (ed.): 'Greek Historiography', Oxford, 1994

JUNG, Reinhard: 'Push and Pull Factors of the Sea Peoples between Italy and the Levant', in: 'An Archaeology of Forced Migration. Crisis-induced mobility and the Collapse of the 13th c. BCE Eastern Mediterranean', Driessen, Jan (ed.), Presses universitaires de Louvain, 2018, pp. 273 – 306

KELDER, Jorrit: 'Royal Gift Exchange Between Mycenae and Egypt: Olives as "Greeting Gifts" in the Late Bronze Age Eastern Mediterranean', in: American Journal of Archaeology 113, Archaeological Institute of America (ed.), 2009, pp. 339 – 352

KELDER, Jorrit: 'The Egyptian Interest in Mycenaean Greece', in: Jaarbericht "Ex Oriente Lux" 42, 2010, pp. 125 – 140

KELDER, Jorrit M.: 'Mycenae, Rich in Silver', in: 'Silver, Money and Credit – A Tribute to Robartus J. van der Spek on the Occasion of his 65th Birthday', Kleber, Kristin and Pirngruber, Reinhard (eds.), Leiden, 2016, pp. 307 – 317

KELDER, Jorrit M. and CLINE, Eric H.: 'In the Midst of the 'Great Green': Egypto-Aegean Trade and Exchange', in: 'Beyond the Nile. Egypt and the Classical World', Spier, Jeffrey, Potts, Timothy and Cole, Sara E. (eds.), Los Angeles, 2018, pp. 24 – 28

KELDER, Jorrit M., COLE, Sara E. and CLINE, Eric H.: 'Memphis, Minos and Mycenae: Bronze Age Contact between Egypt and the Aegean', in: 'Beyond the Nile. Egypt and the Classical World', Spier, Jeffrey, Potts, Timothy and Cole, Sara E. (eds.), Los Angeles, 2018, pp. 9 – 17

KELDER, Jorrit M.: 'From Thutmosis III to Homer to Blackadder – Egypt, the Aegean, and the 'Barbarian Periphery' of the Late Bronze Age World System, presentation at the Getty Foundation, (pre-publishing), 2019

KITCHEN, Kenneth A.: 'The Chronology of Ancient Egypt', in: World Archaeology, Vol. 23, No. 2, Chronologies, 1991, pp. 201 – 208

KITCHEN, Kenneth A.: 'The reliability of the Old Testament', Cambridge, 2006

KITCHEN, Kenneth A.: 'Egyptian and Related Chronologies – Look, No Sciences, No Pots!', in: 'The Synchronisation of Civilisations in the Eastern Mediterranean in the Second Millennium B.C. III', Bietak, M. and Czerny E. (eds.), Proceedings of the SCIEM 2000 – 2nd EuroConference, Vienna, 2007, pp. 163 – 171

KLEINHUBBERT, Guido: 'Italienische Tragoedie – Warum ging Mykene unter?', in: Der Spiegel, Nr. 49, 01.12.2018, pp. 122 – 123

KNAPP, A. Bernard: 'Matter of fact: transcultural contacts in the Late Bronze Age Eastern Mediterranean', in: 'Materiality and Social Practice – Transformative Capacities of Intercultural Encounters', Maran, Joseph and Stockhammer, Philipp W. (eds.), Oxford, 2012, pp. 32 – 50

KNAPP, A. Bernard and MANNING, Sturt W.: 'Crisis in Context: The End of the Late Bronze Age in the Eastern Mediterranean', in: American Journal of Archaeology, 120, Nr. 1, 2016, pp. 99 – 149

KNAPP, A. Bernard: 'Seafaring and Seafarers in the Bronze Age Eastern Mediterranean', Leiden, 2018

KNAPP, A. Bernard: 'Migration Myths and the End of the Bronze Age in the Eastern Mediterranean', Cambridge, 2021

KOCH, John T.: 'Tartessian – Celtic in the South-west at the Dawn of History', 2nd ed, Aberystwyth, 2013

KOPANIAS, Konstantinos: 'Cilicia and Pamphylia during the Early Iron Age – Hiyawa, Mopsos and the Foundation of the Greek Cities', in: Athens University Review of Archaeology (AURA) Volume 1, Athens, 2018, pp. 69 – 95

KOTSONAS, Antonis: 'Early Iron Age Knossos and the development of the city of the historical period', in: Proceedings of the 12th International Congress of Cretan Studies, Heraklion, 2016, pp. 1 – 13

KRISTIANSEN, Kristian and LARSSON, Thomas B.: 'The Rise of Bronze Age Society – Travels, Transmissions and Transformations', Cambridge, 2005

KRISTIANSEN, Kristian and SUCHOWSKA-DUCKE, Paulina: 'Connected Histories: the Dynamics of Bronze Age Interaction and Trade 1500 – 1100 bc', in: Proceedings of the Prehistoric Society, Volume 81, 2015, pp. 361 – 392

KRISTIANSEN, Kristian: 'The Bronze Age expansion of Indo-European languages: an archaeological model', in: 'Becoming European – The transformation of third millennium Northern and Western Europe', Prescott, Christoper and Glorstad, Hakon (eds.), Oxford, 2012, pp. 165 – 181

KRISTIANSEN, Kristian: 'Interpreting Bronze Age Trade and Migration', in: 'Human Mobility and Technological Transfer in the Prehistoric Mediterranean', Kiriatzi, Evangelia and Knappett, Carl (eds.), Cambridge, 2016, pp. 154 – 181

KUIJPERS, Maikel H. G. and POPA, Catalin N.: 'The origins of money: Calculation of similarity indexes demonstrates the earliest development of commodity money in prehistoric Central Europe', in: PLoS ONE 16(1): e0240462., https://doi.org/10.1371/journal.pone.0240462, 20.01.2021

LANE FOX, Robin: 'Travelling Heroes – Greeks and their myths in the epic age of Homer', London, 2009

LATACZ, Joachim; STARKE, Frank: 'Die politische Landschaft im oestlichen Mittelmeerraum in der zweiten Haelfte des 2. Jahrtausends v. Chr.', in: 'Das Schiff von Uluburun – Welthandel vor 3000 Jahren', Katalog der Ausstellung des Deutschen Bergbau-Museums Bochum, Yalcin, Uensal, Pulak, Cemal and Slotta, Rainer (eds.), Bochum, 2005, pp. 187 – 192

LING, Johan; UHNER, Claes: 'Rock Art and Metal Trade', in: Adoranten 2014, Scandinavian Society For Prehistoric Art, pp. 23 – 43

LING, Johan, HJAERTHNER-HOLDAR, Eva, GRANDIN, Lena, STOS-GALE, Zofia, KRISTIANSEN, Kristian, MELHEIM, Anne Lene, ARTIOLI, Gilberto, ANGELINI, Ivana, KRAUSE, Ruediger and CANOVARO, Caterina: ' Moving metals IV: Swords, metals sources and trade networks in Bronze Age Europe', in: Journal of Archaeolgical Science: Reports 26 (2019), pp. 1 – 34

LO SCHIAVO, Fulvia: 'Metallhandel im zentralen Mittelmeer', in: 'Das Schiff von Uluburun – Welthandel vor 3000 Jahren', Katalog der Ausstellung des Deutschen Bergbau-Museums Bochum, Yalcin, Uensal, Pulak, Cemal and Slotta, Rainer (eds.), 2005, pp. 399 – 414

LO SCHIAVO, Fulvia: 'Cyprus and Sardinia, beyond the oxhide ingots', in: Kassianidou, Vasiliki and Papasavas, George (eds.) 'Eastern Mediterranean Metallurgy and Metalwork in the Second Millennium BC', Oxford, 2012, pp. 142 – 150

LURAGHI, Nino: "Local Knowledge in Herodotus' Histories", in: Luraghi, Nino (ed.) 'The Historian's Craft in the Age of Herodotus', Oxford, 2001, pp. 138 – 160

LUBAN, Marianne: 'Manetho Demystified, 3rd ed., 2017

MANNING, Sturt, W. and HULIN, Linda: 'Maritime Commerce and Geographies of Mobility in the Late Bronze Age of the Eastern Mediterranean: Problematisations', in: Blake, Emma and Knapp, Bernard A. (eds.) 'The Archaeology of Mediterranean Prehistory', Chapter 11, https://doi.org/10.1002/9780470773536, 2005

MANNING, Sturt W.: 'Chronology and Terminology', in: Cline, Eric H. (ed.) 'The Oxford Handbook of the Bronze Age Aegean', Oxford, 2010, pp. 11 -28

MANOLEDAKIS, Manolis: 'The Southern Black Sea in the Homeric Iliad: Some Geographical, Philological and Historical Remarks', in: 'Exploring the Hospitable Sea: Proceedings of the International Workshop on the Black Sea in Antiquity' (Thessaloniki, 21-23 September 2012), Manoledakis, Manolis (ed.), Oxford, 2013, pp. 19 – 37

MANTZOURANI, Eleni, KOPANIAS, Konstantinos and VOSKOS, Ioannis: 'A Great King of Alasiya? The archaeological and textual evidence', in: Kelder, Jorrit M. and Waal, Willemijn J.I. (eds.) 'From "Lugal.Gal" to "Wanax" – Kingship and Political Organization in the Late Bronze Age Aegean', Leiden, 2019, pp. 95 – 130

MARAN, Joseph: 'Wessex und Mykene. Zur Deutung des Bernsteins in der Schachtgraeberzeit Suedgriechenlands', in: Haensel, Bernhard and Studenikova, Etela (eds.) 'Zwischen Karpaten und Aegaeis – Neolithikum und aeltere Bronzezeit', Gedenkschrift fuer Viera Nemejcova-Pavukova, Rahden, 2004, pp. 47 – 65

MARAN, Joseph: 'Seaborne contacts between the Aegean, the Balkans and the Central Mediterranean in the 3rd Millennium BC: The unfolding of the Mediterranean world', in: Galanaki, Ioanna, Tomas, Helena, Galanakis, Yannis and Laffineur, Robert (eds.) 'Aegaeum 27 'Between the Aegean and the Baltic Seas – Prehistory across borders', Liege, 2007

MATTHAEUS, Hartmut: 'Kulturaustausch, Handel und Seefahrt im Mittelmeerraum waehrend der Spaeten Bronzezeit', in: 'Das Schiff von Uluburun – Welthandel vor 3000 Jahren', Katalog der Ausstellung des Deutschen Bergbau-Museums Bochum, Yalcin, Uensal, Pulak, Cemal and Slotta, Rainer (eds.), 2005, pp. 333 – 366

McLAUGHLIN, Raoul: 'Rome and the Distant East – Trade Routes to the Ancient Lands of Arabia, India and China', London, 2010

McMILLAN, Gregory: 'Trade relations between the Mycenaean Greeks and the civilizations of the Eastern Mediterranean in the Late Brone Age', Ontario, 2016

MEDEROS MARTIN, Alfredo: 'Ex Occidente Lux: El comerco micenico en el Mediterraneo central y occidental (1625 – 1100 a.C.), Complutum 10, 1999, pp. 229 – 266

MEE, Christopher: 'Anatolia and the Aegean in the late Bronze Age', in: Aegean and the Orient, pp. 137 – 148

MERRILLEES, R. S.: 'Aegean Bronze Age Relations with Egypt', in: American Journal of Archaeology, Archaeological Institute of America (ed.), Vol. 76, No.3, July 1972, pp. 281 -294

MIDDLETON, Guy D.: 'Telling Stories: The Mycenaean Origins of the Philistines', in: Oxford Journal of Archaeology 34 (1), 2015, pp. 45 – 65

MOELLER, Astrid: 'The Beginning of Chronography: Hellanicus' Hiereiai', in: 'The Historian's Craft in the Age of Herodotus', Luraghi, Nino (ed.), Oxford, 2001, pp. 241 – 262

MOELLER, Astrid: 'Greek Chronographic Traditions about the First Olympic Games', in: 'Time and Temporality in the Ancient World', Rosen, Ralph M. (ed.), Pennsylvania, 2004, pp. 169 – 184

MOERNER, Nils-Axel and LIND, Bob G.: 'Long-Distance Travel and Trading in the Bronze Age: The East Mediterranean-Scandinavia Case', Archaeological Discovery, 3, 129-139, (2015), http://dx.doi.org/10.4236/ad.2015.34012

MONDI, Robert: 'Greek Mythic Thought in the Light of the Near East', in: 'Approaches to Greek Myth', in: Edmunds, Lowell (ed.), 2nd ed., Baltimore, 1991, pp. 142 – 198

MORAN, William L. (ed.): 'The Amarna Letters', Baltimore, 1992

MOSENKIS, Iurii: ‚Hellenic Origin of Europe: Formation of the Greeks 4600 – 2600 BC and the first Greek states 2600 – 1450 BC in Cretan hieroglyphs and Linear A Scripts', Kiew, Uman, 2016

MULL, Joerg: 'Mythen und Metalle: Der Trojanische Krieg, die Seevoelker und der Kulturbruch am Ende der Bronzezeit', Leipzig, 2017

MUEHLENBRUCH, Tobias: ‚1200 v. Chr. – Zeit eines kulturellen Umbruchs in der Alten Welt?', in: Wuerzburger Studien zur Vor- und Fruehgeschichtlichen Archaeologie (vol 7); Albers, Gabriele and Falkenstein, Frank (eds.), Wuerzburg, 2021

NAGY, Joseph Falaky: 'Hierarchy, Heroes, and Heads – Indo-European Structures in Greek Myth', in: 'Approaches to Greek Myth', Edmunds, Lowell (ed.), 2nd ed., Baltimore, 1991, pp. 200 – 238

NESSELRATH, Heinz-Guenther: 'Where the Lord of the Sea Grants Passage to Sailors through the Deep-blue Mere no more': The Greeks and the Western Seas', in: Greece and Rome, vol. 52, No. 2, The Classical Association, 2005, pp. 153 – 171

NIEMEIER, Wolf-Dietrich: 'Milet in der Bronzezeit – ein pulsierendes Zentrum zwischen Orient und Okzident', Presseveroeffentlichung der Universitaet Heidelberg, Heidelberg, (2000)

NORGAARD, Heide W., PERNICKA, Ernst and VANDKILDE, Helle: 'Shifting Networks and mixing metals: Changing metal trade routes correlate with Neolithic and Bronze Age transformations', Online Publication; in PLoS ONE 16 (6): e0252376; https://doi.org/10.1371/journal.pone.0252379; 16.06.2021

O' BRIEN, William: 'Prehistoric Copper Mining in Europe 5500 – 500 BC', Oxford, 2015

OLALDE, Inigo (et al.): 'The Beaker phenomenon and the genomic transformation of northwest Europe', in: Nature, vol. 555, doi: 10.1038/nature25738, 08.03.2018, pp. 190 – 196

PANAGIOTOPOULOS, Diamantis: 'Foreigners in Egypt in the Time of Hatshepsut and Thutmose III, in: 'Thutmose III. A New Biography', Cline, Eric and O'Connor, D. (eds.), Ann Arbor, 2006, pp. 370 – 412

PANAGIOTOPOULOS, Diamantis: 'Geschenk oder Handel? Zu den Gaben der Aegaeischen Prozessionen in den Thebanischen Privatgraebern', in: 'Austausch von Guetern, Ideen und Technologien in der Aegaeis und im oestlichen Mittelmeer. Von der praehistorischen bis zu der archaischen Zeit', Kyriatsoulis, A. (ed.), Weilheim, 2008, pp. 167 – 179

PANAGIOTOPOULOS, Diamantis: 'Encountering the foreign. (De-) constructing alterity in the archaeologies of the Bronze Age Mediterranean', in: 'Materiality and Social Practice – Transformative Capacities of Intercultural Encounters', Maran, Joseph and Stockhammer, Philipp W. (eds.), Oxford, 2012, pp. 51 – 60

PARE, Christopher: 'Bronze and the Bronze Age', in: Pare, Christopher (ed.), 'Metals make the World Go Round – The Supply and Circulation of Metals in Bronze Age Europe', Oxford, 2000, pg. 1 – 38

PAUSANIAS: 'Description of Greece', Books 1 – 2 (translated by Jones, W.H.S.), Henderson, Jeffrey (ed.), Loeb Classical Library 93, Harvard, 1918

PAUSANIAS: 'Description of Greece', Books 3 – 5 (translated by Jones W.H.S. and Ormerod H.A.), Henderson, Jeffrey (ed.), Loeb Classical Library 188, Harvard, 1926

PERSSON NILSSON, Martin: 'The Mycenaean Origin of Greek Mythology', Original ed. 1932, republished (www.forgottenbooks.org), 2007

PHILLIPS, Jacke: 'Egypt', in: The Oxford Handbook of the Bronze Age Aegean', Cline, Eric H. (ed.), Oxford, 2010

POLASTRON, Lucien X.: 'Books on Fire – The tumultuous story of the world's great libraries', London 2007

PUHVEL, Jaan 'Comparative Mythology', Baltimore, 2nd ed., 1993

RAHMSTORF, Lorenz: 'Die Nutzung von Booten und Schiffen in der bronzezeitlichen Aegaeis und die Fernkontakte der Fruehbronzezeit', in: Meller, Harald and Bertemes, Francois (eds.) 'Der Griff nach den Sternen', Internationales Symposium in Halle (Saale), Februar 2005, Tagungen des Landesmuseums fuer Vorgeschichte Halle, Band 5, 2010, pp. 675 – 696

RAHMSTORF, Lorenz: 'The Use of Bronze Objects in the 3rd Millennium BC: A Survey between Atlantic and Indus', in: Maran, Joseph and Stockhammer, Philipp (eds.) 'Appropriating innovations. Entangled knowledgement in Eurasia, 5000 -1500 BCE, Oxford, 2015, pp. 184 – 210

RAHMSTORF, Lorenz: 'Die Rahmenbedingungen des bronzezeitlichen Handels in Europa und im alten Orient einschliesslich Aegyptens', in: Dietz, Ute Luise and Jockenhoevel, Albrecht (eds.), 'Praehistorische Bronzefunde', Abteilung XX, Band 14, pgs. 292 – 310, Stuttgart, 2016

RAUSCH, Sven: 'BIlder des Nordens – Vorstellungen vom Norden in der griechischen Literatur von Homer bis zum Ende des Hellenismus', Band 28 'Archaeologie in Eurasien'; Deutsches Archaeologisches Institut, Hansen, Svend (ed.); Darmstadt, 2013

ROBBINS, Manuel: 'Collapse of the Bronze Age – The Story of Greece, Troy, Israel, Egypt and the Peoples of the Sea', Lincoln, 2001

ROEMER, Joerg 'Der groesste Knall der Bronzezeit – Vulkan-Apokalypse von Santorin', in: Spiegel Online (online publication), 13.08.2018 http://www.spiegel.de/wissenschaft/mensch/bronzezeit-streit-um-santorin-vulkan-und-einen-olivenbaum-a-1222364.html

ROHL, David M.: 'The Lords of Avaris – Uncovering the legendary origins of western civilization', London, 2007

ROMER, John: 'A History of Ancient Egypt – From the First Farmers to the Great Pyramid', London, 2012

ROMEY, Kristin: 'The Vogelbarke of Medinet Habu', Thesis submitted to Texas A&M University, 2003

ROMM, James S.: 'The Edges of the Earth in Ancient Thought', Princeton, 1992

ROTSTEIN, Andrea: 'Literary History in the Parian Marble', Cambridge (Ma.)/ London, 2016

SCHOFIELD, Louise: ' The Mycenaeans', London, 2007

SHAW, Ian: 'The Oxford History of Ancient Egypt', Oxford, 2000

SHEPPARD BAIRD, W.: 'The Early Minoan Colonization of Spain', Internet publication, 2007

SHRIMPTON, Gordon S.: 'History and Memory in Ancient Greece', Montreal, Kingston, London, Buffalo, 1997

STRABO: 'The Geography', Roller Duane W. (translation), Cambridge, 2014

STRAUSS, Barry: 'The Trojan War – a new history', New York, 2006

TANDY, David W.: 'Warriors into Traders – The Power of the Market in Early Greece', Berkeley, 1997

TARACHA, Piotr: 'Approaches to Mycenaean-Hittite Interconnections in the Late Bronze Age', in: 'Change, Continuity and Connectivity – North-Eastern Mediterranean at the turn of the Bronze Age and in the early Iron Age', Niesiolowski-Spano, Lukasz and Wecowski, Marek (eds.), Wiesbaden, 2018, pp. 8 – 22

TARTARON, Thomas F.: 'Maritime Networks in the Mycenaean World', Cambridge, 2013

THOMAS, Rosalind: 'Herodotus' Histories and the Floating Gap', in: 'The Historian's Craft in the Age of Herodotus', Luraghi, Nino (ed.), Oxford, 2001, pp. 198 – 210

VAGNETTI, Lucia: 'Western Mediterranean', in: The Oxford Handbook of the Bronze Age Aegean', Cline, Eric H. (ed.), Oxford, 2010

VAN DE MOORTEL, Aleydis: 'A New Typology of Bronze Age Aegean Ships: developments in Aegean shipbuilding in their historical context', in: Baltic and beyond – Change and continuity in shipbuilding, Proceedings of the Fourteenth International

Symposium on Boat and Ship Archaeology, Gdansk, 2015, Litwin, Jerzy (ed.), Gdansk, 2017, pp. 263 – 268

VAN DE NOORT, Robert: 'Exploring the ritual of travel in prehistoric Europe: the Bronze Age sewn-plank boats in context', in: Bronze Age Connections – Cultural Contact in Prehistoric Europe, Clark, Peter (ed.), Oxford, 2009, pp. 159 – 175

VANDKILDE, Helle: 'Bronzization: The Bronze Age as Pre-Modern Globalization', in: Praehistorische Zeitschrift, 91 (1), 2016, pp. 103 – 123

VAN WIJNGAARDEN, Gert Jan: 'Trade goods reproducing merchants? The materiality of Mediterranean Late Bronze Age exchange', in: 'Materiality and Social Practice – Transformative Capacities of Intercultural Encounters', Maran, Joseph and Stockhammer, Philipp W. (eds.), Oxford, 2012, pp. 61 – 72

VARBERG, Jeanette, KAUL, Flemming and GRATUZE, Bernhard: 'Danish Bronze Age glass beads traced back to Egypt – Analyses of glass beads found in Denmark give us new knowledge of Bronze Age trade routes', in: Science Nordic, https://sciencenordic.com/archaeology-bronze-age-denmark/danish-bronze-age-glass-beads-traced-to-egypt/1411142; 08.12.2014

VERBRUGGHE, Gerald P. and WICKERSHAM, John M.: 'Berossos and Manetho – Native Traditions in Ancient Mesopotamia and Egypt', Michigan, 2001

VIANELLO, Andrea: 'Late Bronze Age Aegean Trade Routes in the western Mediterranean', in: The Aegean Bronze Age in relation to the Wider European Context, Papers from a session at the Eleventh Annual Meeting of the European Association of Archaeologists September 2005 (Cork), Whittaker, Helene (ed.), BAR International Series 1745, 2008, pp. 7 – 26

VISSER, Edzard: 'Homers Katalog der Schiffe', Stuttgart and Leipzig, 1997

VON PESSL, H.: 'Das chronologische System Manetho's', Leipzig, 1878, Reprint 2011

VON RANKE-GRAVES, Robert: 'Griechische Mythologie – Quellen und Deutung', Hamburg, 1986

WAAL, Willemijn: 'On the "Phoenician Letters" – The Case for an Early Transmission of the Greek Alphabet from an Archaeological, Epigraphic and Linguistic Perspective', in: Aegean Studies No. 1 (online publication), 2018, pp. 83 – 125

WAAL, Willemijn: '"My brother, a Great King, my peer" – Evidence for a Mycenaean kingdom from Hittite texts', in: Kelder, Jorrit M. and Waal, Willemijn J.I. (eds.) 'From "Lugal.Gal" to "Wanax" – Kingship and Political Organization in the Late Bronze Age Aegean', Leiden, 2019, pp. 9 – 29

WACHSMANN, Shelley, DUNN, Richard K., HALE, John R., HOHLFELDER, Robert L., CONYERS, Lawrence B., ERNENWEIN, G., PIENHEIRO BLOT, Maria Louisa, CASTRO, Filipe and DAVIS, Dan: 'The Palaeo-Environmental Contexts of Three Possible Phoenician Anchorages in Portugal', in: The International Journal of Nautical Archaeology, 08/2009

WANG, Quanyu, STREKOPYTOV, Stanislav, ROBERTS, Benjamin W. and WILKIN, Neil: 'Tin ingots from a probable Bronze Age shipwreck off the coast of Salcombe, Devon: Composition and microstructure', in: Journal of Archaeological Science 67, 2016, pp. 80 – 92

WENTINK, Karsten: 'Stereotype – The role of grave sets in Corded Ware and Bell Beaker funerary practices', Leiden, 2020

WILKINSON, Toby C. 'Tying the Threads of Eurasia – Trans-regional routes and material flows in Transcaucasia, eastern Anatolia and western central Asia, c. 3000 – 1500 BC', Leiden, 2014

WOOD, Michael: 'Jason and the Golden Fleece', Internet publication, 2011

WOUDHUIZEN, Fred C.: 'Minoan and Mycenaean Oversea's Contacts: The Epigraphic Evidence', in: Revue d' Archeologie et d' Histoire Ancienne L III 2010, pp. 5 – 11

WOUDHUIZEN, Fred C.: 'Traces of Ethnic Diversity in Mycenaean Greece', in: Dacia N.S., Tome LVII, Bucarest, 2013, pp. 5 – 21

ZANGGER, Eberhard: 'Ein neuer Kampf um Troia: Archaeologie in der Krise', Munich, 1994

ZUKERMAN, Alexander: 'On Aegean Involvement in Trade with the Near East during the Late Bronze Age', in: 'Ugarit-Forschungen 42, Internationales Jahrbuch fuer die Altertumskunde Syrien-Palaestinas', Dietrich, Manfred and Loretz, Oswald (eds.), Muenster, 2010, pp. 887 – 901